30.00

Current Issues in Lesbian, Gay, Bisexual, and Transgender Health

Current Issues in Lesbian, Gay, Bisexual, and Transgender Health has been co-published simultaneously as *Journal of Homosexuality*, Volume 51, Number 1 2006.

Monographs from the *Journal of Homosexuality*™

For additional information on these and other Haworth Press titles, including descriptions, tables of contents, reviews, and prices, use the QuickSearch catalog at http://www.HaworthPress.com.

12. *The Many Faces of Homosexuality: Anthropological Approaches to Homosexual Behavior,* edited by Evelyn Blackwood, PhD (cand.) (Vol. 11, No. 3/4, 1986). *"A fascinating account of homosexuality during various historical periods and in non-Western cultures." (SIECUS Report)*

13. *Historical, Literary, and Erotic Aspects of Lesbianism,* edited by Monika Kehoe, PhD (Vol. 12, No. 3/4, 1986). *"Fascinating. . . . Even though this entire volume is serious scholarship penned by degreed writers, most of it is vital, accessible, and thoroughly readable even to the casual student of lesbian history." (Lambda Rising)*

14. *Gay Life in Dutch Society,* edited by A. X. van Naerssen, PhD (Vol. 13, No. 2/3, 1987). *"Valuable not just for its insightful analysis of the evolution of gay rights in The Netherlands, but also for the lessons that can be extracted by our own society from the Dutch tradition of tolerance for homosexuals." (The San Francisco Chronicle)*

15. *Integrated Identity for Gay Men and Lesbians: Psychotherapeutic Approaches for Emotional Well-Being,* edited by Eli Coleman, PhD (Vol. 14, No. 1/2, 1987). *"An invaluable tool. . . . This is an extremely useful book for the clinician seeking better ways to understand gay and lesbian patients." (Hospital and Community Psychiatry)*

16. *The Treatment of Homosexuals with Mental Disorders,* edited by Michael W. Ross, PhD (Vol. 15, No. 1/2, 1988). *"One of the more objective, scientific collections of articles concerning the mental health of gays and lesbians. . . . Extraordinarily thoughtful. . . . New thoughts about treatments. Vital viewpoints." (The Book Reader)*

17. *The Pursuit of Sodomy: Male Homosexuality in Renaissance and Enlightenment Europe,* edited by Kent Gerard, PhD, and Gert Hekma, PhD (Vol. 16, No. 1/2, 1989). *"Presenting a wealth of information in a compact form, this book should be welcomed by anyone with an interest in this period in European history or in the precursors to modern concepts of homosexuality." (The Canadian Journal of Human Sexuality)*

18. *Lesbians Over 60 Speak for Themselves,* edited by Monika Kehoe, PhD (Vol. 16, No. 3/4, 1989). *"A pioneering book examining the social, economical, physical, sexual, and emotional lives of aging lesbians." (Feminist Bookstore News)*

19. *Gay and Lesbian Youth,* edited by Gilbert Herdt, PhD (Vol. 17, No. 1/2/3/4, 1989). *"Provides a much-needed compilation of research dealing with homosexuality and adolescents." (GLTF Newsletter)*

20. *Homosexuality and the Family,* edited by Frederick W. Bozett, PhD (Vol. 18, No. 1/2, 1989). *"Enlightening and answers a host of questions about the effects of homosexuality upon family members and the family as a unit." (Ambush Magazine)*

21. *Homosexuality and Religion,* edited by Richard Hasbany, PhD (Vol. 18, No. 3/4, 1990). *"A welcome resource that provides historical and contemporary views on many issues involving religious life and homosexuality." (Journal of Sex Education and Therapy)*

22. *Love Letters Between a Certain Late Nobleman and the Famous Mr. Wilson,* edited by Michael S. Kimmel, PhD (Vol. 19, No. 2, 1990). *"An intriguing book about homosexuality in 18th-Century England. Many details of the period, such as meeting places, coded language, and 'camping' are all covered in the book. If you're a history buff, you'll enjoy this one." (Prime Timers)*

23. *Male Intergenerational Intimacy: Historical, Socio-Psychological, and Legal Perspectives,* edited by Theo G. M. Sandfort, PhD, Edward Brongersma, JD, and A. X. van Naerssen, PhD (Vol. 20, No. 1/2, 1991). *"The most important book on the subject since Tom O'Carroll's 1980 Paedophilia: The Radical Case." (The North American Man/Boy Love Association Bulletin, May 1991)*

24. *Gay Midlife and Maturity: Crises, Opportunities, and Fulfillment,* edited by John Alan Lee, PhD (Vol. 20, No. 3/4, 1991). *"The insight into gay aging is amazing, accurate, and much-needed. . . . A real contribution to the older gay community." (Prime Timers)*

25. *Gay People, Sex, and the Media,* edited by Michelle A. Wolf, PhD, and Alfred P. Kielwasser, MA (Vol. 21, No. 1/2, 1991). *"Altogether, the kind of research anthology which is useful to many disciplines in gay studies. Good stuff!" (Communique)*

26. *Homosexuality and Male Bonding in Pre-Nazi Germany: The Youth Movement, the Gay Movement, and Male Bonding Before Hitler's Rise: Original Transcripts from Der Eigene, the First Gay Journal in the World,* edited by Harry Oosterhuis, PhD, and Hubert Kennedy, PhD (Vol. 22, No. 1/2, 1992). *"Provide[s] insight into the early gay movement, particularly in its relation to the various political currents in pre-World War II Germany." (Lambda Book Report)*

27. *Coming Out of the Classroom Closet: Gay and Lesbian Students, Teachers, and Curricula,* edited by Karen M. Harbeck, PhD, JD, Recipient of Lesbian and Gay Educators Award by the American Educational Research Association's Lesbian and Gay Studies Special Interest Group (AREA) (Vol. 22, No. 3/4, 1992). *"Presents recent research about gay and lesbian students and teachers and the school system in which they function." (Contemporary Psychology)*

28. *Homosexuality in Renaissance and Enlightenment England: Literary Representations in Historical Context,* edited by Claude J. Summers, PhD (Vol. 23, No. 1/2, 1992). *"It is remarkable among studies in this field in its depth of scholarship and variety of approaches and is accessible." (Chronique)*

29. *Gay and Lesbian Studies,* edited by Henry L. Minton, PhD (Vol. 24, No. 1/2, 1993). *"The volume's essays provide insight into the field's remarkable accomplishments and future goals." (Lambda Book Report)*

30. *If You Seduce a Straight Person, Can You Make Them Gay? Issues in Biological Essentialism versus Social Constructionism in Gay and Lesbian Identities,* edited by John P. DeCecco, PhD, and John P. Elia, MA, PhD (cand.) (Vol. 24, No. 3/4, 1993). *"You'll find this alternative view of the age old question to be one that will become the subject of many conversations to come. Thought-provoking to say the least!" (Prime Timers)*

31. *Gay Studies from the French Cultures: Voices from France, Belgium, Brazil, Canada, and the Netherlands,* edited by Rommel Mendès-Leite, PhD, and Pierre-Olivier de Busscher, PhD (cand.) (Vol. 25, No. 1/2/3, 1993). *"The first book that allows an English-speaking world to have a comprehensive look at the principal trends in gay studies in France and French-speaking countries." (André Bèjin, PhD, Directeur, de Recherche au Centre National de la Recherche Scientifique [CNRS], Paris)*

32. *Critical Essays: Gay and Lesbian Writers of Color,* edited by Emmanuel S. Nelson, PhD (Vol. 26, No. 2/3, 1993). *"A much-needed book, sparkling with stirring perceptions and resonating with depth. . . . The anthology not only breaks new ground, it also attempts to heal wounds inflicted by our oppressed pasts." (Lambda)*

33. *Gay and Lesbian Studies in Art History,* edited by Whitney Davis, PhD (Vol. 27, No. 1/2, 1994). *"Informed, challenging . . . never dull. . . . Contributors take risks and, within the restrictions of scholarly publishing, find new ways to use materials already available or examine topics never previously explored." (Lambda Book Report)*

34. *Gay Ethics: Controversies in Outing, Civil Rights, and Sexual Science,* edited by Timothy F. Murphy, PhD (Vol. 27, No. 3/4, 1994). *"The contributors bring the traditional tools of ethics and political philosophy to bear in a clear and forceful way on issues surrounding the rights of homosexuals." (David L. Hull, Dressler Professor in the Humanities, Department of Philosophy, Northwestern University)*

35. *Sex, Cells, and Same-Sex Desire: The Biology of Sexual Preference,* edited by John P. DeCecco, PhD, and David Allen Parker, MA (Vol. 28, No. 1/2/3/4, 1995). *"A stellar compilation of chapters examining the most important evidence underlying theories on the biological basis of human sexual orientation." (MGW)*

36. *Gay Men and the Sexual History of the Political Left,* edited by Gert Hekma, PhD, Harry Oosterhuis, PhD, and James Steakley, PhD (Vol. 29, No. 2/3/4, 1995). *"Contributors delve into the contours of a long-forgotten history, bringing to light new historical data and fresh insight. . . . An excellent account of the tense historical relationship between the political left and gay liberation." (People's Voice)*

37. *Gays, Lesbians, and Consumer Behavior: Theory, Practice, and Research Issues in Marketing,* edited by Daniel L. Wardlow, PhD (Vol. 31, No. 1/2, 1996). *"For those scholars,*

market researchers, and marketing managers who are considering marketing to the gay and lesbian community, this book should be on their required reading list." *(Mississippi Voice)*

38. ***Activism and Marginalization in the AIDS Crisis,*** edited by Michael A. Hallett, PhD (Vol. 32, No. 3/4, 1997). *Shows readers how the advent of HIV-disease has brought into question the utility of certain forms of "activism" as they relate to understanding and fighting the social impacts of disease.*

39. ***Reclaiming the Sacred: The Bible in Gay and Lesbian Culture,*** edited by Raymond-Jean Frontain, PhD (Vol. 33, No. 3/4, 1997). *"Finely wrought, sharply focused, daring, and always dignified.... In chapter after chapter, the Bible is shown to be a more sympathetic and humane book in its attitudes toward homosexuality than usually thought and a challenge equally to the straight and gay moral imagination." (Joseph Wittreich, PhD, Distinguished Professor of English, The Graduate School, The City University of New York)*

40. ***Gay and Lesbian Literature Since World War II: History and Memory,*** edited by Sonya L. Jones, PhD (Vol. 34, No. 3/4, 1998). *"The authors of these essays manage to gracefully incorporate the latest insights of feminist, postmodernist, and queer theory into solidly grounded readings ... challenging and moving, informed by the passion that prompts both readers and critics into deeper inquiry." (Diane Griffin Growder, PhD, Professor of French and Women's Studies, Cornell College, Mt. Vernon, Iowa)*

41. ***Scandinavian Homosexualities: Essays on Gay and Lesbian Studies,*** edited by Jan Löfström, PhD (Vol. 35, No. 3/4, 1998). *"Everybody interested in the formation of lesbian and gay identities and their interaction with the sociopolitical can find something to suit their taste in this volume." (Judith Schuyf, PhD, Assistant Professor of Lesbian and Gay Studies, Center for Gay and Lesbian Studies, Utrecht University, The Netherlands)*

42. ***Multicultural Queer: Australian Narratives,*** edited by Peter A. Jackson, PhD, and Gerard Sullivan, PhD (Vol. 36, No. 3/4, 1999). *Shares the way that people from ethnic minorities in Australia (those who are not of Anglo-Celtic background) view homosexuality, their experiences as homosexual men and women, and their feelings about the lesbian and gay community.*

43. ***The Ideal Gay Man: The Story of Der Kreis,*** by Hubert Kennedy, PhD (Vol. 38, No. 1/2, 1999). *"Very profound.... Excellent insight into the problems of the early fight for homosexual emancipation in Europe and in the USA.... The ideal gay man (high-mindedness, purity, cleanness), as he was imagined by the editor of 'Der Kreis,' is delineated by the fascinating quotations out of the published erotic stories." (Wolfgang Breidert, PhD, Academic Director, Institute of Philosophy, University Karlsruhe, Germany)*

44. ***Gay Community Survival in the New Millennium,*** edited by Michael R. Botnick, PhD (cand.) (Vol. 38, No. 4, 2000). *Examines the notion of community from several different perspectives focusing on the imagined, the structural, and the emotive. You will explore a theoretical overview and you will peek into the moral discourses that frame "gay community," the rift between HIV-positive and HIV-negative gay men, and how Israeli gays seek their place in the public sphere.*

45. ***Queer Asian Cinema: Shadows in the Shade,*** edited by Andrew Grossman, MA (Vol. 39, No. 3/4, 2000). *"An extremely rich tapestry of detailed ethnographies and state-of-the-art theorizing. ... Not only is this a landmark record of queer Asia, but it will certainly also be a seminal, contributive challenge to gender and sexuality studies in general." (Dédé Oetomo, PhD, Coordinator of the Indonesian organization GAYa NUSANTARA: Adjunct Reader in Linguistics and Anthropology, School of Social Sciences, Universitas Airlangga, Surabaya, Indonesia)*

46. ***Gay and Lesbian Asia: Culture, Identity, Community,*** edited by Gerard Sullivan, PhD, and Peter A. Jackson, PhD (Vol. 40, No. 3/4, 2001). *"Superb.... Covers a happily wide range of styles ... will appeal to both students and educated fans." (Gary Morris, Editor/Publisher, Bright Lights Film Journal)*

47. ***Homosexuality in French History and Culture,*** edited by Jeffrey Merrick and Michael Sibalis (Vol. 41, No. 3/4, 2001). *"Fascinating.... Merrick and Sibalis bring together historians, literary scholars, and political activists from both sides of the Atlantic to examine same-sex sexuality in the past and present." (Bryant T. Ragan, PhD, Associate Professor of History, Fordham University, New York City)*

48. ***The Drag King Anthology,*** edited by Donna Jean Troka, PhD (cand.), Kathleen LeBesco, PhD, and Jean Bobby Noble, PhD (Vol. 43, No. 3/4, 2002). *"All university courses on masculinity*

should use this book . . . challenges preconceptions through the empirical richness of direct experience. The contributors and editors have worked together to produce cultural analysis that enhances our perception of the dynamic uncertainty of gendered experience." (Sally R. Munt. DPhil. Subject Chair, Media Studies, University of Sussex)

49. **Icelandic Lives: The Queer Experience,** edited by Voon Chin Phua (Vol. 44, No. 2, 2002). *"The first of its kind, this book shows the emergence of gay and lesbian visibility through the biographical narratives of a dozen Icelanders. Through their lives can be seen a small nation's transition, in just a few decades, from a pervasive silence concealing its queer citizens to widespread acknowledgment characterized by some of the most progressive laws in the world." (Barry D. Adam, PhD, University Professor, Department of Sociology & Anthropology, University of Windsor, Ontario, Canada)*

50. **Gay Bathhouses and Public Health Policy,** edited by William J. Woods, PhD, and Diane Binson, PhD (Vol. 44, No. 3/4, 2003). *"Important. . . . Long overdue. . . . A unique and valuable contribution to the social science and public health literature. The inclusion of detailed historical descriptions of public policy debates about the place of bathhouses in urban gay communities, together with summaries of the legal controversies about bathhouses, insightful examinations of patrons' behaviors and reviews of successful programs for HIV/STD education and testing programs in bathhouses provides. A well rounded and informative overview." (Richard Tewksbury, PhD, Professor of Justice Administration, University of Louisville)*

51. **Queer Theory and Communication: From Disciplining Queers to Queering the Discipline(s),** edited by Gust A. Yep, PhD, Karen E. Lovaas, PhD, and John P. Elia, PhD (Vol. 45, No. 2/3/4, 2003). *"Sheds light on how sexual orientation and identity are socially produced–and how they can be challenged and changed–through everyday practices and institutional activities, as well as academic research and teaching. . . . Illuminates the theoretical and practical significance of queer theory–not only as a specific area of inquiry, but also as a productive challenge to the heteronormativity of mainstream communication theory, research, and pedagogy." (Julia T. Wood, PhD, Lineberger Professor of Humanities, Professor of Communication Studies, The University of North Carolina at Chapel Hill)*

52. **The Drag Queen Anthology: The Absolutely Fabulous but Flawlessly Customary World of Female Impersonators,** edited by Steven P. Schacht, PhD, with Lisa Underwood (Vol. 46, No. 3/4, 2004). *"Indispensable. . . . For more than a decade, Steven P. Schacht has been one of the social sciences' most reliable guides to the world of drag queens and female impersonators. . . . This book assembles an impressive cast of scholars who are as theoretically astute, methodologically careful, and conceptually playful as the drag queens themselves." (Michael Kimmel, author of* The Gendered Society; *Professor of Sociology, SUNY Stony Brook)*

53. **Eclectic Views on Gay Male Pornography: Pornucopia,** edited by Todd G. Morrison, PhD (Vol. 47, No. 3/4, 2004). "An instant classic. . . . Lively and readable." *(Jerry Zientara, EdD, Librarian, Institute for Advanced Study of Human Sexuality)*

54. **Sexuality and Human Rights: A Global Overview,** edited by Helmut Graupner, JD, and Philip Tahmindjis, BA, LLB, LLM, SJD (Vol. 48, No. 3/4, 2005). *"An important resource for anybody concerned about the status of legal protection for the human rights of sexual minorities, especially for those concerned with attaining a comparative perspective. The chapters are all of high quality and are written in a straightforward manner that will be accessible to the non-specialist while containing much detail of interest to specialists in the area." (Arthur S. Leonard, JD, Professor of Law, New York Law School)*

55. **Same-Sex Desire and Love in Greco-Roman Antiquity and in the Classical Tradition of the West,** edited by Beert C. Verstraete and Vernon Provencal (Vol. 49, No. 3/4, 2005). *"This wide-ranging collection engages with the existing scholarship in the history of sexuality and the uses of the classical tradition and opens up exciting new areas of study. The book is an important addition to queer theory." (Stephen Guy-Bray, PhD, Associate Professor, University of British Columbia)*

56. **Sadomasochism: Powerful Pleasures,** edited by Peggy J. Kleinplatz, PhD, and Charles Moser, PhD, MD (Vol. 50, No. 2/3, 2006). *"I would advise anyone interested in doing research on this topic or trying to understand this severely stigmatized behavior to begin with this collection." (Vern L. Bullough, PhD, DSci, RN, Visiting Professor Emeritus, State University of New York; Editor of* Before Stonewall: Activists for Gay and Lesbian Rights in Historical Context)

57. ***Current Issues in Lesbian, Gay, Bisexual, and Transgender Health,*** edited by Jay Harcourt, MPH (Vol. 51, No. 1, 2006). *"A fine addition to our knowledge of LGBT youth adults. The chapter by Dr. Case and her colleagues gives us a wonderful study that supports the addition of sexual orientation to the demographic questions within research studies. Dr. Koh and Dr. Ross's work exploring mental health issues by sexual orientation is also very important." (Suzanne L. Dibble, RN, DNSc, Professor and Co-Director, Lesbian Health Research Center, University of California at San Francisco)*

Current Issues in Lesbian, Gay, Bisexual, and Transgender Health

Jay Harcourt, MPH
Editor

Current Issues in Lesbian, Gay, Bisexual, and Transgender Health has been co-published simultaneously as *Journal of Homosexuality*, Volume 51, Number 1 2006.

Routledge
Taylor & Francis Group

NEW YORK AND LONDON

First published by

Harrington Park Press® is an imprint of The Haworth Press, Inc., 10 Alice Street, Binghamton, NY 13904-1580 USA.

This edition published 2011 by Routledge
711 Third Avenue, New York, NY 10017
2 Park Square, Milton Park, Abingdon, Oxon, OX14 4RN

Current Issues in Lesbian, Gay, Bisexual, and Transgender Health has been co-published simultaneously as *Journal of Homosexuality*, Volume 51, Number 1 2006.

Cover design by Jennifer M. Gaska

Library of Congress Cataloging-in-Publication Data

Current issues in lesbian, gay, bisexual, and transgender health / Jay Harcourt, editor.
      p. cm.
      "Current Issues in Lesbian, gay, and transgender health has been co-published simultaneously as Journal of Homosexuality, Volume 51, Number 1, 2006."
      Includes bibliographical references and index.
      ISBN-13: 978-1-56023-659-7 (hard cover : alk. paper)
      ISBN-10: 1-56023-659-0 (hard cover : alk. paper)
      ISBN-13: 978-1-56023-660-3 (soft cover : alk. paper)
      ISBN-10: 1-56023-660-4 (soft cover : alk. paper)
      1. Lesbians–Health and hygiene. 2. Gays–Health and hygiene. 3. Harcourt, Jay. II. Journal of homosexuality.
RA564.87.C87 2006
613.086′64–dc22

2006000593

ABOUT THE EDITOR

Jay Harcourt, MPH, is completing his doctorate in Public Health at the School of Public Health, University of California, Berkeley where his work focuses on LGBT health, gay men's health and HIV/AIDS prevention, and community organizing. Jay has served for the past 5 years on the Executive Committee of the Lesbian, Gay, Bisexual, and Transgender Caucus of Public Health Workers–in association with the American Public Health Association, and is a founding Community Advisory Board member for Magnet, a gay men's community health center in San Francisco (www.magnetsf.org). Since 1999, he has been the Editorial Assistant at the *Journal of Homosexuality*. He can be reached at <jay.harcourt@gmail.com>.

Current Issues in Lesbian, Gay, Bisexual, and Transgender Health

CONTENTS

Acknowledgments

First, I would like to thank all of the contributors to this volume for their patience with the editorial process, and for their dedication to their work with LGBT populations. I would also like to thank the countless individuals who shared their stories and participated in the research presented here. Without their voices, our work is meaningless. In a time when LGBT research has come under fire from conservatives in government and funding for research has been threatened, it becomes even more important that we continue to do this research and publish the results. Thanks too, to John De Cecco and all of the production and administrative staff at Haworth Press/Harrington Park Press. It has been a pleasure to work with them all over the years and on this specific project. I am especially grateful to my friends and colleagues who, despite being the hardest working bunch of people I know, donated their time to serve as peer reviewers for this volume: Courtney Ahrens, Emilia Lombardi, Monica Mclemore, Meredith Minkler, Lisa Moore, Matthew Moyer, Cheri Pies, Marj Plumb, Kathleen Roe, Michael Shankle, Tony Silvestre, and Jodi Sperber. Without their thoughtful comments and recommendations, this volume would not have been possible.

I am grateful to Jennifer Sarché, Heidi Winig, and Paula Worby for their constant support and encouragement; to Meredith Minkler and Kathleen Roe for showing me, through their inability to do so, when to say "no"; and to Kevin Roe for challenging me to be a better person, for sticking by me, and tolerating my ambitions.

Current Issues in Lesbian, Gay, Bisexual, and Transgender (LGBT) Health: Introduction

Jay Harcourt, MPH

San Francisco, California

Compiling a volume dedicated to Lesbian, Gay, Bisexual, and Transgender (LGBT) health is like putting together a puzzle; some pieces are in full color and have sharp edges and some pieces are black and white and fuzzy. Simply put, although we know a lot about some health issues such as HIV/AIDS among gay and bisexual men, we know little about other health issues effecting LGBT populations. The body of literature on LGBT health issues is still in its infancy. In fact, in a review of the literature indexed in MEDLINE from 1980-1999, Boehmer (2002) found that literature focusing upon LGBT health comprised only 0.1% of all indexed articles. Of those, 56% were focused upon HIV and STDs, primarily among gay and bisexual men (Boehmer, 2002).

Following the publication of a 1999 Institute of Medicine report on lesbian health (Solarz, 1999), and the first ever inclusion of health objectives addressing sexual orientation in 10 of the 28 prevention focus areas for the US included in Healthy People 2010 (HP2010), it has be-

Jay Harcourt is a doctoral student at the School of Public Health, University of California, Berkeley. Correspondence may be addressed: 231 Sanchez Street #5, San Francisco, CA 94114 (E-mail: jay.harcourt@gmail.com).

[Haworth co-indexing entry note]: "Current Issues in Lesbian, Gay, Bisexual, and Transgender (LGBT) Health: Introduction." Harcourt, Jay. Co-published simultaneously in *Journal of Homosexuality* (Harrington Park Press, an imprint of The Haworth Press, Inc.) Vol. 51, No. 1, 2006, pp. 1-11; and: *Current Issues in Lesbian, Gay, Bisexual, and Transgender Health* (ed: Jay Harcourt) Harrington Park Press, an imprint of The Haworth Press, Inc., 2006, pp. 1-11. Single or multiple copies of this article are available for a fee from The Haworth Document Delivery Service [1-800-HAWORTH, 9:00 a.m. - 5:00 p.m. (EST). E-mail address: docdelivery@haworthpress.com].

come apparent that there is a dearth of information about the health issues affecting LGBT populations. In fact, although it was groundbreaking that HP2010 included health objectives directed towards sexual orientation, data are not currently collected to track these objectives. The document actually falls short by failing to identify specific health objectives for eliminating health disparities in LGBT populations and the document ignores entirely transgender populations and gender identity (Sell & Baker, 2001).

Several research challenges contribute to the lack of data on LGBT health. Perhaps the greatest challenge is the issue of generalizability (Dean et al., 2000). Due to the relatively small size of, and the large diversity within, the LGBT population–sexual orientation and gender identity cut across all race/ethnicity and socioeconomic groups–it is difficult to definitively define, making representative sampling in research challenging. Until research is better able to identify and facilitate an understanding of the size and nature of sexual minority populations, we need to rely upon smaller studies to create a picture of these populations.

In the absence of large-scale, federal data collection, researchers have relied upon alternative sampling methods to recruit LGBT study populations (Stein & Bonuck, 2001, Dean et al., 2000). Frequently, they have relied upon targeted advertising and snowball sampling techniques. For example, Meyer (1995), used advertising targeted to the contact lists of gay organizations in New York, and supplemented with snowball sampling of non-affiliated gay men in the city (Meyer, 1995). Such sampling techniques may increase the possibility of bias in the research, in particular selection and volunteer biases (Meyer, 1995).

In addition, methods to assess sexual orientation and gender identity are virtually absent from most population-based surveys making it difficult to measure health issues of LGBT populations on a large-scale basis (Dean et al., 2000). Even when studies use a statistically sound recruitment scheme such as a random-digit-dialed telephone-sampling, the sample may garner very small numbers of LGBT respondents and thus lack power for statistical analysis (Mays & Cochran, 2001). Furthermore, there is no consensus on how to generate questions to capture sexual orientation (Solarz, 1999). Studies have used self-identified orientation, reports of the sex of respondents' sexual partners, or the gender to whom the respondent is attracted as measures of respondents' sexual orientation (Dean et al., 2000). Because of the lack of consensus about how to measure orientation, all authors in this collection have been asked to specify how the orientation and sexual identity of their research participants was measured. Until standardized measures of orientation and identity are validated for large-scale use, we need to be explicit in how we measure such variables.

Until completion of large-scale measurements of LGBT populations' health status, those interested in the health of these populations must rely on smaller descriptive studies. Given that the study of these groups is still relatively new smaller descriptive studies can be informative. For example, we still lack information on LGBT demographics and culture(s). Descriptive qualitative research can contribute to such knowledge and inform the formulation of creation of questions and topics for future larger-scale projects. In addition, because we are just beginning to document the health issues of LGBT people, multiple study methods are appropriate. For health issues that are well documented such as HIV among gay and bisexual men, large quantitative studies can be informative, while qualitative measures may be more able to describe issues that we know little about such as the health care experiences of FTM transgender men (Hussey, in this volume).

Despite the lack of data from federal sources, a growing body of literature focuses on documenting health disparities among LGBT populations. Data suggest that gay men and lesbians face disparities across a broad spectrum of diseases. For example, in addition to the well-documented risks for HIV and other sexually transmitted diseases, Ungvarski and Grossman (1999) found gay men tend to have higher prevalence of Hepatitis A, B, C, E, and G than the general population. Also, gay men may be at increased risk for lung cancer and heart disease due to high rates of cigarette smoking and alcoholism (Ungvarski & Grossman, 1999). In addition, Koblin and colleagues (1996) found that gay men are at excess risk for anal cancer, non-Hodgkin's lymphoma, and Hodgkin's disease.

Among women, lesbian orientations have also been associated with cigarette smoking and heavy alcohol use (Aaron et al., 2001; Diamant et al., 2000a; Gruskin et al., 2001; Valanis et al., 2000) putting them at more risk for malignant neoplasm, coronary artery disease, hypertension, peripheral vascular disease and chronic pulmonary conditions (Diamant et al., 2000a). Although there is no consensus on whether lesbians actually have higher prevalence of cervical and breast cancers (Lee, 2000), many studies have found that they are less likely to get screened for these cancers. Studies have found that lesbian women were less likely than heterosexual women to have had a Pap smear (Aaron et al., 2001; Diamant et al., 2000a; Valanis et al., 2000) or clinical breast exam (Diamant et al., 2000b; Valanis et al., 2000).

If research addressing lesbian, bisexual, and gay people is still in its infancy, research addressing transgender populations is newborn. As Grossman and D'Augelli point out in their article included in this issue, small-scale studies including transgender individuals are just beginning to be published and much of what we know about transgender populations is garnered from case-study reports of the experiences of transgender individuals. In addition, like research on gay and bisexual men, much of what is published about transgender individuals focuses on HIV. For example, several studies have documented increased rates of HIV risk among female-to-male transgender women (Bockting et al., 1998; Clements-Nolle et al., 2001; Kenagy, 2002; Nemoto et al., 1999). There is clearly a need to expand the literature focusing upon transgender populations.

DISCRIMINATION AND HEALTH

Given the newness of research addressing the health of LGBT populations, it is understandable that most of the literature has focused upon describing and documenting health issues within these groups. But some have begun to attempt to conceptualize models that explain and capture reasons for the disparities in health among LGBT populations.

Sodomy laws, which criminalized homosexuality and which were used to justify discriminating against LGBT people (Lambda Legal Defense and Education Fund, 2002) were only overturned by the US Supreme Court in June of 2003. However, insurance companies, governments, hospitals and health clinics may still not recognize LGBT relationships as legitimate family structures and deny LGBT families' privileges granted heterosexual partnerships (O'Hanlan et al., 1997). Clearly, discrimination based upon sexual orientation or gender identity has an impact on the well-being of LGBT persons, and may have an impact on the health of these populations.

Nancy Krieger (2000) provides a framework for conceptualizing and measuring the impact of discrimination on health. She defines discrimination as:

> [A] socially structured and sanctioned phenomenon, justified by ideology and expressed in interactions, among and between individuals and institutions, intended to maintain privileges for members of dominant groups at the cost of deprivation for others. (p. 41)

Drawing from social science literature, Krieger (2000) argues that discrimination can occur on multiple levels: legal and illegal, overt or covert, institutional, and interpersonal discrimination. She suggests three ways in which epidemiology might attempt to measure the health effects of discrimination. First, compare health outcomes between dominant and subordinate groups and control for all risk factors and relevant demographic information. If, after controlling for the above, a difference in health outcomes still exists, then discrimination may be inferred as a possible explanation (Krieger, 2000). Second, compare self-reported experiences of discrimination with their impact on specific health outcomes. Third, measure population-level institutional discrimination such as segregation and lack of political involvement, with group level health outcomes such as mortality and morbidity (Krieger, 2000).

Literature examining discrimination and its health impacts among LGBT populations has employed Krieger's second approach of comparing self-reported experiences of discrimination and specific health outcomes. Of the three studies that could be found that directly compared self-reported experiences of discrimination with health outcomes, Diaz et al., (2001), Meyer (1995), and Mays and Cochran (2001) all used mental health outcomes as their health outcome.

In a sample of gay men living in New York City in 1987, Meyer (1995) found that self-reported Stigma (the expectation of rejection and discrimination) about their orientation and self-reported Prejudice (an experience of antigay violence or discrimination) positively predicted four psychological distress measures: Demoralization, Guilt, Suicidal ideation or behavior, and AIDS-Related Traumatic Stress Response. Among gay and bisexual Latino men in three US cities, Diaz and his colleagues (2001) found high rates of psychological distress such as suicidal ideation, anxiety, and depressed mood. These symptoms were associated with experiences of social discrimination, such as homophobia, poverty, and racism, that influenced the social isolationism and low self-esteem of these men (Diaz et al., 2001).

Mays and Cochran (2001) compared mental health outcomes of the sub-sample of homosexual and bisexual respondents of the National Survey of Midlife Development in the US to the mental health outcomes of the sub-sample of heterosexual respondents of the study. The authors report that more that 75% of the homosexual and bisexual respondents reported discrimination and that they were more likely than heterosexual respondents to have at least 1 of 5 psychiatric disorders assessed (Mays & Cochran, 2001). The authors conclude that discrimination has harmful mental health effects for sexual minorities (Mays & Cochran, 2001).

In addition to the studies cited above that attempted to directly link discrimination with negative (mental) health outcomes, a growing body of literature has investigated gay and lesbian populations' experiences with discrimination in health care settings. While these studies did not measure specific health outcomes, barriers to accessing health care can have an indirect impact on health by limiting people's ability to access care and screening when needed.

This literature has, in general, found that gay men and lesbian women frequently experience culturally insensitive or hostile health care environments (Saunders, 1999; Ungvarski & Grossman, 1999). Many gay and lesbian respondents report negative health care experiences as a result of providers' hostile responses to their sexual orientation (Stevens, 1995; Beehler, 2001; Eliason & Schope, 2001; Schilder et al., 2000; Stein & Bonuck, 2001). As a result, gay and lesbian patients may be reluctant to disclose their orientation to providers (Stevens, 1995; Harrison & Silenzio, 1996; Beehler, 2001; Eliason & Schope, 2001; Schilder et al., 200; Stein & Bonuck, 2001) and fear of being stigmatized by providers may lead to avoidance of care (Cornelson, 1998, Ungvarski & Grossman, 1999). Stein and Bonuk (2001), in a study of gay and lesbian health care consumers in metropolitan New York, found that 17% of their respondents reported avoiding or delaying seeking care because of their sexual orientation.

Although the literature cited above provides suggestive evidence of associations between discrimination and health outcomes, none adequately captures the underlying mechanisms. Further research documenting discrimination and health is clearly needed to further our understanding of how disparities in health may manifest. In order to further the field of LGBT health, we need to both document the health status of LGBT populations and describe factors that may influence health outcomes in LGBT people. To do so, researchers have focused on compiling LGBT literature to answer these data needs. The 2000 publication of the HP2010 companion document focusing on LGBT health (Dean et al., 2000) and the first special issue of the *American Journal of Public Health* (Meyer, ed. 2001) dedicated to LGBT health issues added to our understanding of health issues among LGBT populations. These publications, along with individual articles and other special issues dedicated to LGBT health help to better fill in the gaps in knowledge and to complete the puzzle that is the status of LGBT health. This publication is intended to follow in these footsteps by adding to the body of knowledge about the health issues of LGBT people.

True to the nature of the *Journal of Homosexuality*, this collection is intended to address LGBT health issues from an interdisciplinary and mixed-method framework. This collection presents both quantitative reports and qualitative descriptions of health issues among various population groups. The topics of the articles are diverse, and an attempt was made to focus upon topics that are poorly represented in the extant literature. Specifically, articles focused primarily upon HIV or STDs among gay and bisexual men have been excluded because these issues have been well documented elsewhere. Generally, issues that have been better documented and studied in the past (such as mental health) are approached quantitatively, whereas issues that are less well documented (such as issues of transgender youth) are described qualitatively.

Given the diversity in the articles in this special issue, no single way of arranging them stood out as most logical. Articles could be presented by population group (L, G, B, or T), or by the general age of the study participants (youth vs. adult) or by health issue focused upon, or simply alphabetically by author. Instead, I have arranged the articles in an order that made sense to me in a public health context. In Public Health, we begin with research in order to document and understand the etiology health issues affecting various populations, and end by creating interventions that attempt to address those health issues within the affected groups. This issue loosely follows such a framework. The issue begins with an article that focuses upon doing research that measures the sexual orientation of the study participants, this article is followed by articles that examine and describe various health issues affecting LGBT populations, and the volume ends with a presentation of interventions created to address the health issues affecting MTF Transgenders in San Francisco.

To begin, Patricia Case and her colleagues address concerns about including measures of sexual orientation in large-scale research studies. In their article "Disclosure of Sexual Orientation and Behavior in the Nurses' Health Study II: Results from a Pilot Study," the authors conclude that asking women to report sexual orientation in a pilot was not a deterrent to women's participation in the study. The authors argue that based upon their results, other researchers may be encouraged to add questions about sexual orientation to their research.

Next, Audrey Koh and Leslie Ross report on a comparison of mental health issues between women of different sexual orientations. In "Mental Health Issues: A Comparison of Lesbian, Bisexual and Heterosexual

Women," Koh and Ross report on one of the few studies to Include bisexual women, and to find in their analysis significant differences between these women and lesbian or heterosexual women. The authors find that not only did sexual orientation relate to women's experiencing emotional issues, but also that disclosure of sexual orientation also had an impact on the likelihood that women experienced mental health problems.

In "Factors Associated with 'Feeling Suicidal': The Role of Sexual Identity," Jeanne Abelson and her colleagues examine mental health issues among men of different sexual orientations and HIV status in Australia. This article presents results that confirm previous research that has indicated that sexual orientation is a predictor of suicidality among gay and bisexual men. The authors also report a new finding that experiences of harassment increased the likelihood of feeling suicidal among both heterosexual and gay/bisexual men.

Third, Eric Wright and Brea Perry explore the relationship between sexual identity distress and social support on GLB youth's substance use, psychological distress, and sexual risk behavior in their article, "Sexual Identity Distress, Social Support, and the Health of Gay, Lesbian, and Bisexual Youth." These authors report that sexual identity distress among the youth who participated in the research was associated with less frequent use of alcohol and using fewer illegal drugs. Interestingly, while being out to more people in their social network reduced the youth's sexual identity distress, those youth who reported more social ties to GLB people also reported engaging in more frequent sexual behavior.

In the following article, "Transgender Youth: Invisible and Vulnerable," Arnold Grossman and Anthony D'Augelli contribute to what little we know about the experiences of Transgender youth. In their report of focus groups with transgender youth in New York City, the authors present the youth's experiences of growing up transgender and their exposure to both negative influences like risks, discrimination, and marginalization, and their access to supportive environments. In terms of health-related areas, the youth report a lack of safe environments, poor access to physical health services, and few resources to address their mental health concerns.

Female-to-male (FTM) transsexuals' experiences of accessing health care are powerfully documented in Wendy Hussey's article "Slivers of the Journey: The Use of Photovoice and Storytelling to Examine Female to Male Transsexuals' Experience of Health Care Access." Hussey uses

Photovoice as a method to allow these men to describe their healthcare experiences. By taking pictures telling a story about their accessing healthcare and discussing the images, these men illustrate both visually and through their words their experiences of dealing with the medical system and of provider competence, their feelings of vulnerability and invisibility, and their use of perseverance and activism in their struggle to access adequate healthcare. Recommendations for training of providers, improvements in service provision and future research with transgender populations are discussed.

Next, Danica Bornstein and her colleagues document the experiences of LBT survivors of domestic violence (DV) in their article, "Understanding the Experiences of Lesbian, Bisexual, and Trans Survivors of Domestic Violence: A Qualitative Study." Participants in this research report a lack of awareness within the community about DV, a difficulty in identifying abusive behavior as such, a reluctance to use law enforcement or traditional DV shelters because of fears about disclosing their sexual orientation and identity, and a reliance on services specifically designed for LBT survivors. Participants recommended solutions focused on community organizing and community building that prompted the organization that sponsored the research to develop interventions targeting the community.

The final article in this volume puts research into practice. In "Need for HIV/AIDS Education and Intervention for MTF Transgenders: Responding to the Challenge," Tooru Nemoto and his colleagues describe the health needs of male-to-female (MTF) transgenders of color in San Francisco and the resulting health interventions created to address these needs. The authors report finding high rates of HIV infection and risk, significant amounts of substance use, and reports of discrimination among the responses form the participants. In addition, participants reported a need for sexuality education and health care services. The authors describe three interventions created in San Francisco to meet the needs identified.

While no one volume dedicated to LGBT health issues can present a comprehensive picture of the health of LGBT populations, it continues to be important for research and public health practitioners to contribute to the growing body of literature on LGBT health. Given the evolutionary nature of research it is important that we continue to document and explore LGBT health issues to build upon existing knowledge and to further complete the puzzle.

REFERENCES

Aaron, DJ., Markovic, N., Danielson, ME., et al. (2001). Behavioral Risk Factors for Disease and Preventive Health Practices Among Lesbians. *American Journal of Public Health.* 91(6), 972-975.

Beehler, GP. (2001). Confronting the Culture of Medicine: Gay Men's Experiences with Primary Care Physicians. *Journal of the Gay and Lesbian Medical Association,* 5(4), 135-141.

Bockting, W., Robinsom, B., & Rosser B. (1998). Transgender HIV Prevention: a qualitative needs assessment. *AIDS Care.* 10(4), 505-525.

Boehmer, U. (2002). Twenty Years of Public Health Research: Inclusion of Lesbian, Gay, Bisexual, and Transgender Populations. *American Journal of Public Health.* 92(7), 1125-1130.

Clements-Nolle, K., Marx, R., Guzman, R., & Katz, M. (2001). HIV Prevalence, Risk Behaviors, Health Care Use, and Mental Health Status of Transgender Persons: Implications for Public Health Intervention. *American Journal of Public Health.* 91(6), 915-921.

Cornelson, BM. (1998). Addressing the Sexual Health Needs of Gay and Bisexual Men in Health Care Settings. *Canadian Journal of Human Sexuality,* 7(3), 261-276.

Dean, L., Meyer, I., Robinson, K., et al. (2000). Lesbian, Gay, Bisexual, and Transgender Health: Findings and Concerns. *Journal of the Gay and Lesbian Medical Association,* 4(3), 101-151.

Diamant, AL., Schuster, MA., & Lever, J. (2000a). Receipt of Preventive Health Care Services by Lesbians. *American Journal of Preventive Medicine,* 19(3), 141-148.

Diamant, AL., Wold, C., Spritzer, K., et al. (2000b). Health Behaviors, Health Status, and Access to and Use of Health Care: A Population-Based Study of Lesbian, Bisexual, and Heterosexual Women. *Archives of Family Medicine,* 9, 1043-1051.

Eliason, MJ., Schope, R. (2001). Does "Don't Ask Don't Tell" Apply to Health Care? Lesbian, Gay, and Bisexual People's Disclosure to Health Care Providers. *Journal of the Gay and Lesbian Medical Association,* 5(4), 125-134.

Gruskin, EP., Hart, S., Gordon, N., & Ackerson, L. (2001). Patterns of Cigarette Smoking and Alcohol Usa Among Lesbians and Bisexual Women Enrolled in a Large Health Maintenance Organization. *American Journal of Public Health.* 91(6), 976-979.

Harrison, AE., & Silenzio, VMB. (1996). Comprehensive Care of Lesbian and Gay Patients and Families. *Primary Care,* 21(3), 31-46.

Kenagy, GP. (2002). HIV among transgendered people. *AIDS Care.* 14(1). 127-134.

Koblin, BA., Hessol, NA., Zauber, AG., et al. (1996). Increased incidence of cancer among homosexual men, New York City and San Francisco, 1978-1990. *American Journal of Epidemiology,* 1 44, 916-923.

Krieger, N. (2000). Discrimination and Health. In LF. Berkman & I. Kawachi (Eds.). *Social Epidemiology.* (pp. 36-75). New York, NY: Oxford University Press.

Lambda Legal Defense and Education Fund, Criminal Law. *http://www.lambdalegal. org/cgi-bin/iowa/issues/record?record=11.* Accessed on May 12, 2002.

Lee, R. (2000). Health care problems of lesbian, gay, bisexual, and transgender patients. *Western Journal of Medicine,* 172, 403-408.

Mays, VM., & Cochran, SD. (2001). Mental Health Correlates of Perceived Discrimination Among Lesbian, Gay, and Bisexual Adults in the United States. *American Journal of public Health.* 91(11), 1869-1876.

Meyer, IH. (1995). Minority Stress and Mental Health in Gay Men. *Journal of Health and Social Behavior.* 36, 38-56.

Meyer, IH. (Ed.). (2001). Lesbian, Gay, Bisexual, and Transgender Health. [Special Issue]. *American Journal of Public Health.* 91(6).

Nemoto, T., Luke, D., Mamo, L., Ching, A., & Patria, J. (1999). HIV risk Behaviors among Male-to-Female trangenders in comparison with homosexual or bisexual males and heterosexual females. *AIDS Care.* 11(3), 297-312.

O'Hanlan, K., Gagnon, JH., Michael, RT., & Michael, S. (1994). *The Social Organization of Sexuality: Sexual Practices in the United States.* Chicago University of Chicago Press.

Saunders, JM. (1999). Health Problems of Lesbian Women. *Nursing Clinics of North America,* 34(2), 381-391.

Schilder, AJ., Kennedy, C., Goldstone, IL., et al. (2001). "Being dealt with as a whole person." Care seeking and adherence: the benefits of culturally competent care. *Social Science & Medicine,* 52, 1643-1659.

Sell, RL., & Baker, JB. (2001). Sexual Orientation Data Collection and Progress Toward Healthy People 2010. *American Journal of Public Health.* 91(6), 876-882.

Solarz, AL. (Ed.). (1999). *Lesbian Health: Current assessment and directions for the future.* Washington, DC: National academy.

Stein, GL., & Bonuck, KA. (2001). Physician-Patient Relationships Among the Lesbian and Gay Community. *Journal of the Gay and Lesbian Medical Association,* 5(3), 87-93.

Ungvarski, PJ., & Grossman, AH. (1999). Health Problems of Gay and Bisexual Men. *Nursing Clinics of North America,* 34(2), 313-331.

Valanis, BG., Bowen, DJ., Bassford, T., et al. (2000). Sexual Orientation and Health. *Archives of Family Medicine,* 9, 843-853.

Disclosure of Sexual Orientation and Behavior in the Nurses' Health Study II: Results from a Pilot Study

Patricia Case, ScD

The Fenway Institute

S. Bryn Austin, ScD

Harvard Medical School, Harvard School of Public Health

David J. Hunter, MBBS, ScD

Harvard School of Public Health

Walter C. Willett, MD, DrPH

Harvard School of Public Health

Susan Malspeis, SM

Harvard School of Public Health

JoAnn E. Manson, MD, DrPH

Harvard Medical School,
Harvard School of Public Health

Donna Spiegelman, ScD

Harvard School of Public Health

The authors are indebted to Karen Corsano for her expert programming assistance and to Jarvis Chen for his insightful comments.

[Haworth co-indexing entry note]: "Disclosure of Sexual Orientation and Behavior in the Nurses' Health Study II: Results from a Pilot Study." Case, Patricia et al. Co-published simultaneously in *Journal of Homosexuality* (Harrington Park Press, an imprint of The Haworth Press, Inc.) Vol. 51, No. 1, 2006, pp. 13-31; and: *Current Issues in Lesbian, Gay, Bisexual, and Transgender Health* (ed: Jay Harcourt) Harrington Park Press, an imprint of The Haworth Press, Inc., 2006, pp. 13-31. Single or multiple copies of this article are available for a fee from The Haworth Document Delivery Service [1-800-HAWORTH, 9:00 a.m. - 5:00 p.m. (EST). E-mail address: docdelivery@haworthpress.com].

SUMMARY. *Objective:* To examine disclosure of sexual orientation and response rates in a pilot study of questions on sexual orientation and gender of sexual partners in the Nurses' Health Study II.

Methods: A pilot questionnaire was mailed to random samples of 350 women from each of three marital status strata: never married, previously married, and currently married. We estimated prevalence of each category of sexual orientation in the pilot study. Response rates to the sexual orientation question for the pilot questionnaire and the 1995 cohort questionnaire were compared.

Results: The overall response rate to the pilot study was 78%. In the pilot study, 98% of women reported a sexual orientation of heterosexual, 0.1% bisexual, and 0.9% lesbian, with 0.7% either declining to answer, leaving the question blank, or categorizing themselves as none of the above, weighted for stratified sampling by marital status. The distribution of sexual orientation in the cohort study (N = 91,654) was similar. Asking women to participate in the pilot study of sexual orientation questions did not appear to cause participants to drop out of the cohort. Concordance between reported sexual orientation on the pilot study and the cohort study was high.

Conclusions: Based on our experience, researchers may be encouraged to add questions on sexual orientation to large studies of women. *[Article copies available for a fee from The Haworth Document Delivery Service: 1-800-HAWORTH. E-mail address: <docdelivery@haworthpress.com> Website: <http://www.HaworthPress.com> © 2006 by The Haworth Press, Inc. All rights reserved.]*

KEYWORDS. Lesbian, bisexual, homosexual, women, sexual orientation, sexual behavior, survey research

INTRODUCTION

Published results of studies of lesbian and bisexual women describe a spectrum of increased health risks, including high rates of alcohol consumption,[1-8] cigarette smoking,[1-4,9-11] and higher body-mass index.[1,2,4,5,9,10] Some studies have found lower rates of screening for breast cancer[2,9,12,13] and for cervical cancer,[1,2,9,10,14] though others have not found lower mammography screening rates among lesbians.[1,4] Several studies have documented social issues that could affect the health status of lesbian and bisexual women, including nondisclosure of sexual orientation to health care providers,[9,15] lack of health insurance[2,11,16-18] and failure to seek health care due to experiences of discrimination.[11,19] Homophobia within the health care system, from insensitivity to overt discrimination, and the distrust it engenders directly interferes with lesbian and bisexual women's access to receive adequate and competent care, especially with regard to health screening.[20]

While an increased risk of a range of health conditions among lesbian and bisexual women has been proposed, the validity of published studies has been limited by multiple methodological issues. Recently, the Institute of Medicine issued a report identifying significant gaps in knowledge about lesbian health, calling attention to the need for methodological refinements, and making eight recommendations for research priorities.[21]

The proportion of women in the United States who are lesbian or bisexual is believed to be low. In a national survey using probability sampling methods, Laumann and colleagues reported that the proportion of women with a lesbian sexual orientation was 0.9 percent, a bisexual sexual orientation was 0.5 percent, and overall, 4.3 percent of women surveyed reported sex with a woman in their lifetime.[22]

The Nurses' Health Study II,[23] a prospective cohort of 116,671 female registered nurses between the ages of 25 and 43 when they responded to a mailed survey in 1989, provided an opportunity to assess the health status of women comparing across sexual orientation groups. Every two years after enrollment, participants responded to a mailed questionnaire containing comprehensive questions about health status, behaviors, risks, and disease.

In 1993, Nurses' Health Study II (NHSII) investigators began receiving letters from participants in the study, researchers, and other interested people asking for information on lesbian health. In response to these requests and to the clear need for more information in this area, the investigators considered adding a question on sexual orientation to the 1995 questionnaire. A pilot study of possible questions for inclusion was initiated, and given the generally positive response to the pilot study, a question on sexual orientation was added to the 1995 NHSII questionnaire, allowing an opportunity to examine the reliability of the question.

METHODS

Study Design

In 1993, 80 percent of the women in the Nurses' Health Study II who provided information about their marital status reported that they were currently married. Under the assumption that married women were less likely to have or disclose a lesbian or bisexual orientation, pilot questionnaires were mailed to random samples of 350 from each of three marital status strata–never married, previously married (widowed, separated or divorced) and currently married, for a total sample size of 1,050. By oversampling unmarried women, who made up a small portion of the cohort, a more accurate estimate of the prevalence of lesbian and bisexual women would be possible. The pilot study was sampled from the 93,701 NHSII participants who returned the cohort questionnaire in 1993 and included information on their marital status.

Questions

To contain the cost of pilot-testing new questions for inclusion in the 1995 cohort questionnaire, the pilot survey included two sets of questions for testing. Section I included questions being tested about breast-feeding practices. In a separate group of test questions, Section II asked two questions, one about sexual orientation and the other about gender of sexual partners. Figure 1 shows the Section II question format and wording. In both the cover letter and within the survey itself, every effort was made to distinguish the two sections as separate sets of questions that were unrelated to each other.

The questions on sexual orientation and behavior were adapted from questions proposed by individuals who had written to Nurses' Health Study II investigators requesting information on lesbian health. The question on gender of sexual partners over the adult lifetime is very similar to that used by the Women's Health Initiative,[24] another large cohort study of women. In each section, participants were asked to comment specifically on the structure and content of the questions. The survey was a four-page form, mailed once in October 1994 with a postage-paid return envelope. There were no additional follow-up measures for women who failed to return the pilot survey.

Reliability

As participants' response to the pilot test was very good, the question on sexual orientation was added to the 1995 Nurses' Health Study II cohort questionnaire which was mailed to 116,671 cohort members in June 1995. Follow-up procedures are extensive for nonparticipants who receive two additional mailings of the original full survey, followed by a shortened version with only core questions and finally the set of core

FIGURE 1. Section II Pilot Study Questions

1. Whether you are currently sexually active or not, what is your sexual identity or orientation? Please choose one answer.

a. Heterosexual...................................□

b. Bisexual...□

c. Lesbian, gay, or homosexual..........□

d. None of the above...........................□

e. Prefer not to answer........................□

2. Whether you are currently sexually active or not, which response best describes who you have had sex with over your adult lifetime and over the last five years? Please choose one answer in each column.

	a. Over your adult lifetime	b. Over the last five years
a. Never had sex...................................□		........................□
b. Sex with a woman/women...............□		........................□
c. Sex with a man/men........................□		........................□
d. Sex with both men and women.......□		........................□
e. Prefer not to answer........................□		........................□

3. Do you have any comments on the structure or content of the preceding questions? Please use the space below for comments.

questions as a telephone survey. The sexual orientation question was included on the original full survey, mailed up to three times, but excluded from the set of core questions. By comparing answers on both the pilot survey and the cohort questionnaire, we were able to evaluate the reliability of the question.

Statistical Methods

The data were analyzed using the SAS statistical package.[25] We examined frequencies, and compared lesbian and heterosexual women using the χ^2 test for the difference between proportions. Where cell sizes were small, Fisher's exact test was used. We estimated prevalence within sexual orientation groups in the pilot study and constructed confidence intervals using techniques for stratified sampling.[26] Responses to the sexual orientation question of women who returned both the pilot questionnaire and the 1995 cohort questionnaire were used to determine the percent concordance in their answers on the two forms.

Data from the pilot study were linked to further data on participants in the cohort study. Data from both the pilot study and the cohort study are presented for comparative purposes. Information on ancestry was obtained from the 1989 questionnaire. Participants were allowed to indicate more than one category of ancestry, and a previously developed algorithm was applied to assign one major ethnicity to each participant.[27]

Data on marital status, information about whom the participant was living with, whether the participant was employed in nursing, was obtained from the 1993 questionnaire. Age was calculated to reflect age in June 1995. Region of residence in 1995 was derived by grouping the state listed in the participant's current address into four regions–Northeast, Midwest, South, and West.

RESULTS

The overall response rate was 78 percent for the pilot study and 91 percent for the cohort study. Response rates significantly differed by marital status in the pilot study ($p = 0.04$) with 81 percent of the currently married, 80 percent of the previously married, and 74 percent of the never married participants responding. There was no difference in response rates by marital status in the cohort study ($p = 0.18$). The pilot test questionnaire was mailed in October 1994 and responses were received over the next eight months. Of the 824 who responded to the pilot study, 97 percent (799) of the participants returned their questionnaires within four months.

The proportion of the sample in each sexual orientation group in the pilot study, weighted for stratified sampling by marital status, was calculated. Responding participants were willing to state their sexual orientation, with 788 reporting that they were heterosexual, four bisexual, and 26 lesbian. Five respondents either declined to state their sexual orientation or left the question blank, and one participant identified herself as none of the above. Thus, only six respondents failed to classify themselves as heterosexual, bisexual or lesbian in the pilot study. Weighted estimates for each sexual orientation group in the pilot group were 98.2 percent heterosexual, 0.1 percent bisexual, and 0.9 percent lesbian. Prevalence within sexual orientation groups in the pilot and the cohort studies was similar, with 1.0 percent of participants in the pilot study and 1.1 percent in the cohort reporting themselves to be either lesbian or bisexual.

Fifteen percent of women responding to the pilot survey commented on the sexual orientation and behavior questions, compared to 22 percent who commented on the breast-feeding questions in section 1. Comments about the sexual orientation and behavior questions ranged from a simple "O.K." to more in-depth comments on the validity, structure, and grammar of the questions, as well as providing personal contexts for answers. Overall, most comments were constructive with the rest about equally divided between positive and critical comments.

Constructive comments included many thoughtful suggestions for clarifying the questions and suggesting additional areas of research. Other research questions were suggested, including questions assessing monogamy, number of sexual partners, and questions on sexually transmitted disease. Women also suggested modifications to the questions and identified concerns and confusion with the structure and wording of the questions. For example, there were comments that the term "adult lifetime" didn't include the teenage years or that the definition of "sex" was unclear. Grammar was corrected, in particular the construction of question 2, with the suggestion that "with whom you have had sex" be substituted for "who you have had sex with." One area of confusion for several women that should be considered for change in adapting these questions was the confusion of the singular/plural construction of "man/men" and "woman/women." One participant wrote asking "Does this mean 1 man and then another man or more than 1 man at a time?" Despite our best efforts to indicate that the two pilot test sections, Section I on breast-feeding practices and Section II on sexual orientation, were separate, some participants questioned the connection between breast-feeding and sexual orientation and were confused by the two sections.

Critical comments included the feeling that the questions were too personal, none of our business, a complaint that the questions would not produce valid data, and a comment that suggested the questions might not be appropriate for Christians to answer. One woman wrote " I don't feel that questions about my sexual identity and activity are appropriate. But since I am committed to the study, I have answered." Another participant wrote simply "I don't like #2. It's too personal" and others wondered what sexual orientation had to do with women's health.

Positive comments included participants thanking us for exploring this aspect of women's health. One woman said "I am pleased to see that this study finally recognizes that a woman's sexuality is an important factor to consider." Heterosexual women wrote positive comments such as "I'm glad you're looking into this" and "happy to participate" and "tastefully done for the information needed" as did lesbians who wrote similar comments such as "very nicely designed" and one lesbian who wrote " I'm very excited you are asking about sexual orientation! In any good relationship–hetero or homo–stress is much reduced in life (I think) and health is better due to less stress."

Table 1 shows the distribution of selected demographic variables for both the pilot study and cohort study. In the pilot study, there were no significant differences between lesbians and heterosexuals in age, ancestry, country of birth, region of residence in the United States, living arrangements, and work situation. In the cohort study, lesbians were significantly older (41 years, ± 5) compared to heterosexuals (40 years, ± 5). Sixty-six percent of lesbians had never been married compared to 9 percent of heterosexuals in the cohort study. In the cohort study, lesbians were also more likely to be white, live in the western United States, and live either alone or in arrangements other than with a partner or husband compared to heterosexuals.

Table 2 shows the relationship between gender of sexual partners over the participant's lifetime and in the last five years with self-reported sexual orientation. After weighting for stratified sampling, the overall estimate of lifetime sexual experience with women is 1.9 percent (95 percent confidence interval [95% CI]: 1.0, 2.8) and the overall estimate of sexual experience with women in the last five years is 1.3 percent (95% CI: 0.6, 1.9). Overall, a small proportion of the sample did not provide information on gender of sexual partners: 1.9 percent (95% CI: 0.7, 3.0) of the women in the pilot study did not answer the question about gender of sexual partners over their adult lifetime, and 5.3 percent (95% CI: 3.3, 7.3) did not answer the question with respect to the last five years. Among women who described themselves as heterosexual, 1.2 percent declined to answer gender of sexual partners over their lifetime and 4.7 percent did not provide data on sexual partners in the last five years. All of the women who described themselves as lesbian answered both questions on gender of sexual partners.

Reliability of the sexual orientation question is shown in Table 3. Of the 824 women who responded to the pilot study mailing, 782 (95.0%) also responded to the 1995 cohort questionnaire. The percent concordance in the lesbian and heterosexual categories was nearly perfect: 100 percent of women who classified themselves as lesbians and 99.3 percent of those who classified themselves as heterosexual on the pilot study placed themselves in the same categories on the cohort questionnaire eight months later. Of the four women who identified themselves as bisexual on the pilot study, three reclassified themselves, two as het-

TABLE 1. Prevalence of Demographic Variables by Sexual Orientation

| | Pilot Study[1,2,3] | | | Cohort Study[1] | | | | |
| | Hetero-sexual n = 788 | Lesbian n = 26 | | Hetero-sexual n = 89,812 | Lesbian n = 694 | | Bisexual n = 317 | |
	%	%	p-value	%	%	p-value	%	p-value
Age in 1995			0.07			< 0.01		0.08
30-35	18.7	19.0		18.4	13.1		12.9	
36-40	34.2	11.6		32.6	31.1		33.1	
41-45	30.5	42.3		32.8	33.9		36.6	
>45	16.6	27.1		16.1	21.9		17.4	
Ancestry			0.3			< 0.01		1.0
White	93.2	96.2		92.4	95.7		92.4	
Non-white	6.8	3.8		7.6	4.3		7.6	
Country of birth			0.9			0.3		0.3
U.S.	96.0	96.2		96.8	96.1		97.9	
Non-U.S.	4.0	3.8		3.2	3.9		2.1	
Current residence			0.9			< 0.01		< 0.01
Northeast	36.8	30.6		33.9	32.3		34.7	
Midwest	30.2	27.1		33.4	21.3		21.5	
South	18.4	15.4		17.8	18.4		17.7	
West	14.6	26.8		14.9	28.0		26.2	

TABLE 1 (continued)

| | Pilot Study[1,2,3] | | | Cohort Study[1] | | | | |
	Heterosexual n = 788 %	Lesbian n = 26 %	p-value	Heterosexual n = 89,812 %	Lesbian n = 694 %	p-value	Bisexual n = 317 %	p-value
Marital status								
Never married	29.6	80.8	< 0.01	8.5	65.6	< 0.01	30.1	< 0.01
Previously married	34.5	19.2		10.2	26.7		29.8	
Married	36.0	0.0		81.4	7.7		40.1	
Living Arrangements								
Alone	8.3	34.5	0.1	8.7	22.7	< 0.01	19.7	< 0.01
With husband/ partner	83.1	26.8		83.4	49.6		57.4	
Other arrangement	8.6	38.7		7.9	27.7		22.8	

[1]Missing data excluded from the analysis.

[2]Due to the small number of women who described their sexual orientation as other than lesbian or heterosexual, in the pilot study, only lesbians and heterosexual women were compared.

[3]Pilot data are adjusted for sample produced by stratified sampling by marital status in three equal groups with marital status data presented unweighted.

TABLE 2. Sexual Orientation and Gender of Sexual Partners in the Last Five Years and Lifetime (n = 823)[1]

	Gender of Sexual Partners				
Sexual Orientation	No partners %	Women only %	Men only %	Both women and men %	Other[2] %
In Last Five Years					
Heterosexual	2.6	0.0	92.3	0.4	4.7
Bisexual	24.5	0.0	51.0	0.0	24.5
Lesbian	3.8	96.2	0.0	0.0	0.0
Other[3]	0.0	0.0	0.0	0.0	100.0
In Lifetime					
Heterosexual	1.5	0.0	96.3	1.0	1.2
Bisexual	24.5	0.0	24.5	51.0	0.0
Lesbian	3.8	42.0	7.9	46.4	0.0
Other[3]	0.0	0.0	0.0	0.0	100.0

[1]Data weighted for stratified sampling by marital status.
[2]Other category for last five years and lifetime partners includes those who responded "prefer not to answer" and those who left the question blank.
[3]Other category for sexual orientation includes those who responded "prefer not to answer" and those who left the question blank. One woman responded "none of the above" and was excluded.

erosexual and one as a lesbian. One woman reported a heterosexual orientation on the pilot and a bisexual orientation on the cohort study. Of the six women who declined to state a sexual orientation on the pilot study, three classified themselves as heterosexual on the cohort study.

DISCUSSION

Some investigators were concerned that asking questions about a sensitive topic such as sexual orientation would increase the rate of attrition from the cohort. Contrary to fears that women might be reluctant to disclose their sexual orientation, only 0.7 percent of responding participants in the pilot study and 0.8 percent of participants in the cohort study declined to classify themselves in one of three sexual orientation categories–lesbian, bisexual and heterosexual. In contrast, Bradford and her colleagues reported that 6 percent of 520 women participating

TABLE 3. Reliability of Sexual Orientation Over Eight-Month Period: Concordance Between Responses on the Pilot Study and Cohort Questionnaires (n = 781)

	Cohort Study			
	Heterosexual %	Bisexual %	Lesbian %	Other[2] %
Pilot Study				
Heterosexual	**99.3**	0.1	0.0	0.5
Bisexual	50.0	**25.0**	25.0	0.0
Lesbian	0.0	0.0	**100.0**	0.0
Other[3]	50.0	0.0	0.0	**50.0**

[1]Only subjects who responded to both the pilot and cohort questionnaire are included.

[2]Other category for cohort study includes those who responded "prefer not to answer" and those who left the question blank. The 124 women who responded "none of the above" were excluded.

[3]Other category for the pilot study includes those who responded "prefer not to answer" and those who left the question blank. One woman responded "none of the above" and was excluded.

in a telephone survey declined to disclose their sexual orientation.[28] Participants were willing to state their sexual orientation and the question as written appeared acceptable to the vast majority of participants. Many women who participated in the pilot study offered thoughtful comments on the structure of the pilot question and suggestions for future research. Reliability of the question was high.

In the pilot study, participants were slightly more willing to state their sexual orientation than they were to answer the question about gender of sexual partners. This difference is primarily explained by heterosexual women declining to answer the question about gender of sexual partners in the past five years: Almost 5 percent of heterosexual women did not report the gender of partners in the previous five years, compared to only 1 percent who did not provide this information on lifetime partners. Among lesbian women, 100 percent answered both questions.

There is no evidence in our data that women stopped participating in the cohort study due to either pilot testing of the sexual orientation and behavior questions or because of the addition of the question on sexual orientation to the cohort questionnaire. The overall response rates to the cohort questionnaire mailings remained high after the introduction of the question. Between 1991 and 1993, before the inclusion of the question about sexual orientation on the form, there was an increase of 1.3 percent in the return of mailed study forms (from 93.3 percent in 1991 to 94.6 percent in 1993), and in 1995, after the inclusion of the sexual orientation question on the study form there was a 1.6 percent increase in return of study forms (from 94.6 percent in 1993 to 96.2 percent in 1995).

In the cohort study, 0.8 percent of the women were lesbians and 0.3 percent were bisexual, figures generally consistent with other reported population estimates.[22,28] In studies using probability sampling, reported prevalence of a lesbian or bisexual orientation was 1.4 percent in a national study (0.9 percent lesbian, 0.5 percent bisexual),[22] and 1.8 percent in a telephone study of women.[28] The Women Physicians Health Study, a stratified random sample of women ages 30 to 70 with medical degrees in the United States, found 2% identified as lesbians and 1.2% as bisexual.[29] Higher prevalence estimates of lesbian and bisexual sexual orientation have been reported in special populations, for example, cohorts of women at high risk for HIV infection,[30] but these groups are not representative of the U.S. general population nor comparable with the present study population.

Overall, an estimated 1.9 percent of women in the pilot study reported sex with another woman in their lifetime, nearly twice the number that reported a sexual orientation of lesbian or bisexual. This estimate is consistent with results from the Women's Health Initiative (WHI), a large cohort of older women ages 50-79 that uses a mailed survey. WHI found 1.4 percent of women reported same-sex partners during their lifetime.[4] The NHS estimate is lower than some other reported lifetime prevalence figures for homosexual behavior among women. Laumann and his colleagues found that, among women ages 18-59, 4.3 percent of women reported a female partner in their adult lifetime.[22] In the 1993 General Social Survey, a national cross-section constructed using probability sampling, 4 percent of sexually active women report at least one female partner since age 18.[31] The Women Physicians Health Study, found 2.3% of the sample reported currently being sexually active with women, but information on lifetime sexual partners was not collected.[29]

The willingness to disclose sexual orientation is a prerequisite for prevalence estimates, and thus unmeasured are the social factors such as fear of stigma, which prevent disclosure. A limitation of the pilot study is that 22 percent of the sample did not return the study form. This could result in biased estimates of the prevalence of sexual orientation groups if the response rate differed significantly by sexual orientation. The response rate to the pilot study differed by marital status. Among never married participants, where 81 percent of the lesbians were found, the response rate was 7 percent lower than in the married participants. However, this difference was not observed eight months later in the cohort study, when the response rates to the first mailing of study forms were not significantly different by marital status, and the response rate of never married participants was 0.2 percent lower than married participants. One explanation for the lower response rate by never married women in the pilot study might relate to the ordering of the pilot questions. Women were first asked about breast-feeding, then about sexual orientation. It is possible that women who had not breast-fed thought the pilot questions did not pertain to them and skipped the second part with the sexual orientation items. Disclosure fears may also have contributed to the lower response rate by never married women in the pilot study. While most participants answered the question, fear of disclosure was illustrated by one respondent in the pilot study who categorized herself as a lesbian, carefully tore off her identification number, and mailed the study form back. The cost of long-standing societal discrimination for our research is seen in the tension implicit in the response of a woman who was willing to respond to the study and yet took precautions against identification.

While the rates of disclosure are encouraging, researchers should be cautioned against overgeneralizing the results. Members of the Nurses' Health Study Cohort have a longstanding relationship with the researchers. Participants have responded to questionnaires, mailed back biological specimens such as blood samples, and regularly been asked to assess their health and respond to detailed questions about their medical history. Participants have had many opportunities to assess the confidentiality standards of the project and tend to be loyal and well motivated. The response rates may in part be attributed to this loyalty and it is difficult to say whether participants in other types of studies will be as responsive.

Another limitation of the Nurses Health Study II is to be found in the homogeneity of the cohort with respect to the race/ethnicity of the participants, occupational class, educational levels, and access to health care. It is impossible to say how different or similar participants in the NHS II are from all lesbian or bisexual women in the United States. However our estimate of the prevalence of lesbian sexual orientation is similar to those obtained by national surveys using probability sampling techniques[22] and our estimate of the prevalence of same-sex sexual behavior is consistent with that of an older, more heterogeneous study population (the WHI).[32] These points suggest that there are important similarities between the lesbian and bisexual women in the Nurses' Health Study II and in the general population.

As presented in Table 1, few differences were found comparing lesbians and heterosexual women in the pilot study, while many were observed in the cohort study. Importantly, the cohort study's power to detect differences between the two groups was orders of magnitude larger than that of the pilot study.

Sexual orientation is understood to be a multidimensional construct with three primary dimensions: identity, behavior, and attraction.[29,33-37] Each domain covers a constellation of experiences relating to sexual orientation that are overlapping but not identical. People may respond differently to questions tapping the different domains. For example, someone who reports same-sex sexual behavior or attraction may not identify as gay, lesbian, or bisexual. Similarly, someone may report same-sex sexual attractions and identity but may not have yet had sex with someone of the same sex. Mechanisms underlying associations between sexual orientation and health behaviors will vary depending on which domain of sexual orientation is under study. In this pilot study, the two domains of identity and behavior were measured, with one question on identity and another on gender of sexual partners.

While reliability of the questions on sexual orientation was extremely high, validity of the questions remains unmeasured. In addition to being multidimensional, sexual orientation is dynamic and may change over the life course.[38] Five women reported a different sexual orientation on the cohort study than they reported eight months previously on the pilot study. It is possible that these women misclassified themselves unintentionally on either the pilot or the cohort questionnaires, misreading the word bisexual to mean heterosexual, for example, or that they felt their sexual orientation changed over the eight-month period. Sexual orientation was stable for the vast majority of women responding to the pilot and cohort surveys; however, it is possible that in earlier phases of their lives, their sexual orientation was different. In some ways, the question is a proxy for an individual's willingness to publicly disclose her orientation, and the degree to which, for example, lesbians may have intentionally misclassified themselves as heterosexual is unknown and unmeasured.

In this study, 3.8 percent of lesbian women reported no sex partners in the last five years. Sole reliance on a behavioral definition of sexual orientation, defining a lesbian as one who reported same-sex behavior, would not have captured these women or their heterosexual and bisexual counterparts without current partners.

After the pilot test of potential questions for inclusion, we chose to include the item on sexual orientation rather than gender of partners on the 1995 cohort questionnaire. For studies of sexually transmitted infections, gender of sexual partners is important data to gather because whether a sexual partner is male or female has direct relationship to the mode and probability of disease transmission. In contrast, our study is focused on illnesses and conditions such as cancer and heart disease with multiple causal behavioral factors that are largely socially patterned, such as smoking, alcohol use, and exercise. Compared to the more narrowly focused item on gender of sexual partners, the item on sexual orientation is expected to serve as a better proxy for categorizing study participants in terms of their social experience as a lesbian, bisexual, or heterosexual woman in our society.

However, we also found a high degree of concordance between sexual identity and gender of sexual partners in the previous five years, with an estimated 96 percent of lesbians reporting sex with women only (none reported male partners within the last five years) and an estimated 92 percent of heterosexuals reporting sex with men only (0.4 percent reported female partners within the last five years). While there was more variation in gender of sexual partners when the time frame included the participant's adult lifetime, a single question about gender of sexual partners without more detailed questions about sexual history, frequency, and behaviors might be too broad to capture possible variations in health related to sexual behavior. Future research measuring validity of various ways to assess sexual identity and behavior would contribute much to an understanding of lesbian and bisexual women's health.

Our results have many implications for future research. The question about sexual orientation was asked once, in 1995, and may be re-asked in the future, which could lead to comparisons in the cohort study of sexual orientation over time. Analyses of health risk factors relative to sexual orientation have been conducted and future papers are planned that will describe differences by sexual orientation in breast cancer and cardiovascular risk factors, mental health, physical functioning, experiences of childhood violence and other topics. Other researchers may be encouraged to add questions on sexual orientation to questionnaires who have more diverse study populations with respect to race and ethnicity, social class, and in more general populations in an effort to contribute to knowledge of all women's health.

AUTHOR NOTE

Patricia Case is Senior Research Scientist at The Fenway Institute, Fenway Community Health. S. Bryn Austin is Assistant Professor in the Division of Adolescent and Young Adult Medicine, Children's Hospital, Harvard Medical School, and in the Department of Society, Human Development, and Health and Social Behavior, Harvard School of Public Health. David J. Hunter is the Vincent L. Gregory Professor in Cancer Prevention in the Departments of Epidemiology and Nutrition at the Harvard School of Public Health. Walter C. Willett is Professor of Epidemiology and Nutrition, and Chair of the Department of Nutrition at the Harvard School of Public Health. Susan Malspeis is a Biostatistician for the Nurses' Health Study II. JoAnn E. Manson is Chief of the Division of Preventive Medicine at Brigham and Women's Hospital, Professor of Medicine at Harvard Medical School, and Professor of Epidemiology at the Harvard School of Public Health. Donna Spiegelman is Professor of Epidemiologic Methods in the Departments of Epidemiology and Biostatistics at the Harvard School of Public Health. Correspondence may be addressed: Patricia Case, The Fenway Institute, Fenway Community Health, 7 Haviland Street, Boston MA 02115.

The work reported in this manuscript was supported by CA50385, the main Nurses' Health Study II grant. The Nurses' Health Study II is supported for other specific projects by the following NIH grants: CA55075, CA67262, AG/CA14742, CA67883, CA65725, DK52866, HL64108, HL03804. In addition, for activities related to the Nurses' Health Study, we have received modest additional resources at various times and for varying periods since January 1, 1993, from the Alcoholic Beverage Medical Research Foundation, the American Cancer Society, Amgen, the California Prune Board, the Centers for Disease Control and Prevention, the Ellison Medical Foundation, the Florida Citrus Growers, the Glaucoma Medical Research Foundation, GlaxoSmithKline, Hoffmann-LaRoche, Kellogg's, Lederle, the Massachusetts Department of Public Health, Mission Pharmacal, the National Dairy Council, Rhone Poulenc Rorer, the Robert Wood Johnson Foundation, Roche, Sandoz, the U.S. Department of Defense, the U.S. Department of Agriculture, the Wallace Genetics Fund, Wyeth-Ayerst, and private contributions.

REFERENCES

1. Aaron DJ, Markovic N, Danielson ME, Honnold JA, Janosky JE, Schmidt NJ. Behavioral risk factors for disease and preventive health practices among lesbians. *Am J Public Health.* 2001;91(6):972-975.

2. Cochran SD, Mays VM, Bowen D, et al. Cancer-related risk indicators and preventive screening behaviors among lesbians and bisexual women. *Am J Public Health.* 2001;91(4):591-597.

3. Gruskin EP, Hart S, Gordon N, Ackerson L. Patterns of cigarette smoking and alcohol use among lesbians and bisexual women enrolled in a large health maintenance organization. *Am J Public Health.* 2001;91(6):976-979.

4. Valanis BG, Bowen DJ, Bassford T, Whitlock E, Charney P, Carter RA. Sexual orientation and health: comparisons in the women's health initiative sample. *Arch Fam Med.* 2000;9(9):843-853.

5. Deevy S. Older lesbian women: An invisible minority. *J Gerontol Nurs.* 1990; 16:35-39.

6. Fifield LH, Latham JD, Phillips C. *Alcoholism in the Gay community: The price of alienation, isolation, and oppression.* Los Angeles, CA: The Gay Community Services Center; 1977.

7. Israelstam S, Lambert S. Homosexuality and alcohol: Observations and research after the psychoanalytic era. *The Int J Addict.* 1986;21(4 & 5):509-537.

8. Saghir MT, Robins E, Walbran B, Gentry KA. Homosexuality. IV. Psychiatric disorders and disability in the female homosexual. *Am J Psychiatry.* 1970;127(2): 147-154.

9. Bradford J, Ryan C. *The National Lesbian Health Care Survey.* Washington, DC: National Lesbian and Gay Health Foundation.; 1988.

10. Biddle BS. *Health Status Indicators for Washington Area Lesbians and Bisexual Women: A Report on the Lesbian Health Clinic's First Year, 1993.* Washington, DC: Whitman-Walker Clinic; 1993.

11. Bybee D. *The Michigan Lesbian Health Survey: A Report to the Michigan Organization for Human Rights.* Lansing, MI: Michigan Department of Public Health; 1991.

12. Johnson SR, Smith EM, Guenther SM. Comparison of gynecologic health problems between lesbian and bisexual women. *J Reprod Med.* 1987;32:805-811.

13. Rankow EJ. Breast and cervical cancer among lesbians. *Womens Health Issues.* 1995;5:123-129.

14. Robertson P, Schacter J. Failure to identify venereal disease in a lesbian population. *Sex Transm Dis.* 1981;8:75-77.

15. Cochran SD, Mays VM. Disclosure of sexual preference to physicians by black lesbian and bisexual women. *West J Med.* 1988;149:616-619.

16. Denenberg R. Report on lesbian health. *Womens Health Issues.* 1995;5(2):1995.

17. Michigan Organization for Human Rights. *The Michigan Lesbian Health Survey.* Lansing, MI 1991.

18. Price JH, Easton AN, Telljohann SK, Wallace PB. Perceptions of cervical cancer and Pap smear screening behavior by women's sexual orientation. *J Community Health.* 1996;21(2):89-105.

19. Rankow EJ, Tessaro I. Cervical cancer risk and Papanicolaou screening in a sample of lesbian and bisexual women. *J Fam Pract.* 1998;47(2):139-143.

20. O'Hanlan KA. A review of the medical consequences of homophobia with suggestions for resolution. *Journal of the Gay and Lesbian Medical Association.* 1997; 1(1):25-39.

21. Solarz AL, ed. *Lesbian Health: Current Assessment and Directions for the Future.* Washington, DC: Institute of Medicine; 1999.

22. Laumann EO. *The Social Organization of Sexuality: Sexual Practices in the United States.* Chicago: University of Chicago Press; 1994.

23. Solomon CG, Willett WC, Carey VJ, et al. A prospective study of pregravid determinants of gestational diabetes mellitus. *JAMA.* 1997;278(13):1078-1083.

24. Women's Health Initiative Study Group. Design of the Women's Health Initiative clinical trial and observational study. *Control Clin Trials.* 1998;19:61-109.

25. SAS Institute Inc. *SAS Procedures Guide, Release 6.03 Edition.* Cary, NC: SAS Institute Inc.; 1988.

26. Cochran WG. *Sampling Techniques.* 2nd ed. New York City: John Wiley & Sons; 1963.

27. Holmes MD, Stampfer MJ, Wolf AM, et al. Can behavioral risk factors explain the difference in body mass index between African-American and European-American women? *Ethn Dis.* 1998;8(3):331-339.

28. Bradford J, Honnold JA, Ryan C. Disclosure of sexual orientation in survey research on women. *Journal of the Gay and Lesbian Medical Association.* 1997;1(3): 169-177.

29. Brogan D, Frank E, Elon L, O'Hanlan KA. Methodologic concerns in defining lesbian for health research. *Epidemiology.* 2001;12(1):109-113.

30. Barkan SE, Melnick SL, Preston-Martin S, et al. The Women's Interagency HIV Study. *Epidemiology.* 1998;9(2):117-125.

31. Smith TW. *The Demography of Sexual Behavior.* Henry J. Kaiser Foundation; 1994.

32. Valanis BG, Bowen DJ, Bassford T, Whitlock E, Charney P, Carter RA. Sexual orientation and health: comparisons in the Women's health initiative sample [In Process Citation]. *Arch Fam Med.* 2000;9(9):843-853.

33. Chung YB, Katayama M. Assessment of sexual orientation in lesbian/gay/bisexual studies. *J Homosex.* 1996;30(4):49-62.

34. Institute of Medicine. *Lesbian Health: Current Assessment and Directions for the Future.* Washington DC: National Academy Press; 1999.

35. Sell RL, Petrulio C. Sampling homosexuals, bisexuals, gays, and lesbians for public health research: a review of the literature from 1990 to 1992. *J Homosex.* 1996;30(4):31-47.

36. Sell RL, Becker JB. Sexual orientation data collection and progress toward Healthy People 2010. *Am J Public Health.* 2001;91(6):876-882.

37. Shively M, Jones D, De Cecco J. *Research on sexual orientation: definitions and methods.* New York: Harrington Park Press; 1985.

38. Chung YB, Katayama M. Assessment of sexual orientation in lesbian/gay/bisexual studies. *J Homosex.* 1996;30(4):49-62.

Mental Health Issues:
A Comparison of Lesbian, Bisexual and Heterosexual Women

Audrey S. Koh, MD

School of Medicine, University of California, San Francisco

Leslie K. Ross, PhD

School of Nursing, University of California, San Francisco

SUMMARY. This study examines mental health issues among women of different sexual orientations. An anonymous survey was administered at 33 health care sites across the United States; the sample (N = 1304) included lesbians (n = 524), bisexual (n = 143) and heterosexual women (n = 637). Not only did sexual orientation influence the probability of experi-

Audrey S. Koh is on the Clinical Faculty, Department of Obstetrics, Gynecology and Reproductive Sciences, School of Medicine, University of California, San Francisco. Leslie K. Ross is Specialist, Institute for Health and Aging, School of Nursing, University of California, San Francisco, and Advisory Council member for the National Center for Lesbian Health Research, University of California, San Francisco. Correspondence may be addressed: Audrey S. Koh, MD, 2100 Webster Street, Suite 427, San Francisco, CA 94115. Data analysis was supported by the Lesbian Health Fund of the Gay and Lesbian Medical Association. The authors wish to thank Suzanne L. Dibble, DNSc, Co-Director, Center for Lesbian Research, University of California, San Francisco for her inspiration and encouragement of this analysis.

[Haworth co-indexing entry note]: "Mental Health Issues: A Comparison of Lesbian, Bisexual and Heterosexual Women." Koh, Audrey S., and Leslie K. Ross. Co-published simultaneously in *Journal of Homosexuality* (Harrington Park Press, an imprint of The Haworth Press, Inc.) Vol. 51, No. 1, 2006, pp. 33-57; and: *Current Issues in Lesbian, Gay, Bisexual, and Transgender Health* (ed: Jay Harcourt) Harrington Park Press, an imprint of The Haworth Press, Inc., 2006, pp. 33-57. Single or multiple copies of this article are available for a fee from The Haworth Document Delivery Service [1-800-HAWORTH, 9:00 a.m. - 5:00 p.m. (EST). E-mail address: docdelivery@haworthpress.com].

encing emotional stress, but also whether a bisexual woman or lesbian had disclosed her sexual orientation (was "out") impacted the likelihood of having or having had mental health problems. Bisexual women and lesbians experienced more emotional stress as teenagers than did heterosexual women. Bisexual women were more than twice as likely to have had an eating disorder compared to lesbians. If a bisexual woman reported being out she was twice as likely to have had an eating disorder compared to a heterosexual woman. Lesbians who were not out and bisexual women who were out were 2-2.5 times more likely to experience suicidal ideation in the past 12 months. Lesbians and bisexual women who were not out were more likely to have had a suicide attempt compared to heterosexual women. Lesbians used psychotherapy for depression more commonly than did heterosexual or bisexual women. This is one of the few studies that compares lesbians, bisexual and heterosexual women. The implications of these findings are discussed. *[Article copies available for a fee from The Haworth Document Delivery Service: 1-800-HAWORTH. E-mail address: <docdelivery@haworthpress.com> Website: <http://www.HaworthPress.com> © 2006 by The Haworth Press, Inc. All rights reserved.]*

KEYWORDS. Sexual orientation, mental health, lesbian, bisexual women, sexual orientation disclosure, suicidality, eating disorders, methodology

A large body of epidemiological research has identified factors that place people at risk for mental health problems. Gender differences–with women affected at higher rates than men–exist for many of these problems, including anxiety, eating disorders, depression and suicidality (Kessler et al., 1994). However, information on sexual orientation has not been routinely included in this research, so it is not possible to draw conclusions about how or whether a woman's sexual orientation impacts her mental health status (Institute of Medicine, 1999; Rothblum, 1994).

Women who self-identify as lesbian or bisexual may experience stressors as members of a minority group in a heterosexual macro-culture, namely, stigmatization, discrimination and isolation. A study by Krieger and Sidney (1997) found that among 25 to 37 year-olds who had at least one same-sex sexual partner, 33% of African-American women and 56% of Caucasian women reported experiencing discrimination based on sexual orientation. The impact of these negative influences has been posited to adversely affect the mental health of lesbians (Institute of Medicine, 1999). This hypothesis was verified in a study by Mays and Cochran (2001) wherein lesbian and bisexual women–as compared to heterosexual women–reported higher frequencies of discrimination, which in turn, was associated with psychiatric morbidity.

The research that has been done on lesbians and mental health issues paints a mixed picture. Several studies suggest that disorders such as stress/anxiety and depression are equally common in the lesbian and heterosexual women populations (Bradford, Ryan and Rothblum, 1994; Hughes, Haas and Avery, 1997; Cochran and Mays, 1999; Rothblum and Factor, 2001). Despite equal rates of depressive illness, lesbians utilize psychotherapy and counseling services at higher rates than the general population (Bradford et al., 1994; Hughes et al., 1997; Cochran and Mays, 1999; Sorensen and Roberts, 1997; Rothblum and Factor, 2001). Teen stress, and suicidality–including suicide attempts–are reported at higher rates among lesbians compared to heterosexual women in some studies (Garofalo, Wolf, Kessel, Palfrey and DuRant, 1998; Hughes et al., 1997). However, in population-based studies, equal rates of suicidality are reported among teen women respondents (Remafedi, French, Story, Resnick and Blum, 1998; Garofalo, Wolf, Wissow, Woods and Goodman, 1999). Finally, eating disorders are reported to afflict lesbians at a lower rate than heterosexual women (Brand, Rothblum and Solomon, 1992; Siever, 1994).

Many of the studies done on lesbians and mental health have methodological problems. Many studies lack a comparison group, or the comparison group is a non-matched sample or the sample size is small. There are very few studies whatsoever evaluating bisexual women and their mental health.

The largest survey of lesbians and mental health issues to date is the National Lesbian Health Care Survey of 1,925 lesbians from 50 states. The conclusions from this convenience sample study are limited by the lack of a heterosexual comparison group. Prevalences of mental disorders for heterosexual women in this study were based on published figures for women in the general population.

Three recent studies begin to address some of these methodological problems by including valid comparison groups. Hughes, Haas and Avery (1997) administered a survey to 284 lesbians and a control group of heterosexual women in three US metropolises. Lesbian respondents were instructed to give a second copy of the survey to a heterosexual woman friend, acquaintance or colleague with a work role similar to her own. Lesbian and heterosexual women had equal rates of: a history of depression; and having had serious thoughts of killing themselves in the past. However, significantly more lesbians than heterosexual women reported previous suicide attempts (18% vs. 8%, respectively).

An analysis of the 1996 National Household Survey of Drug Abuse, a population-based survey, compared psychiatric disorders in 5,792 heterosexual women and 96 women with at least one female sexual partner (Cochran and Mays, 1999). No clear differences between the heterosexual women and the lesbian/bisexual women were found in one-year prevalence for generalized anxiety disorders or major depression. Women with a history of having been with female sexual partners did use mental health and substance abuse services more often compared to heterosexual women (15% vs. 6%). This is one of the few population-based surveys to look at mental health issues of women of different sexual orientations. However, lesbian and bisexual women were not separately evaluated, but rather, grouped together.

Rothblum and Factor (2001) conceived a novel design methodology to obtain comparable samples when examining how sexual orientation may impact mental health. They studied 314 lesbians and used the respondents' sisters as a control group. Demographic and mental health factors were compared. They found that bisexual women (some of the control group sisters were bisexual) had poorer mental health than the heterosexuals (who comprised most of the control group) or lesbians on two measures of overall mental health.

It has been theorized that lesbians who make their sexual orientation known to family, friends and/or coworkers (i.e., those who are "out of the closet"), have better mental health than lesbians who are closeted. Disclosure of lesbian identity has been associated with less anxiety, more positive affectivity and higher self-esteem (Jordan and Deluty, 1998). Further, lesbians who are out are more likely to align with peer groups and receive social support, which can diminish the likelihood of mental disorders (Morris et al., 2001; Oetjen and Rothblum, 2000). Thus, being out can be associated with positive mental health. An alternative theory is that lesbians who come out are more prone to experience anti-lesbian discrimination or violence, and therefore experience increased mental stress (Herek, Gillis, Cogan and Glunt, 1997). There is no known data on bisexual women and outness.

This study was designed to compare the mental health status of lesbian, bisexual and heterosexual women and to examine the effect of sexual orientation disclosure or outness on mental health. It is an analysis of a large data set that examined preventive health behaviors and health care access issues of 1,304 women attending health care offices in 1996-97 (Koh, 2000; van Dam, Koh and Dibble, 2001). The following outcome variables were analyzed: (a) feeling stressed and anxious, as a teen, or as an adult; (b) history of eating disorders; (c) history of receiving treatment for depression; (d) frequency of suicidal ideation in the past 12 months; (e) history of suicide attempt(s) and (f) use of treatment interventions such as counseling, psychotropic medications or psychiatric hospitalizations.

METHOD

The data set consisted of 1,304 completed surveys entitled "Promoting Women's Health: Measuring Preventive Health Behaviors and Improving Health Care Access." The written survey instrument was developed by a panel of experts and refined after two pilot tests that resulted in 98 questions about: a patient's access to health care; medical screening tests; general health status; substance use; sexual behaviors and demographic factors. The survey did not state that sexual orientation was a characteristic of interest. There were approximately equal numbers of heterosexual and nonheterosexual women studied. The study protocol was approved by the Institutional Review Board of California Pacific Medical Center in San Francisco.

In an effort to obtain a varied sample of women seeking healthcare, the surveys were distributed to outpatients at 33 health care sites across the United States. This mix of private medical offices and lesbian health clinics were predominantly purveyors of primary care services. Site recruitment was via personal communication between one of the authors (A.K.) and clinicians and via announcements in newsletters and conferences of national lesbian and gay health organizations. At sites known to have a prevalence of lesbians of greater than 30% of women patients (which applied to approximately one half of the sites) surveys were offered to all women patients. At the remaining sites, surveys were distributed to the known lesbian patient and to the next two women patients This distribution method with a 30% threshold was used in an effort to gather heterosexual women respondents in approximately equal numbers to lesbian and bisexual women respondents. A drop box at the clinical site and/or individual business reply envelopes were supplied for the anonymous return of the completed surveys.

Sexual orientation was defined by the patient's self-identification to the following question: "How do you define your sexual orientation?" (Four possible responses were available to choose from: "heterosexual/ straight," "bisexual," "lesbian/gay/homosexual," "unsure.") The sexual orientation item was the primary independent variable in all of the analyses. However, additional analyses were conducted that examined the relationship of self-identified sexual orientation with sexual behavior. Thus, the lifetime gender of sexual partners as well as the current sexual partners (sexual behaviors within the past 12 months) were analyzed. Questions that related to mental health and the sexual orientation question were selected for analysis (see Table 1).

To quantify the self-reports of being "depressed," questions regarding treatment modalities for depression and the duration of such treatments were included. To quantify the self-reports of prior suicidality, questions regarding the presence and number of suicide attempts were included.

DATA ANALYSIS

Statistical Analysis of Study Aims

SAS™ version 8.0 was used for all analyses. Data entry was done with 100% verification via double-keyed entry by a commercial data processing service. Demographic variables and descriptive information regarding drug, alcohol and tobacco use; stress, depression, suicide attempts, psychiatric issues; and eating disorder, weight issues and exercise patterns among the lesbian, bisexual and heterosexual groups were compared via chi-square analysis or ANOVAs (depending on the level of the data). Since history of an eating disorder was a dependent variable, nicotine history, or cigarette smoking, was included because cigarettes are sometimes used as an aid to weight loss or maintenance. Multivariate logistic regressions were conducted to determine the relationship of sexual orientation to several outcome variables that included self reports of: (a) feeling stressed and anxious, as a teenager or as an adult; (b) having had an eating disorders; (c) history of receiving treatment for depression; (d) frequency of suicidal ideation in the past 12 months; (e) history of suicide attempt(s). Multiple regression procedures were used to analyze the use of treatment interventions such as, counseling, medication or hospitalization, since these variables are continuous. If there was a significant difference between the groups on any of the demographic variables or other predictor variables, that variable was included in the multivariate logistic analysis. In addition, duration identified as a lesbian or bisexual and degree of outness was included in all the models. Duration identified with a sexual orien-

TABLE 1. Items Used in the Logistic Regression Analyses from the "Promoting Women's Health: Measuring Preventive Health Behaviors and Improving Health Care Access" Survey

Category	Item	Responses
Sexual Orientation	How do you define your sexual orientation?	Heterosexual/straight; bisexual; lesbian/gay/homosexual; unsure
Ever Stressed and Anxious as a Teenager	As a teenager how do you feel your emotional stress or emotional problems compared to those of your peers?	0 = had none, fewer, about the same emotional stress as others 1 = had more emotional stress/problems than others
Ever Stressed and Anxious as an Adult	During the *past twelve months*, how often have you felt stressed, anxious, or worried?	0 = never, rarely, or sometimes 1 = often or very often
Ever Had an Eating Disorder	Have you ever had an eating disorder?	0 = no 1 = yes (includes anorexia, bulimia, and binge eating)
History of Receiving Treatment for Depression	If you are depressed *now* or have been *in the past*, are you being or have you been treated?	0 = no 1 = yes
Frequency of Suicidal Ideation in the Past 12 Months	In the *past 12 months* have you had thoughts of suicide/ ending your life?	0 = never 1 = occasionally, often, or very often
Ever Attempted Suicide	How you *ever* tried to commit suicide/end your life?	0 = yes 1 = no
Use of Counseling Services	If you are depressed *now* or have been *in the past*, are you being or have you been treated?	Total number of months of psychotherapy, counseling
Use of Psychiatric Medications	If you are depressed *now* or have been *in the past*, are you being or have you been treated?	Total number of months of medication
Use of Psychiatric Hospitalizations	If you are depressed *now* or have been *in the past*, are you being or have you been treated?	Total number of months of hospitalization

tation was dichotomized between less than five years versus greater than or equal to five years. Degree of outness was also dichotomized between being out to less than or equal to 50% of family, friends and co-workers versus being out to more than 50% of family, friends and co-workers.

RESULTS

Demographics. Of 2716 distributed surveys, 1,362 were returned, yielding a 50% response rate. After excluding those surveys with incomplete information about sexual orientation, 1,304 surveys (48%) were available for analysis. This sample of 1,304 women was comprised of three groups: lesbians n = 524; bisexual women n = 143; and heterosexual women n = 637 (see Table 2). The heterosexual women were significantly older than the lesbians and bisexual women, and the lesbians were significantly older than the bisexual group. Lesbians and bisexual women had more education than the heterosexual women. Lesbians had identified with their sexual orientation longer and were more out than the bisexual women. There were significant differences between the groups for race/ethnicity, household and individual income. Significantly more lesbians and heterosexual women than bisexual women were in a married or committed relationship. There were also significant differences between the groups regarding the duration of the committed relationship. Regarding illicit drug use in the past 12 months, not including intravenous drug use, significantly more bisexual women used illicit drugs compared to lesbians and bisexual women (see Table 3). Table 3 also shows that although the bisexual group reported a greater frequency of having had an eating disorder, and the bisexual and heterosexual women had a higher rate of trying to lose weight compared to lesbians, the three groups did not differ in their body mass index or in self-perception of their weight.

Table 4 shows the relationship between self-identified sexual orientation and sexual behaviors. The majority of women, regardless of sexual orientation considered their gender identity to be female. The three groups significantly differed in who they have had sex with over their lifetime. While the majority of heterosexual women have had sex with men and the majority of bisexual women in this study have had sex with both men and women, lesbians are almost equally divided between having had sex only with women (42%) and having had sex with both men and women (54%). The majority of women in this study have

TABLE 2. Demographic Information

	Heterosexual N = 637 %(n)	Bisexual N = 143 %(n)	Lesbian N = 524 %(n)
Age [yrs: mean (sd)]	41.08 (13.08)	36.25 (9.71)	39.02 (8.63)***
Education [yrs: mean (sd)]	15.94 (2.54)	16.59 (2.52)	16.89 (2.46)***
Gender Identity: Female	98.3 (619)	97.9 (137)	96.9 (499)
Transgender	1.7 (11)	2.1 (3)	3.1 (16)
Duration Identified with Sexual Orientation: < 5 yrs.	.32 (2)	21.99 (31)	7.54 (39)
≥ 5 yrs.	99.68 (607)	78.01 (110)	92.46 (478)***
Degree of "Outness" "Out" to more than 50% of family, friends, and coworkers	91.85 (541)	49.30 (70)	71.29 (370)***
Race/Ethnicity:			
American Indian	1.4 (9)	2.1 (3)	1.9 (10)
Hispanic	1.9 (12)	5.7 (8)	3.4 (18)
Asian	4.1 (26)	3.5 (5)	2.7 (14)
Caucasian	82.1 (518)	81.6 (115)	85.2 (445)
African American	8.7 (55)	4.3 (6)	3.4 (18)
Other	1.7 (11)	2.8 (4)	3.3 (17)**
Individual Income: < 20k	34.5 (212)	34.1 (46)	22.8 (119)
20k-< 40k	35.5 (218)	32.6 (44)	34.1 (178)
40k-< 60k	19.5 (120)	22.2 (30)	24.5 (128)
60k-100k	6.8 (42)	8.1 (11)	14.0 (73)
> 100k	3.6 (22)	8.0 (4)	4.6 (24)***
Location of Residence:			
Major City	77.4 (490)	83.9 (120)	80.1 (418)
Small City	14.2 (90)	9.8 (14)	11.9 (62)
Rural	5.8 (37)	4.2 (6)	5.9 (31)
Military Base	.2 (1)	.7 (1)	.2 (1)
Other	2.4 (15)	1.4 (2)	1.9 (10)
Married or in a Committed Relationship	68.8 (436)	60.3 (85)	77.7(405)***
Length of Committed Relationship: < 1 yr.	8.5 (52)	10.2 (14)	10.9 (55)
1-2 yrs.	8.3 (51)	10.9 (15)	12.9 (65)
3-5 yrs.	13.7 (84)	16.8 (23)	19.9 (100)
> 6 yrs.	37.3 (229)	21.2 (29)	33.2 (167)***

*$p < .05$. **$p < .01$. ***$p < .001$.

been sexually active within the past year, with lesbians indicating a greater frequency of having had sex within the past year than bisexual or heterosexual women. Interestingly, there was not a difference between the three groups and their having had a sexual partner within the past year. This may have been due to small sample sizes for this analysis.

TABLE 3. Descriptive Information for Drug, Alcohol, and Tobacco Use; Stress, Depression, Suicide Attempts, Psychiatric Issues; Eating Disorder, Weight Issues, and Exercise Patterns

	Heterosexual N = 637 %(n)	Bisexual N = 143 %(n)	Lesbian N = 524 %(n)
Used Illicit Drugs in the Past 12 mos. (not including IDU)	13.7 (84)	25.5 (35)	16.0 (81)**
# of Drinks per Month [mean (sd)]	13.19 (25.22)	11.46 (19.05)	12.06 (23.26)
Current Smoker	17.90 (114)	21.68 (31)	18.55 (97)
Cigarette Pack [yrs: mean (sd)]	12.00 (16.88)	9.70 (12.96)	11.93 (16.51)
Perceived Mental Health as a Teenager:			
No Problems/Fewer/About the Same as Others	56.63 (316)	40.60 (54)	42.06 (204)
More Problems	43.37 (242)	59.40 (79)	57.94 (281)
Frequency of Currently Feeling Stressed:			
Never, Rarely, or Sometimes	38.51 (243)	31.91 (45)	35.19 (183)
Often or Very Often	61.49 (388)	68.09 (96)	64.81 (337)
Currently Depressed	17.8 (95)	24.3 (28)	11.3 (89)
Ever Treated for Depression	42.1 (268)	53.2 (76)	56.7 (297)***
Ever Tried Suicide	10.2 (63)	21.3 (30)	16.7 (85)***
Freq. Think About Suicide Past 12 mos.			
Never	78.4 (486)	63.4 (90)	71.2 (366)
Occasionally	19.8 (123)	28.2 (40)	23.3 (120)
Often	1.1 (7)	2.8 (4)	3.5 (18)
Very Often	.6 (4)	5.6 (8)	1.9 (10)***
Days Lost Due to Poor Mental Health	3.32 (6.08)	4.43 (7.12)	3.46 (6.15)
# of Suicide Attempts	0.32 (2.34)	0.49 (2.20)	0.34 (1.06)
Age at 1st Suicide Attempt	21.55 (9.11)	16.46 (4.62)	17.88 (6.86)***
Counseling Received (mos)	15.90 (39.73)	20.92 (41.86)	27.30 (49.87)***
Psychiatric Medications Taken (mos)	8.19 (32.49)	8.75 (30.70)	8.08 (21.85)
Psychiatric Hospitalizations (mos)	0.44 (5.52)	0.31 (2.24)	0.37 (3.13)
Body Mass Index [mean (sd)]	25.62 (6.25)	26.10 (7.02)	26.17 (6.16)

	Heterosexual N = 637 %(n)	Bisexual N = 143 %(n)	Lesbian N = 524 %(n)
Ever Had an Eating Disorder (e.g., anorexia, bulimia, binge eating)	12.72 (71)	25.20 (31)	14.38 (68)**
Weight Perception: Underweight	1.9 (12)	2.1 (3)	1.9 (10)
Just right	44.7 (284)	44.4 (63)	45.5 (237)
Overweight	53.5 (340)	53.5 (76)	52.6 (274)
Try to Change Weight: Lose weight	56.0 (349)	50.4 (71)	42.8 (219)
Stay at the same weight	22.6 (141)	24.1 (34)	26.8 (137)
Gain weight	2.2 (14)	2.8 (4)	1.6 (8)
Not trying to change weight	19.1 (119)	22.7 (32)	28.9 (148)***
Frequency of Strenuous Exercise: Never	6.8 (43)	4.9 (7)	4.8 (25)
< 1/mo.	8.0 (51)	6.3 (9)	8.8 (46)
1-3 times/mo.	8.0 (51)	12.6 (18)	10.2 (53)
< 1/wk.	13.9 (88)	14.7 (21)	11.5 (60)
1-2 times/wk.	25.2 (160)	28.0 (40)	27.8 (145)
3+ times/wk.	38.0 (241)	33.6 (48)	37.0 (193)

*$p < .05$. **$p < .01$. ***$p < .001$

Within the past 12 months, bisexual women had significantly more male partners than heterosexual women and lesbians. Heterosexual women had significantly more male partners than lesbians. Bisexual women and lesbians had significantly more gay and bisexual male sexual partners than heterosexual women.

Logistic Regression Analyses

Ever Stressed and Anxious as a Teenager. Bisexual women were slightly more than twice as likely to report having experienced more emotional stress and problems as a teenager than heterosexual women, whereas lesbians were 97% more likely to have experienced teenage stress than heterosexual women (see Table 5). There was no difference between lesbians and bisexual women in the stress and problems they may have experienced as a teenager. There was a slight effect of education level, suggesting that women with more education were slightly less likely to experience emotional stress as a teenager, regardless of sexual orientation.

Ever Stressed and Anxious as an Adult. There was no difference among lesbians, bisexuals and heterosexual women in the frequency of

TABLE 4. Gender Identity and Sexual Behaviors Among Lesbian, Bisexual, and Heterosexual Women

	Heterosexual N = 637 %(n)	Bisexual N = 143 %(n)	Lesbian N = 524 %(n)
Gender identity: Female	98.25 (619)	97.86 (137)	96.89 (499)
Transgender	1.75 (11)	2.14 (3)	3.11 (16)
Sexual Partner as an Adult			
Never	1.74 (11)	0 (0)	0.38 (2)
Men	89.72 (567)	7.25 (10)	3.26 (17)
Women	2.85 (18)	5.80 (8)	42.23 (220)
Men and Women	5.70 (36)	86.96 (120)	54.13 (282)***
Sexually Active Within the Past Year	84.06 (522)	88.24 (120)	91.68 (463)***
# of Female Partners Within the Past Year [mean (sd)]	0.55 (1.21)	1.32 (1.49)	1.57 (4.88)
# of Male Partners Within the Past Year [mean (sd)]	1.44 (1.37)	1.93 (3.05)	0.46 (1.24)***
# of Male Partners Who Were Gay or Bisexual Within the Past Year [mean (sd)]	0.04 (0.28)	0.34 (0.75)	0.31 (0.61)***

TABLE 5. Summary of Logistic Regression Analyses: Level of Stress Experienced as a Teenager and Level of Stress Experienced as an Adult

		95% Confidence Limits	
	Odds Ratio Estimate	Lower Limit	Upper Limit
Level of Stress Experienced as a Teenager (N = 1,095)			
Lesbian vs. Heterosexual	1.96	1.49	2.59***
Bisexual vs. Heterosexual	2.10	1.74	3.28***
Bisexual vs. Lesbian	1.07	.70	1.62
Age	0.99	0.98	1.00*
Education	0.92	0.87	0.97**
Level of Stress Experienced as an Adult (N = 1,148)			
Lesbian vs. Heterosexual	1.01	.76	1.34
Bisexual vs. Heterosexual	1.01	.64	1.60
Bisexual vs. Lesbian	1.00	.65	1.55
Age	0.99	0.97	1.00**
In a Committed Relationship	0.66	0.50	0.88**

*p < .05. **p < .01. ***p < .001

stress they experienced in the past 12 months (see Table 5). Being in a relationship, regardless of sexual orientation, was shown to decrease the likelihood by approximately 34% of often/very often experiencing stress during the past 12 months.

Ever Had an Eating Disorder. Bisexual women were almost twice as likely to have or have had an eating disorder compared to lesbians (see Table 6). Furthermore, if a bisexual woman reported being out to a majority of family, friends and co-workers she had a two-fold increased risk for having had an eating disorder compared to a heterosexual woman. The following variables were significant for increasing the likelihood of having or having had an eating disorder, regardless of sexual orientation: history of or current depression; Hispanic women compared to Caucasians; having experienced teen stress.

History of Receiving Treatment for Depression. Lesbians are 56% and 82% more likely to have received treatment for depression than heterosexual and bisexual women, respectively (see Table 7). In addition, lesbians who are out to a majority of family, friends and co-workers were 63% more likely to have received treatment for depression compared to heterosexual women. Regardless of sexual orientation the following variables were significant for an increased likelihood of having

TABLE 6. Summary of Logistic Regression Analyses: History of an Eating Disorder

		95% Confidence Limits	
	Odds Ratio Estimate	Lower Limit	Upper Limit
Ever Had An Eating Disorder (N = 1,007)			
Lesbian vs. Heterosexual	.79	.52	1.20
Bisexual vs. Heterosexual	1.55	0.89	2.70
Bisexual vs. Lesbian	1.96	1.14	3.39*
"Out" Bisexual vs. Heterosexual	2.02	1.04	3.92*
Age	0.97	0.96	.99**
Depression: Current or History	3.00	1.97	4.71***
Hispanic (reference group = Caucasian)	2.37	1.01	5.56*
Experienced Stress as a Teenager	2.04	1.38	3.04***

*p < .05. **p < .01. ***p < .001

TABLE 7. Summary of Logistic Regression Analyses: History of Receiving Treatment for Depression

	Odds Ratio Estimate	95% Confidence Limits	
		Lower Limit	Upper Limit
Hx of Receiving Treatment for Depression (N = 936)			
Lesbian vs. Heterosexual	1.56	1.12	2.19**
Bisexual vs. Heterosexual	.86	.50	1.46
Lesbian vs. Bisexual	1.82	1.10	3.02*
"Out" Lesbians vs. Heterosexuals	1.63	1.17	2.27**
Experienced Stress as a Teenager	2.73	2.02	3.68***
Suicidal Ideation–Occasionally or very frequently within the past 12 mos.	2.57	1.77	3.72***
History of an Eating Disorder	2.06	1.34	3.18***
Income < $20,000 (reference group = Income > $100,000)	2.08	1.03	4.11*
Experience Stress as an Adult	1.94	1.43	2.64***
African-American (reference group = Caucasian)	0.40	0.19	0.82*
Age	1.02	1.01	1.04***
Education	1.09	1.02	1.17**

$*p < .05.$ $**p < .01.$ $***p < .001$

been treated for depression: experience of stress as an adult in the past 12 months; experience of stress as a teen; have or had an eating disorder; occasional to very frequent suicidal ideation within the past year; income less than $20,000; age and education showed a slight effect. African-Americans were 60% less likely to have received treatment for depression, regardless of sexual orientation.

Frequency of Suicidal Ideation in the Past 12 Months. Lesbians who are undisclosed regarding their sexual orientation are more than 2.5 times more likely to have reported suicidal ideation occasionally or very often compared to heterosexual women (see Table 8). For lesbians who were out, the odds ratio approached significance (OR = 1.47, p = .06). Bisexual women who are "out" are twice as likely to have reported suicidal ideation occasionally or very often compared to heterosexual

TABLE 8. Summary of Logistic Regression Analyses: Frequency of Suicidal Ideation

	Odds Ratio Estimate	95% Confidence Limits	
		Lower Limit	Upper Limit
Freq. of Suicidal Ideation in the Past 12 Mos. (N = 936)			
"Out" Lesbians vs. Heterosexuals	1.47	.991	2.18
Not "Out" Lesbians vs. Heterosexual	2.64	1.62	4.33***
"Out" Bisexuals vs. Heterosexuals	2.17	1.14	4.13*
Not "Out" Bisexuals vs. Heterosexuals	1.83	.901	3.73
Experience Stress as an Adult	3.39	2.30	5.00***
Experienced Stress as a Teenager	2.38	1.70	3.34***
History of an Eating Disorder	1.57	1.05	2.37*
In a Committed Relationship	0.44	0.31	0.61***
Age	0.98	0.96	1.00*
Education	0.93	0.86	1.00*

$*p < .05.$ $**p < .01.$ $***p < .001$

women. Regardless of sexual orientation the following variables significantly increased the likelihood of experiencing suicidal ideation in the past 12 months: experiencing stress often or very often within the past 12 months; having experienced stress as a teenager; and having an eating disorder. The following characteristics decreased the likelihood of occasionally or very often having suicidal ideation within the past 12 months: being older; having more education; and being in a relationship.

Ever-Attempted Suicide. Lesbians who are undisclosed regarding their sexual identity are 90% more likely to have had a suicide attempt, and bisexual women who are not out are three times more likely to have had a suicide attempt than heterosexual women (see Table 9). Regardless of sexual orientation the following variables significantly increased the likelihood of having had attempted suicide: suicidal ideation that is experienced occasionally or very often; experience of teen stress; having or having had an eating disorder; women whose ethnic background is American Indian.

Use of Counseling Services. If a woman's identified sexual orientation is lesbian, this predicted greater use of counseling services (see Table 10). Although lesbian sexual orientation was significant, it explained the least amount of variance in the overall model.

TABLE 9. Summary of Logistic Regression Analyses: History of Suicide Attempts

	Odds Ratio Estimate	95% Confidence Limits	
		Lower Limit	Upper Limit
Ever Attempted Suicide (N = 925)			
Lesbian vs. Heterosexual	1.84	1.01	3.08*
Bisexual vs. Heterosexual	1.95	.95	3.99
Bisexual vs. Lesbian	1.06	.57	1.97
"Not Out" Lesbians vs. Heterosexuals	1.90	1.02	3.54*
"Not Out" Bisexuals vs. Heterosexuals	3.17	1.46	6.87**
American-Indian (reference group = Caucasian)	10.19	3.09	33.61***
Experienced Stress as a Teenager	7.10	4.10	12.30***
Suicidal Ideation–Occasionally or very frequently within the past 12 mos.	2.30	1.52	3.50***
History of an Eating Disorder	2.37	1.49	3.76***

*$p < .05$. **$p < .01$. ***$p < .001$

TABLE 10. Summary of Stepwise Regression Analyses for Variables Predicting Use of Counseling Services (N = 964)

	B	*SE B*	β
Step 1: Ever Had a Suicide Attempt	25.01	4.15	0.19***
Step 2: Suicidal Ideation Occasionally to Very Frequently in the Past 12 Months	22.39	3.28	0.21***
Step 3: Experienced Teen Stress	15.88	2.89	0.17***
Step 4: Age	.54	0.12	0.12***
Step 5: Education	2.05	0.58	0.10***
Step 6: Have an Eating Disorder	10.21	3.87	0.08**
Step 7: Lesbian Sexual Orientation	6.95	2.78	0.07*

Note. $R^2 = .09$ for Step 1; $\Delta R^2 = .05$ for Step 2; $\Delta R^2 = .03$ for Step 3; $\Delta R^2 = .02$ for Step 4; $\Delta R^2 = .01$ for Step 5; $\Delta R^2 = .005$ for Step 6; $\Delta R^2 = .005$ for Step 7 ($ps < .05$).
*$p < .05$. **$p < .01$. ***$p < .001$

Use of Psychiatric Medications/Psychiatric Hospitalizations. The interaction effects of sexual orientation by degree of "outness" or duration a women identified with her sexual orientation was nonsignificant, as was the main effect for sexual orientation (see Tables 11 and 12).

DISCUSSION

The results of this study suggest that sexual orientation per se, does not result in psychiatric disorders or symptoms. Rather, the development of psychiatric disorders or symptoms appears to be associated

TABLE 11. Summary of Stepwise Regression Analyses for Variables Predicting Use of Psychiatric Medications (N = 964)

		B	SE B	β
Step 1:	Experienced Teen Stress	7.77	1.78	0.14***
Step 2:	Ever Had a Suicide Attempt	10.13	2.57	0.13***
Step 3:	Age	.27	0.08	0.11***
Step 4:	Individual Income Less Than 20K	5.67	1.92	0.09***
Step 5:	Experiences Significant Stress as an Adult in the Past 12 Months	4.50	1.75	0.08**
Step 6:	Have an Eating Disorder	5.96	2.42	0.08**
Step 7:	Used Illicit Drugs in the Past 12 Months	−4.71	2.33	−0.06*

Note. R^2 =.04 for Step 1; ΔR^2 = .02 for Step 2; ΔR^2 = .01 for Step 3; ΔR^2 = .01 for Step 4; ΔR^2 = .01 for Step 5; ΔR^2 = .01 for Step 6; ΔR^2 = .004 for Step 7 (*ps* < .05).

TABLE 12. Summary of Stepwise Regression Analyses for Variables Predicting Use of Psychiatric Hospitalizations (N = 964)

		B	SE B	β
Step 1:	Ever Had a Suicide Attempt	1.44	0.28	0.17***
Step 2:	Suicidal Ideation Occasionally to Very Frequently in the Past 12 Months	.48	0.22	0.07*

Note. R^2 = .03 for Step 1; ΔR^2 = .005 for Step 2 (*ps* < .05).

*p < .05. **p < .01. ***p < .001

with stigmatization. The degree of outness can be taken as an indirect measure of level of comfort a lesbian or bisexual woman feels with her sexual orientation and can influence the degree of stigmatization she may experience. One hypothesis is that when a women discloses her sexual orientation to others, she is more likely to align with peer groups and receive social support that can diminish the likelihood of mental disorders or symptoms (Morris, Waldo and Rothblum, 2001). Conversely, women who are free of psychological disorders may be more able or more empowered to come out. Thus, being out can be associated with positive mental health. An alternative hypothesis is that if a lesbian or bisexual woman is out, she is more prone to experience discrimination or even violence against her, and therefore, experience increased emotional stress (McLeod and Crawford, 1998; Herek et al., 1997).

This study found that the extent to which a lesbian or bisexual woman is out to her family, friends and coworkers is of greater significance to mental health than the duration of time she has identified with a particular sexual orientation. This was especially evident for the experience of suicidal ideation within the past 12 months, history of a suicide attempt(s) and history of an eating disorder.

The results show that lesbians and bisexual women experience more stress than heterosexual women during their teenage years. Teen stress was associated with a 7-fold increase in the likelihood of a suicide attempt. This is consistent with some of the extant literature showing suicide attempts to be 3-7 times higher among gay and lesbian youth as compared to heterosexual youth (Garofalo et al., 1998; Hershberger, Pilkington and D'Augelli, 1997). In this study, lesbian and bisexual women reported suicide attempts at a higher rate than heterosexual women (16.7% and 21.3% vs. 10.2%, respectively). These prevalences are remarkably consistent with suicide attempts by lesbians as reported by Bradford, et al. (18%), Hughes et al. (18%) and Sorenson and Roberts (18%).

The rates of current stress and anxiety were equivalent among the sexual orientation subgroups. Those respondents in a committed relationship were 34% less likely to experience stress often or very often compared to those not in a relationship. This complements the finding by Oetjen and Rothblum (2000) that lesbians in committed relationships have decreased levels of depression. It is unclear whether a committed relationship is protective regarding stress and anxiety, or whether experiencing less stress allows one to maintain a relationship.

An eating disorder history also demonstrated a relationship to being out. Out bisexuals were more likely to have an eating disorder than heterosexual women. It is unclear why this association would be found. Regardless of degree of outness, bisexual women were twice as likely to have had an eating disorder than lesbians. There is no other existing data on bisexual women and eating disorders. Despite the differing rates of eating disorder histories, the B.M.I.s and current self-perceptions of weight were equal among the lesbian, bisexual and heterosexual women subgroups. The findings of this study with respect to the bisexual population and the influence of outness and eating disorders highlight the need for further research in this area.

Lesbians were more likely to utilize or have utilized counseling services for depression compared to the bisexual and heterosexual women respondents (50% versus 45% and 35%, respectively). This held true whether or not the lesbian was out with her sexual identity. Other researchers have also found that lesbians seek counseling for depression at high rates (Bradford et al. −37% and Hughes et al. −37%). Lesbians may seek psychotherapy more readily due to higher levels of trust in the mental health profession or in greater valuation placed on introspective growth compared to heterosexual women (Morgan, 1992). Additionally, lesbians may need and seek more counseling due to their experiences of anti-gay discrimination and stigmatization.

In this study, both lesbian and bisexual women respondents thought about suicide at higher rates than heterosexual women. This contrasts with the only other study with a matched control group, in which equal rates of prior or current suicidal ideation were found between lesbian and heterosexual women (Hughes et al., 1997). There were higher rates of recent suicidal ideation in bisexual women who were disclosed regarding their sexual orientation versus bisexuals who were undisclosed, and in lesbians who were undisclosed versus out lesbians. Additional research should be done to explore the robustness of this result as well as to study why outness might affect bisexual women differently than lesbians. One possible explanation is that bisexual women may feel particularly isolated due to stigmatization from both the heterosexual and lesbian communities. Bisexual women–who might "pass" relatively easily as heterosexuals–may experience more discrimination after disclosing their sexual orientation, thus leading to increased stress and suicidality *after* coming out. In this study, bisexual women were significantly less disclosed than lesbians (49% versus 71%, respectively were out to more than 50% of family, friends and coworkers). Lesbians and bisexual women who are undisclosed are more likely to have had a suicide attempt compared to heterosexual women. This finding conforms to the model presented by Morris, Waldo and Rothblum (2001) wherein greater degrees of outness predicts better psychological health which in turn predicts less suicidality.

The study methodology is a new approach to finding sexual orientation minorities and obtaining a valid control (the sexual orientation majority) group. Due to the preponderance of heterosexuals in the general population, a population-based study yielding a sizable number of lesbian and bisexual women would be an ambitious and expensive (but worthwhile) undertaking.

Thus, studies–including this one–have sought convenience sampling with a valid comparison group. Hughes, Haas and Avery (2001) distributed surveys in lesbian social and organizational settings. Lesbian respondents solicited a work-role control to fill out a second copy of the survey. Rothblum and Factor (2001) distributed surveys in lesbian social settings and by advertising in lesbian periodicals. Lesbian respondents gave a second copy of the survey to their sister. In this study, participants came from health care offices with a diverse sexual orientation clientele; a built-in heterosexual comparison group was thus ensured.

STRENGTHS AND LIMITATIONS

Several factors highlight the importance of this study and the contribution it can make to better understanding lesbian, bisexual and heterosexual women's health. This is the first large study to compare the mental health of lesbian, bisexual and heterosexual women in the health care setting. This study is one of only three that is a convenience sample of lesbians with a heterosexual control group. It is a new approach to obtaining such a sample. By choosing a convenience sample with a significant proportion of women of each sexual orientation, analysis of all three sexual orientation subgroups of women was possible. This is critical given that so little is known about bisexual women's health and that even less is known in direct comparison to lesbian and heterosexual women.

This study is unique among the three studies with heterosexual controls in that an attempt was made to blind the respondents to the fact that sexual orientation was a primary factor of interest. Most of the questions related to sexual orientation were within a subsection on sexual behaviors near the end of the survey. The single sexual orientation self-identification question was immersed in the demographics subsection at the end of the survey. Respondents may have suspected that sexual orientation minorities were being sought due to the study distribution or survey contents, but this was not stated. This strategy may have mitigated sampling bias that might occur when a sub-population (lesbians) know that they are being selected.

The survey was administered in 33 health care settings across the United States, thus, increasing the generalizability of the findings. Multivariate logistic analysis was used to explore the relationship of sexual orientation to the outcome variables. The use of multivariate statistical techniques permits a better understanding of how sexual orientation impacts mental health issues since confounding variables, such as demographic information, can be controlled in the multivariate logistic analysis. Previous studies have relied primarily on bivariate analysis that does not control for potentially confounding variables.

Despite its strengths, most studies have weaknesses that limit the generalizability of the findings and this study is no exception. This is a non-probability sample of women going to health care providers and as such is not representative of women in general (whether heterosexual, bisexual or lesbian). By sampling women attending medical offices, women of higher socioeconomic status are over-represented, compared to the overall population. This is reflected in the study's lesbian composition of primarily Caucasian (83%), highly educated (42% with some graduate school education) and health insured women (88%).

An effort was made to get a more economically and racially diverse sample by including community health and lesbian health clinics. While such clinics made up one-fifth of the sites (7 of 33 sites), their respondents made up only 12% of the total study respondents. The response rate from community health clinics may be related to the economically-diverse clientele at these sites. Caucasian race, higher socioeconomic and higher education levels are all associated with participating in research–these are characteristics that may have been less prevalent among community health clinic attendees. There may be factors at the community clinic sites themselves that contributed to a lower response rate (e.g., an overburdened staff; staff turnover; a plethora of forms and/ or surveys to fill out or non-prominent placement of study materials). Community clinics probably represent a unique environment that requires specific outreach to the populations that they serve. This is a challenge that all research should strive to meet in order to obtain representative samples. The experiences from this study provide some direction to what future studies will need to consider to obtain a more diverse sample.

Additional potential weaknesses of the sample pertain to a predominance of urban sites and a predominance of a few sites: 80% of the respondents came from only 12 of the 33 sites and only half of the 33 sites had significant sexual orientation diversity among their clientele. There is also potential bias from the practitioners who decided to participate in this research. That is, some practitioners may have been more "lesbian-conscious" or "research-conscious" than others and these factors might contribute to a biased sample in some manner. This sample may have an over-abundance of women who feel comfortable about their sexual identities within these health care sites–either because of their own comfort and outness or because they believe the setting is tolerant of all sexual identities. Such women may differ from women in the general population. Finally, due to the sensitive nature of the questions, there might be a reporting bias (i.e., under-reporting) of the mental health issues addressed in this study. Although under-reporting is a potential weakness, it would not lessen the results from this study; rather it emboldens the significance of the findings.

CONCLUSIONS

This study highlights the need for mental health support services for all teenagers, and specifically teenagers who may have a sexual orientation different from the majority. Interventions to help teens respond to homophobic discrimination–both at home, and in society, in general–are crucial given the high reported rates of teenage mental distress, and both suicidal ideation and attempts by bisexual and lesbians respondents. Interventions to help the broader society appreciate the impact of anti-gay and lesbian discrimination are needed (e.g., advocacy programs for lesbian/gay youth; anti-discrimination policies that include sexual orientation in schools and recreational centers; education and support groups for parents of lesbian/gay youth). It is also important for primary care providers to inquire about their patients' sexual orientation and to function as an initial intervention point for mental health services for lesbian, bisexual and "questioning" (those who are unsure of their sexual orientation) patients.

The results from this study demonstrate the importance of examining lesbians and bisexual women as distinct populations in medical research. These two groups of women–but particularly bisexual woman–experienced significantly more emotional stressors as teens and as adults than heterosexual women. There is very little extant research on the mental health of bisexual women. The bisexual women in this study were significantly more closeted and experienced significantly more emotional stressors than lesbians and heterosexual women. This finding of worse mental health in several areas for bisexual women is consistent with the only other controlled sample of women of different sexual orientations (Rothblum et al., 2001).

Additional research is greatly needed to better understand the differences between lesbians, bisexual and heterosexual women, as well as to determine if these differences are reliable and what factors contribute to this dynamic.

This study shows that it cannot be assumed that if a woman is disclosed about her sexual orientation, that she is receiving the social support she needs. Being out can have different implications for lesbians and bisexual women. Further investigation is needed into the interplay of mental health characteristics that predispose to coming out; whether and how being out affects lesbians differently than bisexual women; and how the degree of outness affects both mental and physical health.

Research on lesbian and bisexual women inclusive of a valid (heterosexual women) comparison group is in its early, exciting stages. Additional studies are needed to further examine the mental health conclusions presented here. Exploration of other sampling modalities is needed to continue to piece together the complex, "whole" picture of women's sexual orientation as it relates to their health.

REFERENCES

Bradford, J., Ryan, C., and Rothblum, E. D. (1994). National Lesbian Health Care Survey: Implications for Mental Health Care. *J Consult Clin Psychol*, 62(2), 228-42.

Brand, P.A., Rothblum, E.D., and Solomon, L.J. (1992). A Comparison of Lesbians, Gay Men, and Heterosexuals on Weight and Restrained Eating. *International Journal of Eating Disorders*, *11*(3), 253-259.

Cochran S.D. and Mays V.M. (1999. Are Lesbians More at Risk for Psychiatric Disorders? Evidence from the 1996 National Household Survey of Drug Abuse. Proceedings from the National Conference on Health Statistics, Washington DC. Department of Health and Human Services.

Fergusson, D. M., Horwood, J., and Beatrais, A. L. (1999). Is sexual orientation related to mental health problems and suicidality in young people. *Archives of General Psychiatry*, 56, 876-880.

Garofalo, R., Wolf, R.C., Kessel. S., Palfrey, J. and DuRant, R.H. (1998). The Association Between Health Risk Behaviors and Sexual Orientation among a School-based Sample of Adolescents. *Pediatrics 101*(5), 895-902.

Garofalo, R., Wolf, C., Wisso, L.S., Woods, W.R. and Goodman, E. (1999). Sexual Orientation and Risk of Suicide Attempts Among a Representative Sample of Youth. *Arch Pediatr Adolesc. Med.*153, 487-493.

Herek, G.M., Gillis, J.R., Cogan, J.C. and Glunt, E.K. (1997). Hate Crime Victimization among Lesbian, Gay and Bisexual Adults. *Journal of Interpersonal Violence*, 12, 195-215.

Herrel, R., Goldberg, J., True, W. R., Ramakrisnan, V., Lyons, M., Eison, S., and Tsuang, M. T. (1999). Sexual orientation and suicidality. *Archives of General Psychiatry*, 56, 867-874.

Hershberger, S.L., Pilkington, N.W., D'Augelli, A.R. (1997). Predictors of suicide attempts among gay, lesbian and bisexual youth. *Journal of Adolescent Res.*, 12, 477-497.

Hughes, T. L., Haas, P., and Avery, L. (1997). Lesbians and mental health: Preliminary results from the Chicago Women's Health Survey. *Journal of the Gay and Lesbian Medical Association*, 1(3), 137-148.

Institute of Medicine, Committee of Lesbian Health Research Priorities. (1999). *Lesbian Health: Current Assessment and Directions for the Future*. Washington, DC.: National Academy Press.

Jordan K.M., Deluty R.H. (1988). Coming out for Lesbian Women: Its Relation to Anxiety, Positive Affectivity, Self-Esteem and Social Support. *Journal of Homosexuality*, 35. 41-63.

Kessler R.C., McGonagle K.A., Zhao S., Nelson, C.B., Hughes, M., Eshleman, S., Wittchen, H.U., Kendler, K.S. (1994). Lifetime and 12-month Prevalence of DSM-III-R Psychiatric Disorders in the United States: Results from the National Comorbidity Survey. *Arch Gen Psychiatry*, 51, 8-19.

Koh, A. (2000).Use of Preventive Health Behaviors by Lesbian, Bisexual and Heterosexual Women: Questionnaire Survey. *Western Journal of Medicine*, 172, 379-384.

Krieger, N., and Sidney, S. (1997). Prevalence and health implications of anti-gay discrimination: a study of black and white women and men in the CARDIA cohort. Coronary Artery Risk Development in Young Adults. *Int J Health Serv*, 27(1), 157-76.

Mays, V.M. and Cochran, S.D. (2001). Mental Health Correlates of Perceived Discrimination Among Lesbian, Gay, and Bisexual Adults in the United States. *American Journal of Public Health*, 91(11), 1869-1876.

Morgan, K.S. (1992). Caucasian lesbians' use of psychotherapy: A matter of attitude? *Psychology of Women Quarterly*, 16, 127-130.

Morris, J.F., Waldo, C.R., and Rothblum, E.D. (2001). A model of predictors and outcomes of outness among lesbian and bisexual women. *Am J of Orthopsychiatry*, 71, 61-71.

Oetjen, H., Rothblum, E.D. (2000) When Lesbians aren't Gay: Factors Affecting Depression Among Lesbians. *J of Homosexuality*, 39, 49-73.

Remafedi, G., French, S., Story, M., Resnick, M. and Blum, R.(1998).: The Relationship Between Suicide Risk and Sexual Orientation: Results of a Population-based Study. *Am J Public Health*, 88, 57-60.

Roberts, S. J., and Sorensen, L. (1995). Lesbian health care: a review and recommendations for health promotion in primary care settings. *Nurse Pract*, 20(6), 42-7.

Rothblum, E.D. (1994) "I Only Read About Myself on Bathroom Walls": The Need for Research on the Mental Health of Lesbians and Gay Men. *J of Consulting and Clinical Psychology*, 62(2), 213-220.

Rothblum, E. D. and Factor, R. (2001) "Lesbians and Their Sisters as a Control Group: Demographic and Mental Health Factors. *Psychological Science*, 12(1), 63-69.

Siever, M.D. (1994) "Sexual Orientation and Gender as Factors in Socioculturally Acquired Vulnerability to Body Dissatisfaction and Eating Disorders. *Journal of Consulting and Clinical Psychology*, 62(2), 252-260.

Sorensen, L., Roberts, S.J. (1997) "Lesbian Uses of and Satisfaction with Mental Health Services: Results from Boston Lesbian Health Project" *J of Homosexuality*, 33(1), 35-49.

van Dam, M.A., Koh, A.S., Dibble, S.L. (2001). "Lesbian Disclosure to Health Care Providers And Delay of Care." *Journal of the Gay and Lesbian Medical Society*, 5(1), 11-19.

Factors Associated with 'Feeling Suicidal': The Role of Sexual Identity

Jeanne Abelson, DPhil

National Centre in HIV Social Research

Sasho Lambevski, PhD

National Centre in HIV Social Research, Australia

June Crawford, PhD

National Centre in HIV Social Research, Australia

Michael Bartos, PhD

Joint United Nations Program on HIV/AIDS (UNAIDS)

Susan Kippax, PhD

National Centre in HIV Social Research, Australia

SUMMARY. This paper examines factors associated with feeling suicidal in a large sample of urban men in Sydney and Melbourne, aged

---

Jeanne Abelson is a consultant with the National Centre in HIV Social Research (NCHSR) at the University of New South Wales, Sydney, Australia. Sasho Lambevski is affiliated with the NCHSR. June Crawford is a research consultant with the NCHSR. Michael Bartos is currently affiliated with the Joint United Nations Program on HIV/AIDS (UNAIDS), Geneva, Switzerland. Susan Kippax is Director of the NCHSR. Correspondence may be addressed: Dr. J. Abelson, National Centre in HIV Social Research, Sir Robert Webster Building, Faculty of Arts and Social Sciences, University of New South Wales, Sydney 2052, Australia (E-mail: J.Abelson@unsw.edu.au).

[Haworth co-indexing entry note]: "Factors Associated with 'Feeling Suicidal': The Role of Sexual Identity." Abelson, Jeanne et al. Co-published simultaneously in *Journal of Homosexuality* (Harrington Park Press, an imprint of The Haworth Press, Inc.) Vol. 51, No. 1, 2006, pp. 59-80; and: *Current Issues in Lesbian, Gay, Bisexual, and Transgender Health* (ed: Jay Harcourt) Harrington Park Press, an imprint of The Haworth Press, Inc., 2006, pp. 59-80. Single or multiple copies of this article are available for a fee from The Haworth Document Delivery Service [1-800-HAWORTH, 9:00 a.m. - 5:00 p.m. (EST). E-mail address: docdelivery@haworthpress.com].

Available online at http://www.haworthpress.com/web/JH
© 2006 by The Haworth Press, Inc. All rights reserved.
doi:10.1300/J082v51n01_04

18-50, including heterosexual, gay and bisexual men, HIV antibody positive and HIV antibody negative. As in previous research, sexuality (being homosexual or bisexual) was found to be a major predictor of suicidality. The research went some way towards explaining the close relationship between feeling suicidal and sexual orientation. Sexuality interacts with feeling bad in that, once men feel moderately bad/depressed, they are more likely to feel suicidal if they are homosexual or bisexual than if they are heterosexual. In addition, the research found that experience of verbal abuse and physical assault (harassment) increased feeling suicidal for both heterosexual and gay/bisexual men, not just for homosexual men as suggested by previous research, and that social isolation in the form of living alone is a further risk factor. Seeking counseling help and taking sexual risks were also independently associated with feeling suicidal. These actions may result from feeling suicidal rather than the reverse, and their association with feeling suicidal warrants further research. Many of the 46 independent variables examined in the research, including HIV antibody status and closeness to the HIV/AIDS epidemic, were related to feeling suicidal only through their association with being gay/bisexual. Celibacy and general risk taking were not related to feeling suicidal in this study. *[Article copies available for a fee from The Haworth Document Delivery Service: 1-800-HAWORTH. E-mail address: <docdelivery@haworthpress.com> Website: <http://www.HaworthPress.com> © 2006 by The Haworth Press, Inc. All rights reserved.]*

KEYWORDS. Feeling suicidal, suicidality, men's sexuality, harassment, social isolation, sexual risk taking, counseling, HIV/AIDS

It is generally accepted that there is a higher risk of 'suicidality,' including suicidal behaviours, thoughts, feelings, and ideation, among gay/bisexual men than among heterosexual men. Two recent reviews, covering the literature of the last three decades, have come to this conclusion, and have ruled out the possibility of cohort effects (Kulkin, Chauvin & Percle, 2000; McDaniel, Purcell & D'Augelli, 2001). Indeed, the higher risk among gay/bisexual men of 'suicidality' in its broadest definition is now thought to pertain to the whole of the life-cycle and not just to the vulnerable years of adolescence and 'coming out,' although actual suicide and attempts at self-harm may peak during this early period (Savin-Williams, 1994; Remafedi, 1999; Herrell, Goldberg, William, Ramakrishnan, Lyons, Eisen & Tsuang, 1999).

The reasons for the higher prevalence of suicidality among male homosexuals and bisexuals compared with other men is the subject of much debate. One possibility is that suicidality has been confounded with affective disorders and illicit drug use. However, psychiatric disorders and illicit drug use have not always been found to be higher among gay, lesbian and bisexual persons than in the general population (McDaniel et al., 2001; compare Kauth & Prejean, 1997), and two recent studies have shown that the association between homosexuality and suicidality in men is independent of both mental health problems and illicit drug use. Herrell, Goldberg, William and colleagues (1999), in a co-twin study, consisting of homosexual men having a heterosexual twin brother and aged between 44 and 62 years, used five measures of suicidality including, thoughts about death, wanting to die, thoughts about suicide, attempted suicide, and the presence of any of these symptoms. They found that, after adjusting for illicit drug use and depressive symptoms, all except one of their suicidal measures (wanting to die) remained significantly associated with same-gender sexual orientation. Fergusson, Horwood and Beautrais (1999), in a 21-year longitudinal study in New Zealand, examined a variety of separate outcome measures, including suicidal ideation, suicidal attempts, depression, generalized anxiety disorder, conduct disorder and substance use disorders. They found that gay and bisexual persons were at increased risk for each of these problems, but had particularly high scores for suicidality and multiple disorders.

If higher rates of suicidality among gay/bisexual men cannot be explained by depression or illicit drug use, what, it has been asked, can account for its higher prevalence (Remafedi, 1999)? A large number of risk factors pertaining to suicide have been identified. Some of these, including social isolation, homelessness, interpersonal conflict, and psychiatric disorders, may be the same for homosexual and heterosexual men, while others, such as conflict over nonconformist sexuality, gender nonconformity, and nondisclosure of sexual orientation, may be unique to homosexual men, or may interact with factors shared by the general population (McDaniel et al., 2001; Remafedi, 1999; Friedman, 1999; Kulkin et al., 2000).

Three predictors have been suggested as particularly warranting further research in all age groups of men. These are: victimization and experience of homophobic acts, presence of the immunodeficiency virus, and sexual celibacy (McDaniel et al., 2001). Homophobia is widespread in our society and, in homosexual persons, it is internalized and manifested as shame, hostility and self-hatred (Herek, 1996; Kauth & Prejean, 1997). Consequently, homophobia may underlie many of the factors associated with suicidality in homosexual men, including illicit drug use, depression, isolation and violence (DuRant, Krowchuk & Sinal, 1998; Kulkin et al., 2000; Gilman, Cochran, Mays, Hughes, Ostrow & Kessler, 2001). From the perspective of Durkheim's theory of suicide, society's homophobia could provide fertile ground for suicidality in homosexual men through lack of social support, a sense of alienation or estrangement from social norms, and the stress and negative emotion that these experiences would engender. Saunders and Valente (1987) in their review of suicide among gay and lesbian persons, concluded that low self-acceptance and poor social integration may have a greater influence on suicidal behaviour among these groups than sexual orientation. More recently, Diaz, Ayala, Bein, Henne and Marin (2001) reported that, in their sample of Latino men, social isolation compounded the mental health risks resulting from a lifelong history of discrimination, while family acceptance, community involvement and social activism reduced these risks.

Only a few studies have looked at a possible association between HIV/AIDS and suicidality. Results have been mixed and are complicated by factors such as disease stage, pain levels, mental health status and new medical treatments (McDaniel et al., 2001; compare Mishara, 1998). While McDaniel and colleagues conclude that persons with AIDS 'may have a modestly elevated risk for suicide' (p. 96), Mishara cites at least one study (Joseph, Caumartin, Tal, Kirscht, Kessler, Ostrow & Wortman, 1990) which found that HIV positive gay men were no more likely to have suicidal ideation than other gay men.

Celibacy, or level of sexual activity, is a relatively new variable to be considered. Bagley and Tremblay (1997) found that adult gay men who were celibate reported more self-harming behaviours, suicide attempts and depression than sexually active gay men or heterosexual men. Interestingly, the reverse may be true for schoolboys: for them, multiple male sex partners has been found to increase risk of suicide (DuRant et al., 1998).

Another variable that has been found to be associated with suicidality, at least in the 18- to 24-year-old age group, is risk taking. Barrios, Everett, Simon and Brener (2000) noted a clustering of injury-related risk behaviours among students who reported suicidal ideation. These students were significantly more likely than other students to engage in a variety of risky behaviours such as carrying a weapon, engaging in physical fights, boating and swimming after drinking alcohol, and not using seat belts.

Finally, there is evidence that gay men seek professional help for emotional distress (including depression and suicidal ideation) more often, or more readily, than heterosexual men. Bell and Weinberg (1978; cited by Kauth & Prejean, 1997) found that 50-58% of adult gay men sampled (N = 686) had sought professional help while only 13 to 30% of heterosexual men had done so.

The study on which this paper is based was designed to examine a range of issues covering current life experiences of men living in large cities. 'Feeling suicidal' was included as one item tapping into the important area of emotions. Many variables known or suspected to contribute to the higher risk of suicidal ideation among homosexual men (as opposed to heterosexual men) were included in the study, including illicit drug use, social connectedness, health status, risk taking, experience of verbal and/or physical harassment, HIV status and levels of sexual activity.

This paper examines factors associated with feeling suicidal in a sample of urban men that included a high proportion of homosexual/bisexual men, both HIV antibody positive and HIV antibody negative. The main research question of interest was: What are the important predictors of feeling suicidal? In addition, it was asked, Can the association between homosexual/bisexual identity and feeling suicidal (if such an association is found) be accounted for by sexual identity differences in other variables associated with feeling suicidal?

METHOD

Sample and Instrument

The sample was a volunteer sample recruited in Sydney and Melbourne through dance clubs or nightclubs, gyms, and social and political organisations including charities, political parties, human rights organisations, and organisations supporting people with chronic illnesses. Recruitment was designed to obtain roughly equal numbers of heterosexual and homosexual men. Although there were some differences in the composition of the Sydney and Melbourne samples, preliminary data analysis found no meaningful associations between city of residence and any of the key variables. Consequently, city of residence is not included as an independent variable in the analyses reported in this paper.

Questionnaires were distributed at gyms and dance clubs, and social and political organisations, and were mailed to men on various nightclub mailing lists in Sydney and Melbourne. The response rate was around 20 percent. Apart from information about city of residence, there is no way of determining the source of recruitment of individual respondents.

The self-complete questionnaire was 25 pages long. Responses provided information across a wide range of domains of interest including: age; educational status; economic status (house ownership, income, nature of investments, and insurance); employment status and occupation; sexual identity; coping behaviours; attitudes towards doctors and health; goals in life; ways of spending free time; exercise; body satisfaction; social interaction; self concepts; experiences of illness and death; sexual behaviour; illicit drug use; risk activities; and, finally, emotions.

The sample consisted of 529 heterosexual, 656 gay or homosexual, and 115 bisexual men. There were 238 men who were HIV positive, of whom only eight were heterosexual and 19 bisexual. There was a wide range of ages (18-50 years) and income, with the average age being 34.2 years. On the whole the sample was well educated, a large percentage (48 percent) having tertiary education.

Measures

The dependent variable (feeling suicidal) was the response to just one item from the questionnaire, namely: How often do you feel suicidal? This item was scored 0 (never) 1 (rarely) 2 (sometimes) 3 (often) and treated as a numeric variable. Twelve men did not respond to the question. Therefore, the sample size for data analyses was 1,288.

Sexual identity was divided into three categories, namely heterosexual, gay, and bisexual, for all analyses except the multivariate analysis, in which a binary (heterosexual versus gay/bisexual) categorization was used. Sexual identity/orientation was defined principally by sexual behaviour. Men were asked whether they engaged in 'heterosexual vaginal or anal intercourse' or in 'homosexual anal intercourse' or had had sex with women or men, or both, in the last six months. They were also asked whether they sexually identify as 'straight,' 'gay,' 'bisexual,' 'homosexual,' 'heterosexual,' 'camp,' etc. In the very small number of cases where responses to these questions did not agree, behaviour was given priority.

Values for the following independent variables were available directly from the questionnaire: age, employment (full-time, part-time, unemployed), experience of illness, goals in life, household composition (living alone or with others), HIV status, experience of verbal abuse and/or physical assault 'as a result of appearance or manner,' self-labelling[1] (macho, snag, ocker, regular guy, etc.), being celibate for the six months prior to the survey. Sexual risk of transmission of HIV and of sexually transmitted infections (here referred to as 'sexual risk taking') was assessed from responses to a number of questions about sexual intercourse, condom use, serostatus of regular partners, and involvement in casual sex with male/female partners. Sexual risk taking was divided into three categories: definite risk, possible risk and no risk.[2] Social class was inferred from income, home ownership and education.

A further set of independent variables was constructed from the questionnaire using scale analysis. In each case, responses to a series of questions were numerically coded and added together to form a scale score. Each scale was analysed to assess reliability, and in some cases items were deleted in order to improve reliability. For scales with more than two items, reliabilities range from 0.43 (body satisfaction) to 0.87 (anxiety or worry about environmental or political matters). The scales, with coefficients alpha, are given in Table 1.

Analysis

The data were analysed in three stages.

First, to address the question of which variables are associated with feeling suicidal, bivariate analyses were carried out to examine relationships between the dependent variable and each of the independent variables. One way ANOVA was used to examine the relationship between feeling suicidal and categorical variables. Product-moment correlations (Pearson's r) were used to assess the significance of the relationships between feeling suicidal and each of the numeric independent variables.

Second, since the main independent variable of interest was sexual identity, relationships between sexual identity and each of the other independent variables were examined. For this purpose, chi-squared tests were used for categorical independent variables, and one-way ANOVAs for numeric independent variables.

Finally, having established which variables, taken one at a time, were significantly related to feeling suicidal and to sexual orientation, a multiple regression analysis was carried out to test the null hypothesis that, after adjusting for other variables, men who identified as gay or bisexual were no more likely than heterosexual men to report feeling suicidal. Due to the relationships observed in the literature between suicidality and depression, on the one hand, and suicidality and homophobia, on the other, two interaction terms were included in the multiple regression

TABLE 1. Scales, Items, and Reliability Coefficient Alpha

Scale	Scale Description	Number of Items	Coefficient Alpha
Planning	Having detailed plans & planning far ahead	2	0.64
Unwise coping	Coping with stress/conflict by getting drunk, running away from problem, taking it out on others	6	0.70
Seeking professional help	Coping with stress/conflict by seeking help from doctors, professionals, or higher authorities	3	0.60
Political activism	Involvement in political & social organisations	17	0.85
Confiding in others	Confiding in friends, relatives, colleagues, etc.	11	0.65
Social interaction	Spending leisure time with people in a variety of activities	9	0.74
Fitness activity	Attending gym, jogging, swimming, and other exercise activities	5	0.63
Spectator sport	Play or watch team sport, live, or on TV	3	0.78
Body satisfaction	How satisfied are you with your body? How sexually attractive do you think you are?	2	0.43
Drug use	Frequency of use of a variety of drugs, inc. marijuana, amphetamines, ecstasy, heroin, cocaine, etc. (not inc. alcohol)	13	0.77
General risk taking	Variety of risk taking activities engaged in in past year, from bungee jumping to eating junk food, gambling, and breaking regulations (excludes sexual risk and drug taking other than alcohol)	17	0.72
Anxiety/worry	Degree of feeling 'at risk,' e.g., from pollution, nuclear war, etc.	7	0.87
Feeling good	Responses to items concerning positive affect, e.g., 'How often do you feel: calm, happy, etc.?'	4	0.76
Feeling bad	Responses to items concerning negative affect, e.g., 'How often do you feel: sad, depressed, angry, etc.'	6	0.79

analysis, namely, sexual identity by 'feeling bad,' and sexual identity by experience of verbal abuse and/or physical assault ('harassment').

A reduced model was obtained by eliminating variables, using a combination of theory-driven model reduction in conjunction with backward elimination.

A Type I error rate of 0.01 was used in tests of statistical significance.

RESULTS

Feeling suicidal had a mean of 0.49 with a standard deviation of 0.71. Thus, on average, the sample reported feeling suicidal somewhere between 'never' (0) and 'rarely' (1).

Variables Related to Feeling Suicidal

Feeling suicidal was significantly related to sexual identity (p < 0.001). For heterosexual men, the mean was 0.31, compared with 0.61 for gay men and 0.62 for bisexual men (Table 2). Thus bisexual men and gay men had similar levels of feeling suicidal, with a mean twice as high as that of heterosexual men.

Feeling suicidal was significantly related to many other independent variables. Significant relationships with categorical variables are shown in Table 2. The results indicate: those more likely to feel suicidal are men who are unemployed, live alone, have the goals of making a difference or spiritual enlightenment, but not of being a good father or a good partner, are not sports mad, have not cared for someone with AIDS, are HIV antibody positive. Non-significant relationships tested included the goals of financial security, being successful, having fun, and getting rich. In addition, being celibate, and the self labels of 'macho,' 'ocker,' 'sensitive new age guy,' 'traditional Aussie male,' 'yuppie,' 'regular guy,' 'surfie' and 'nerd' were not significantly related to feeling suicidal among the men in this study. Note that, of all the categorical variables investigated, sexual identity had the greatest separation of mean values. In other words, identifying as homosexual or bisexual had the strongest association with feeling suicidal.

Feeling suicidal was also significantly related to many of the numeric independent variables. Table 3 shows correlations and levels of significance. Significant relationships, in order of magnitude, were with: feeling bad, harassment, feeling good, unwise coping, seeking help with coping, body satisfaction, planning, illicit drug use, sexual risk taking, experience of death, spectator sport, socio-economic class, experience of illness, fitness activity, confiding in others, age, leisure-time spent with people, number of people known who died of AIDS. Most of these relationships were in the expected direction, with negative relationships for: feeling good, body satisfaction, planning, spectator sport, class, fitness activity, and leisure time spent with people. Feeling suicidal was not related to active involvement in social and political organisations,

TABLE 2. Statistically Significant Relationships Between Feeling Suicidal and Categorical Independent Variables

	n	mean	s.d.	p-value
Demographic variables				
Employment status				< 0.001
Not employed	190	0.73	0.85	
Part-time employed	237	0.53	0.70	
Full-time employed	861	0.43	0.67	
Living alone				< 0.001
Alone	311	0.67	0.80	
Not alone	977	0.43	0.67	
(Celibacy, not significant, n.s.)				
Sexuality				
Sexual Identity				< 0.001
Heterosexual	524	0.31	0.60	
Gay	652	0.61	0.75	
Bisexual	112	0.62	0.79	
Planning variables				
Goal: 'To make a difference'				0.003
Chose this goal	435	0.57	0.72	
Did not choose this goal	853	0.45	0.71	
Goal: 'Spiritual enlightenment'				< 0.001
Chose this goal	290	0.65	0.69	
Did not choose this goal	998	0.44	0.78	
Goal: 'To be a good father'				<0.001
Chose this goal	320	0.35	0.64	
Did not choose this goal	968	0.54	0.73	
Goal: 'To be a good partner'				< 0.001
Chose this goal	810	0.40	0.66	
Did not choose this goal	478	0.65	0.78	

(Other goals, n. s.)

	n	mean	s.d.	p-value
Image variables				
Self label: Sports mad	255	0.38	0.65	0.006
Not Sports mad	1,033	0.52	0.73	
(Other self labels, n.s.)				
Mortality variables				
Having cared for HIV/AIDS victim				< 0.001
Cared for person with AIDS	965	0.45	0.69	
Not cared for person with AIDS	323	0.63	0.78	
HIV status				< 0.001
Negative/unknown	1,055	0.45	0.68	
Positive	233	0.69	0.81	

general risk taking behaviour, or anxiety/worry about environmental and political issues. The positive relationship between feeling suicidal and frequent confiding in others suggests that men with problems impart confidences more frequently and to more categories of people, or are more willing to acknowledge confiding in others.

Most of the relationships between feeling suicidal and numeric variables are weak (less than r = .300). The only moderately strong relationship is with feeling bad (r = .515). Thus, feeling suicidal is related to having a range of negative emotions, including depression. The relationship between feeling suicidal and feeling bad explains around one-quarter of the variance in feeling suicidal.

To summarise the results of the first analysis: a number of the variables that were suggested by previous research as likely correlates of measures of 'suicidality,' such as negative emotion, illicit drug use, harassment, age, social class, and employment status, and living alone (a possible indicator of social isolation) were related to our measure of feeling suicidal. Feeling bad, a possible indicator of depression, was the strongest single predictor, while sexual identity (specifically, self-identifying as gay, queer, or other identity associated with homosexuality) was the next most important single predictor.

In addition, a number of variables not investigated by previous research were significantly related to feeling suicidal. These included: sexual risk taking, social and leisure activities, sport and fitness, satis-

TABLE 3. Statistically Significant Correlations Between Feeling Suicidal and Numeric Independent Variables

Variable	r	p-value
Demographic variables		
Age	0.081	0.004
Social class	−0.117	< 0.001
(Education, n.s.)		
Planning variables		
Unwise coping	0.230	< 0.001
Professional help seeking	0.229	< 0.001
Planning ahead	−0.172	< 0.001
(Doctor, n.s.)		
Social interaction variables		
Leisure-time with people	−0.077	0.006
Confiding in others	0.080	0.004
(Political/social activity, n.s.)		
Exercise variables		
Spectator sports	−0.111	< 0.001
Fitness activity	−0.082	0.003
Image variables		
Body satisfaction	−0.183	< 0.001
Harassment	0.264	< 0.001
Risk variables		
Drug use	0.128	< 0.001
Sexual risk taking	0.124	< 0.001
(General risk taking, n.s.)		
Mortality variables		
Illness experience	0.096	0.001
No. of deaths experienced	0.115	< 0.001
No. of AIDS deaths experienced	0.075	0.007
Emotions variables		
Feeling good	−0.247	< 0.001
Feeling bad	0.515	< 0.001
(Anxiety, n.s.)		

faction with one's body, planning ahead, personal goals, experience of illness, and exposure to death and to the HIV/AIDS epidemic.

Celibacy and general risk taking, two variables found by previous research to be related to suicidality, were not associated with feeling suicidal in this study.

Variables Related to Sexual Identity

As expected, many variables related to feeling suicidal were also related to sexual identity. In particular, being gay (and often also being bisexual[3]) was associated with many of the variables positively related to feeling suicidal, including feeling bad, living alone, seeking professional help, confiding in others, experience of harassment, illicit drug use, sexual risk taking, and contact with the HIV/AIDS epidemic (for example, being HIV antibody positive, or having known a large number of people who died). See Table 4.

Variables related to feeling suicidal but not associated with sexual identity were: unwise coping strategies (such as excessive drinking, quitting work, etc.), body satisfaction, experience of personal illness or injury, and feeling good. There were no significant differences in relation to these variables among gay, bisexual and heterosexual men.

A few variables that were not directly related to feeling suicidal were associated with sexual identity. Compared with heterosexual and bisexual men, gay men were: less likely to have been celibate in the six months prior to the survey, more likely to choose the life-goals of 'financial security' and 'having fun,' more likely to have been actively involved in social and political organisations, and more likely to self label as 'a regular guy.' Gay and bisexual men were less likely than heterosexual men to self label as 'ocker' and more likely to self-label as 'snag.'

One variable was not related to either feeling suicidal or sexuality. This was anxiety about environmental issues.

Multivariate Regression Analysis

The multivariate regression analysis for feeling suicidal, comprised all of the independent variables mentioned above, including some which were not related to feeling suicidal but which were related to sexual identity, such as celibacy, general risk taking, and political activity. It also included the interaction variables: sexual identity by feeling bad, and sexual identity by harassment. The analysis was carried out using

TABLE 4. Table of Means for Correlates of Feeling Suicidal by Sexual Identity

Correlate of Feeling Suicidal	Heterosexual n = 529	Gay n = 656	Bisexual n = 115	p-value
Demographic variables				
Employment[a]	2.59	2.51	2.27	< 0.001
Living alone[b]	0.15	0.31	0.32	< 0.001
Social class[a]	2.12	2.11	1.91	< 0.001
Age[c]	31.66	36.47	33.18	< 0.001
Planning variables				
Goal: 'To make a difference'[d]	0.28	0.37	0.37	0.002
Goal: 'Spiritual enlightenment'[b]	0.15	0.28	0.30	< 0.001
Goal: 'To be a good father'[e]	0.51	0.02	0.24	< 0.001
Goal: 'To be a good partner'[b]	0.74	0.56	0.50	< 0.001
Unwise coping	4.07	4.43	4.59	n.s.
Prof. help seeking[b]	1.76	2.48	2.48	< 0.001
Planning ahead[d]	1.98	1.72	1.63	0.001
Social interaction variables				
Leisure-time with people[d]	19.59	21.37	20.43	< 0.001
Confiding in others[b]	8.04	9.32	9.37	< 0.001
Exercise variables				
Spectator sport[e]	4.90	2.01	2.98	< 0.001
Fitness activity	4.87	4.24	4.26	n.s.
Image variables				
Self label: Sports mad[c]	0.33	0.02	0.22	< 0.001
Body satisfaction	3.48	3.39	3.32	n.s.
Harassment[d]	1.49	1.93	1.79	< 0.001
Risk variables				
Drug use[b]	2.64	6.80	5.62	< 0.001
Sexual risk[b]	1.12	1.47	1.44	< 0.001

Correlate of Feeling Suicidal	Heterosexual n = 529	Gay n = 656	Bisexual n = 115	p-value
Mortality variables				
Cared for someone with HIV/AIDS	0.02	0.42	0.25	< 0.001
HIV status[e]	0.02	0.32	0.17	< 0.001
Illness experience	0.97	0.86	1.10	n.s.
Number of deaths experienced[e]	5.50	8.97	7.24	< 0.001
Number AIDS deaths experienced[d]	0.35	8.24	3.81	< 0.001
Emotions variables				
Feeling good	7.90	7.60	7.47	n.s.
Feeling bad[d]	7.41	8.08	8.30	< 0.001

[a]Bisexual group significantly different from each of the other two groups.

[b]Heterosexual group significantly different from each of the other two groups.

[c]Gay group significantly different from each of the other two groups.

[d]The only significant difference is between heterosexual and gay groups.

[e]All groups differ significantly from each other.

the Manova program of SPSS 8.00. The full model included 46 predictors, all with a single degree of freedom since both sexual identity and employment status were reduced to two categories (gay/bisexual versus heterosexual; employed versus unemployed).

The full model accounted for 35.0 percent of the variation in feeling suicidal. The distribution of the residuals from the full model was non-normal, but was uni-modal and only slightly skewed. Due to large numbers of intercorrelations between variables, the model was reduced systematically to determine which variables were truly redundant. Although caution is needed in interpreting levels of significance, the analysis is appropriate given the large sample size and the robustness of multiple regression.

The final model is shown in Table 5. It accounts for 32 percent of the variance in feeling suicidal. The variables which remained significant at the 0.01 level after adjusting for all the other variables in the full model were: feeling bad, harassment (experience of verbal abuse and/or physical assault), living alone, leisure-time spent with people or in social interaction, coping by seeking help from professionals or superiors, sexual risk taking, and the interaction between feeling bad and sexual identity.

TABLE 5. Results of Multiple Regression Analysis. Variables Independently Related to Feeling Suicidal. Mutiple R^2 0.32

Predictor	df	Univariate R^2	Multivariate B Coefficient (95% C.I.) (Unstandardized)	B Coefficient (Standardized)
Harassment	1	0.070**	.059 (.033, .085)	.109**
Sexual risk taking	1	0.021**	.058 (.019, .097)	.071*
Prof. help coping	1	0.053**	.036 (.016, .055)	.089**
Living alone	1	0.020**	.131 (.054, .208)	.078*
Social interaction	1	0.006*	−.010 (−.017, −.003)	−.066*
Feeling bad	1	0.265**	.088 (.068, .108)	.334**
Sexuality[a]	1	0.043**	−.190 (−.392, .012)	−.131
Interaction: Sexuality by feeling bad[b]	1		.042 (.017, .066)	.264*

**p < 0.001 *p < 0.01
[a]Coded as '0' for heterosexual, '1' for gay or bisexual.
[b]Interaction not included in univariate analyses.

Since one of the key research questions in this study related to the role of sexual identity as a predictor of feeling suicidal, it is an important finding that, after adjustment for all other variables, sexual identity in interaction with feeling bad, remained statistically significant. The significant interaction term means that the relationship between feeling bad and feeling suicidal (after adjustment for living alone, leisure-time spent with people, sexual risk taking, professional help seeking and harassment) is different according to sexuality. The model predicts that, as feeling bad increases, gay/bisexual men's suicidality increases more rapidly than that of heterosexual men. In other words, the difference between gay/bisexual and heterosexual men in feeling suicidal becomes greater as the level of feeling bad rises. Since feeling bad itself is on average higher for homosexual men (8.12) than for heterosexual men (7.41), it is clear that the multivariate analysis confirms that gay/bisexual men are more likely to report feeling suicidal than heterosexual men. This difference between gay/bisexual and heterosexual men is not accounted for by differences between the two groups on any of the other variables included in this study, specifically, differences in harassment, living alone, or the other variables remaining in the final model.

The interaction term for sexual identity and harassment did not remain in the final model. The final model predicts that men who experience harassment–or live alone, lack leisure-time with others, use professional help seeking, or engage in sexual risk taking–are more likely to feel suicidal than other men, *irrespective of sexuality*. In other words, after adjusting for other variables including sexuality, experience of harassment has much the same effect on heterosexual as on gay/bisexual men, and increases their feelings of suicidality to about the same extent.

It is worth noting that, after adjusting for other variables, HIV antibody status does not remain in the model: men who are HIV antibody positive are no more likely than other gay or bisexual men to report feeling suicidal.

With the possible exception of professional help seeking, all the variables remaining in the final model, are related to feeling suicidal in the expected direction.

DISCUSSION

The sample used in this research is of interest since it included both heterosexual men as well as gay/bisexual men. Furthermore, it included a relatively large proportion of men who were HIV antibody positive as well as gay and bisexual men who had been close to the centre of the HIV/AIDS epidemic in Australia. It was thus possible to examine whether having a life-threatening condition oneself, or having known or cared for people who died of HIV/AIDS or other conditions, was related to feeling suicidal. Also, it was possible to look at these issues in a multivariate analysis where the inter-relationships between sexuality, HIV antibody status and experience of death could be taken into account.

A large number of variables included in this study were found to be associated with feeling suicidal in bivariate analysis. Many of these variables, such as advancing age, low social class, unemployment, living alone, unwise coping, low levels of social interaction and fitness, high levels of non-prescription illicit drug use, and feeling bad, have been found in previous research to be associated with measures of suicidality, and their association with feeling suicidal is consistent with our general understanding of the risk factors for mental health in the population as a whole (McDaniel et al., 2001).

The research confirmed the finding of previous research (Herrell et al., 1999; Fergusson et al., 1999) that sexual identity is related to feeling suicidal, and that men who identify as gay or bisexual are more likely to report feeling suicidal than men who identify as heterosexual. The research sought to address this issue, and to explain why gay and bisexual men tend to report higher levels of suicidality than heterosexual men (Remafedi, 1999).

A number of variables in this study were related to both feeling suicidal and sexual identity. These included variables concerned with planning, coping, social interaction of various kinds, spectator sport, fitness activity, body satisfaction, illicit drug use, and variables indicative of closeness to the HIV/AIDS epidemic, such as HIV antibody status, having cared for a person living with HIV/AIDS, experience of illness and death. For all but one of these variables, the association with feeling suicidal was in the same direction as the association with being gay or bisexual. The exception was having cared for someone living with HIV/AIDS. Although almost all those who had cared for someone with HIV/AIDS were gay or bisexual, these carers reported lower levels of feeling suicidal than other men who had not been carers.

Surprisingly, and contrary to the predictions of previous research (Barrios et al., 2000), feeling suicidal was not related to general risk taking, even though this variable was related to sexuality. Also contrary to the findings of previous research (Bagley & Tremblay, 1997), feeling suicidal was not related to celibacy, although this variable was related to sexuality.

With so many variables being associated with feeling suicidal, both ones which were associated with sexual identity, and ones which were not, it was necessary to clarify which associations were most important and what is the role of sexuality in these relationships. A multivariate analysis was conducted for these purposes.

The results of the multivariate analysis were that feeling bad, and sexual identity together with its interaction with feeling bad, remained two of the most important predictors of feeling suicidal after adjustment for other variables. Only five of the other correlates of feeling suicidal–experience of harassment, living alone, leisure-time spent with people, professional help seeking and sexual risk taking–remained significant after adjusting for other independent variables. This indicates that most of the bivariate correlations between independent variables and feeling suicidal that were found in this study, were based on a mutual relationship with sexual identity. Once sexual identity, or sexual identity in interaction with feeling bad, was taken into account, most of these relationships, including the relationship with closeness to the HIV/ AIDS epidemic, ceased to be significant.

At least two of the variables that continued to predict feeling suicidal independently, after sexuality had been taken into account, have been documented previously in the literature. Experience of harassment (being verbally abused or physically assaulted because of the way one looks, walks, talks, etc.), especially in the form of homophobia, has previously been found to be associated with suicidality (Herek, 1996; McDaniel et al., 2001). In the present research, harassment was shown to increase suicidality in heterosexual as well as gay/ bisexual men. This is a new finding. Similarly, social isolation has been found by previous research to be an important predictor of suicidality (DuRant et al., 1998; Kulkin et al., 2000). In the present study, social isolation, in the form of (a) living alone and (b) lack of leisure-time spent with others/in social interaction, increased the likelihood of feeling suicidal for both gay/bisexual and heterosexual men. Therefore, it is not accurate to say that social isolation is more important than sexual orientation in influencing men's suicidality (Saunders and Valente, 1987). Rather, social isolation would seem to compound men's despair, irrespective of sexuality.

Seeking professional help and taking sexual risks were also found to be predictors of feeling suicidal after taking into account sexual orientation. It may be that taking sexual risks and seeking counseling result from feeling suicidal rather than the reverse: as mentioned above, it has been found previously that homosexual men seek counseling for emotional distress more often, or more readily, than heterosexual men (see Kauth & Prejean, 1997). The relationship between these variables and feeling suicidal warrants further research.

Feeling bad, which includes feeling depressed, increased feeling suicidal in both heterosexual and homosexual men. This has been found previously, but the relationship between these variables has not been well understood (Remafedi, 1999; McDaniel et al., 2001). It turns out that the relationship between feeling bad and feeling suicidal is complex. Sexual identity and feeling bad interact significantly and, as levels of feeling bad increase, homosexual men (both gay and bisexual) feel suicidal more rapidly and at higher levels than heterosexual men. In other words, the relationship between feeling bad and feeling suicidal is closer for homosexual men than for heterosexual men, although the relationship is positive for both groups.

CONCLUSION

There are limitations to this study. The sample was not random and came from relatively well-connected locations (bars, social and political organisations, etc.). It did not include socially isolated individuals or those seeking mental health services. Also, the dependent variable, 'feeling suicidal,' might be considered somewhat simplistic. Nevertheless, the findings themselves are quite strong. It is unusual to have such a large sample of both heterosexual and gay/bisexual men, and questions of suicidality have not often been addressed by comparing these two groups.

The results confirm that men who identify as gay or bisexual are more likely to report feeling suicidal than men who identify as heterosexual. Indeed, the sexual identity differences on most variables included in this study explain why so many of the variables in the study are related to feeling suicidal. Thus, one important finding of the research is that HIV antibody status and closeness to the HIV epidemic are related to feeling suicidal only through their association with being gay/bisexual. Men who are HIV antibody positive and men who are close to the HIV/AIDS epidemic are not more likely than other gay and bisexual men to feel suicidal. This finding supports the conclusion of Joseph and colleagues (1990; cited by Mishara, 1998), in their longitudinal study, that HIV positive men were no more likely to have suicidal ideation than negative gay men. This does not mean, however, that differences do not exist in terms of disease stage, as noted by McDaniel and colleagues (2001).

The findings suggest that Durkheim's analysis of suicide is the one most likely to explain why gay and bisexual men have higher levels of suicidality. The confirmation in the present study of the importance of experience of harassment indicates that homophobia and discrimination may well play an important role. Further, social isolation, in the form of living alone and/or a lack of leisure-time social interaction, is also a risk factor.

The closer relationship between feeling suicidal and feeling bad among gay and bisexual men than among heterosexual men may merely mean that gay and bisexual men use the term 'feeling suicidal' more readily than their heterosexual counterparts. On the other hand, this closer relationship could mean that gay and bisexual men are more vulnerable to feeling suicidal. Moderate levels of depression among gay and bisexual men may more readily lead to suicidal feelings, and therefore may need to be taken more seriously than comparable levels of depression and negative emotion in heterosexual men.

NOTES

1. Labels included were: macho, ocker, snag, regular Aussie guy, surfie, sports-mad, nerd. The term 'ocker' refers to a type of 'over-the-top' Australian, loud, badly and casually clothed, beer-drinking, somewhat insensitive. 'Snag' is an acronym for sensitive new-age guy. 'Surfie' refers to someone who looks like a frequenter of beaches, with sun-bleached hair. All of the labels were derived from descriptions of self and others used fairly frequently in the open-ended interviews carried out to assist in designing the questionnaire.

2. Patterns of sexual practice and condom use were varied, and a rough index of risk of HIV transmission was derived from questions regarding condom use and sexual behaviour in the six months prior to completing the questionnaire. High risk was defined as reporting unprotected intercourse with a known serodiscordant partner or unprotected anal intercourse with casual partners. Low risk was defined as having no unprotected anal intercourse with casual partners and/or unprotected anal intercourse only with a seroconcordant regular partner. All other patterns of practice were classified in the middle ('possible risk') category.

3. Almost all of the significant results show that heterosexual men differed significantly from gay men, with bisexual men's scores between those of heterosexual and gay men, but most often resembling gay men's. Notable exceptions to this are employment and social class: bisexual men in this sample were more likely than either heterosexual or gay men to be unemployed and of low social class. The sample was slightly skewed in terms of age with heterosexual and bisexual men younger on average (32-33 years) than gay men (36.5 years).

REFERENCES

Bagley, C. & Tremblay, P. (1997). Suicidal behaviors in homosexual and bisexual males. *Crisis*, 18, 24-34.

Barrios, L. C., Everett, S.A., Simon, T.R. & Brener, N.D. (2000). Suicide ideation among US college students: Associations with other injury risk behaviors. *Journal of American College Health*, 48:5, 229-233.

Bell, A. & Weinberg, M. (1978). *Homosexualities: A study of diversity among men and women*. New York: Simon & Schuster.

Diaz, R.M., Ayala, G. Bein, E., Henne, J. & Marin, B.V. (2001). The impact of homophobia, poverty, and racism on the mental health of gay and bisexual Latino men: findings from 3 US cities. *American Journal of Public Health*, 91:6, 927-932.

DuRant, R.H., Krowchuk, D.P. & Sinal, S.H. (1998). Victimization, use of violence, and drug use at school among male adolescents who engage in same-sex sexual behavior. *Journal of Pediatrics*, 132, 113-118.

Durkheim, E. (1952). *Suicide: A study in sociology*. London: Routledge & K. Paul.

Fergusson, D.M., Horwood, L.J. & Beautrais, A.L. (1999). Is sexual orientation related to mental health problems and suicidality in young people? *Archives of General Psychiatry*, 56:10, 876-880.

Friedman, R.C. (1999). Homosexuality, psychopathology, and suicidality. *Archives of General Psychiatry, 56:10*, 887-888.

Gilman, S.E., Cochran, S.D., Mays, V.M., Hughes, M., Ostrow, D. & Kessler, R.C. (2001). Risk of psychiatric disorders among individuals reporting same-sex sexual partners in the National Comorbidity Survey. *American Journal of Public Health, 91:6*, 933-939.

Herek, G.M. (1996). Heterosexism and homophobia. In R.P. Cabaj & T.S. Stein (Eds.), *Textbook of Homosexuality and Mental Health*, Washington, D.C.: American Psychiatric Press, pp. 101-113.

Herrell, R., Goldberg, J., William, R., Ramakrishnan, V., Lyons, M, Eisen, S. & Tsuang, M. T. (1999). Sexual orientation and suicidality: A co-twin control study in adult men. *Archives of General Psychiatry, 56:10*, 867-874.

Joseph, J.G., Caumartin, S.M., Tal, M., Kirscht, J.P., Kessler, R.C., Ostrow, D.G. & Wortman, C.B. (1990). Psychological functioning in a cohort of gay men at risk for AIDS: A three-year descriptive study. *The Journal of Nervous and Mental Disease, 178*, 607-615.

Kauth, M.R. & Prejean, J. (1997). Health behavior in gay men. In D.S. Gochman (Ed.), *Handbook of Health Behavior Research*. New York: Plenum Press, vol 1, pp. 303-328.

Kulkin, H.S., Chauvin, E.A. & Percle, G.A. (2000). Suicide among gay and lesbian adolescents and young adults: A review of the literature. *Journal of Homosexuality, 40:1*, 1-29.

McDaniel, J.S., Purcell, D. & D'Augelli, A.R. (2001). The relationship between sexual orientation and risk for suicide: Research findings and future directions for research and prevention. *Suicide & Life-Threatening Behavior, 31*, 84-105.

Mishara, B.L. (1998). Suicide, euthanasia and AIDS. *Crisis, 19:2*, 87-96.

Remafedi, G. (1999). Suicide and sexual orientation: Nearing the end of controversy? *Archives of General Psychiatry, 56:1*, 885-886.

Saunders, J. M. & Valente, S.M. (1987). Suicide risk among gay men and lesbians: A review. *Death Studies, 11*, 1-23.

Savin-Williams, R.C. (1994). Verbal and physical abuse as stressors in the lives of lesbian, gay male, and bisexual youths: Associations with school problems, running away, substance abuse, prostitution, and suicide. *Journal of Consulting and Clinical Psychology, 62:2*, 261-269.

Sexual Identity Distress, Social Support, and the Health of Gay, Lesbian, and Bisexual Youth

Eric R. Wright, PhD

Indiana University, Purdue University, Indianapolis

Brea L. Perry, BA, BS

Indiana University, Bloomington

Eric R. Wright received his PhD in sociology from Indiana University, Bloomington. Currently, he is appointed as Associate Professor and Director of Health Policy at Indiana University, Purdue University, Indianapolis (IUPUI). He also serves as Associate Director of the Indiana Consortium for Mental Health Services Research, a research center at Indiana University dedicated to conducting research on mental health services research and policy. As a medical sociologist, his primary research and teaching interests center on mental health, sexually transmitted disease, social networks, and human sexuality. Brea L. Perry holds a master's degree in sociology from Indiana University, Bloomington, where she is currently a doctoral student. Her research interests are in sexuality, mental health, medical sociology, and social networks. In 2001, she was awarded a graduate fellowship from the National Science Foundation. Correspondence may be addressed: Eric R. Wright, Department of Sociology, Indiana University Purdue University Indianapolis (IUPUI), Cavanaugh Hall 303, 425 University Blvd., Indianapolis, IN 46202-5140 (E-mail: ewright@iupui.edu).

This research was supported by a grant from the Health Resources and Services Administration's (HRSA) Special Projects of National Significance (SPNS) Program (BRH9700152) to the Indiana State Department of Health (ISDH), the Indiana Youth Group, Inc. (IYG), and Indiana University. The views and interpretations presented here are solely those of the authors and do not necessarily reflect the opinions of HRSA, ISDH, IYG, or Indiana University. The authors would like to thank the youth and staff at IYG for their participation and assistance in conducting this research. In addition, the authors thank the anonymous reviewers for their thought provoking comments and suggestions on an earlier version of this paper.

[Haworth co-indexing entry note]: "Sexual Identity Distress, Social Support, and the Health of Gay, Lesbian, and Bisexual Youth." Wright, Eric R., and Brea L. Perry. Co-published simultaneously in *Journal of Homosexuality* (Harrington Park Press, an imprint of The Haworth Press, Inc.) Vol. 51, No. 1, 2006, pp. 81-110; and: *Current Issues in Lesbian, Gay, Bisexual, and Transgender Health* (ed: Jay Harcourt) Harrington Park Press, an imprint of The Haworth Press, Inc., 2006, pp. 81-110. Single or multiple copies of this article are available for a fee from The Haworth Document Delivery Service [1-800-HAWORTH, 9:00 a.m. - 5:00 p.m. (EST). E-mail address: docdelivery@haworthpress.com].

SUMMARY. Sex researchers and mental health clinicians have long recognized that the stigma surrounding homosexuality plays an important role in shaping the social psychological adjustment of gay, lesbian, and bisexual (g/l/b) people. In recent years, researchers have suggested that sexual identity-related distress may influence the physical health status of g/l/b people, primarily because of the ways these self-related feelings and beliefs impact patterns of health-related behavior. This study examines the influence of sexual identity distress and social support on g/l/b youth's drug and alcohol use, psychological distress, and risky sexual behavior. The data come from a services research demonstration program conducted at the Indiana Youth Group, Inc., a g/l/b youth development agency based in Indianapolis, Indiana. Results indicate that sexual identity distress is strongly associated with psychological distress, less frequent use of alcohol, and using fewer types of illegal drugs. Being out to more people in one's support network, however, attenuates the severity of youth's sexual identity-related distress. Youth who report more support ties to g/l/b people indicate engaging in more frequent risky sexual behavior. The implications of these findings for theories of g/l/b youth's sexual identity development are discussed. *[Article copies available for a fee from The Haworth Document Delivery Service: 1-800-HAWORTH. E-mail address: <docdelivery@haworthpress.com> Website: <http://www.HaworthPress. com> © 2005 by The Haworth Press, Inc. All rights reserved.]*

KEYWORDS. Gay, lesbian, bisexual youth, social support, health risk behavior, internalized homophobia, sexual identity distress

The stigma of homosexuality has long been theorized to be a central force affecting the mental health status of gay, lesbian, and bisexual (g/l/b) people (Frabel, Wortman, & Joseph, 1997; Meyer, 1995; Miranda & Storms, 1989; Savin-Williams, 1990; Wagner, Brondolo, & Rabkin, 1996; Walters & Simoni, 1993; Weinberg & Williams, 1974). More recently, researchers have argued that internalization of these stigmatizing beliefs, or what is often referred to as "internalized homophobia" (Gonsiorek, 1982; Malyon, 1982), also may have serious negative consequences for g/l/b people's physical health. While the specific mechanisms linking stigma and physical health remain unclear, most researchers believe that internalized homophobia, measured in a variety of ways, is causally related, directly or indirectly, to g/l/b adult's and youth's health status and/or health behavior (French, Story, Remafedi, Resnick, & Blum, 1996; Meyer & Dean, 1998; Rosario, Hunter, & Gwadz, 1997; Rotheram-Borus, Rosario, Reid, & Koopman, 1995; Savin-Williams,

1990; Savin-Williams & Lenhart, 1990; Winters, Remafedi, & Chan, 1996).

This paper examines sexual identity distress in the early phases of "coming out" and its relationship to drug and alcohol use, psychological distress, and risky patterns sexual activity in a sample of self-identified g/l/b youth in Indianapolis, Indiana. We build on prior research in two important ways. First, we propose a new, more specific measure of *sexual identity distress* designed to assess the negative affect associated with an individual's sexual identity. Prior efforts to measure internalized homophobia have suffered from a lack of conceptual clarity primarily because of the use of omnibus measures that make it difficult to disentangle the particular theoretical dimensions of minority-related stress that are related to particular health or social outcomes. Second, we emphasize the importance of considering g/l/b youth's health, mental health, and related behaviors within a developmental framework. Most theoretical models suggest that sexual identity-related distress declines as individuals develop a positive g/l/b identity and a supportive social network. Yet, most empirical studies in this area do not give systematic consideration to these developmental processes in the analysis or interpretation of health-related findings (see Hetrick & Martin, 1987 for an exception). Our principal aim is to improve scientific understanding of the relationship between sexual identity distress, social support, and health risk behavior during the early phases of the coming out process.

THE STIGMA OF HOMOSEXUALITY AND THE HEALTH OF GAY, LESBIAN, AND BISEXUAL PEOPLE

For decades, social scientists have documented serious negative health consequences of the stigma of homosexuality (Gay and Lesbian Medical Association and LGBT Health Experts, 2001). The internalization of stigmatizing beliefs, for example, has been found to be a significant source of psychological distress for both adolescent and adult g/l/b people (Hetrick & Martin, 1987; Meyer, 1995). These feelings are characterized typically by guilt, self-loathing, shame, a delay in identity formation, poor psychosexual development, poor self-esteem, and a myriad of other threats to a positive self-concept (Allen & Oleson, 1999; Grossman & Kerner, 1998; Shidlo, 1994). Gonsiorek (1982) and others (Frabel et al., 1997; French et al., 1996; Malyon, 1982; Miranda & Storms, 1989; Walters & Simoni, 1993) have suggested that mental health professionals focus special attention on addressing internalized homophobia as it often can cause symptoms of psychological distress and even psychopathology in g/l/b clients. This special group of stressors has also been judged to be an important cause of suicide attempts by youth struggling with sexual orientation issues (Gibson, 1989; Remafedi, Farrow, & Deisher, 1991). Still others have argued that internalized homophobia can help explain some g/l/b people's problems in finding and maintaining intimate relationships and developing adequate support systems (Barranti, 1998; Hardin, 1999; Meyer & Dean, 1998; Pimental-Habib, 1999; Wagner et al., 1996).

In recent years, researchers have extended this theoretical argument to the physical health of g/l/b youth. Rosario et al. (1997), for example, found relatively high levels of alcohol and illicit drug use in a sample of g/l/b youth in New York City and, after controlling for other possible theoretical causes, concluded that stress and difficulties of growing up gay were the most likely cause of the elevated rates of substance use. Similarly, others argue that internalized homophobia and the social stigma surrounding homosexuality also may have a direct effect on g/l/b youth's risky sexual behavior by decreasing their motivations and/or limiting their opportunities to engage in less risky sexual behavior (Remafedi, 1994a; Remafedi, 1994b; Rotheram-Borus & Koopman, 1991; Savin-Williams, 1990; Savin-Williams & Lenhart, 1990). In contrast, Rotheram-Borus et al. (1995), in one of the few longitudinal studies in this area, examined several competing theoretical models of risk behavior and were unable to document a direct link between the stress of coping with being g/l/b and risk behavior; however, they did find a direct effect of gay-related stress on emotional distress.

While there is a growing consensus that societal stigma regarding homosexuality affects the health of g/l/b youth and adults, there is much less theoretical or empirical agreement on how best to conceptualize or measure its social or psychological manifestations in the lives of g/l/b people. Prior efforts to measure internalized homophobia, for example, have included questions covering a number of conceptually distinct dimensions of the stigma experience, including perceptions of community attitudes, congruency between community and personal views, religious beliefs, anxiety about interacting with g/l/b people, and identity-related self-assessments (Nungesser, 1983; Shidlo, 1994). More often researchers have used proxy indicators (e.g., self-esteem, homosexuality-related attitudes) or other measures believed to reflect stigma-related psychological outcomes (i.e., psychological distress, depression) (Allen & Oleson, 1999; Grossman & Kerner, 1998; Mays & Cochran, 1988; Shidlo, 1994).

Recently, Meyer and others have applied the concept of "minority stress" to describe the array of social and psychological stressors associated with being g/l/b (DiPlacido, 1998; Meyer, 1995). DiPlacido (1998) emphasizes that these stressors are rooted in both external and internal sources. That is, g/l/b youth and adults may experience stress as the direct result of negative social interactions with prejudiced individuals, ranging from everyday hassles associated with people assuming one is heterosexual to overt harassment (D'Augelli, 1998; DiPlacido, 1998; Meyer, 1995; Russell, Franz, & Driscoll, 2001; Savin-Williams, 1994). Internally, minority stress can manifest itself through the social psychological internalization of negative societal attitudes, the psychological pressures associated with maintaining a concealed identity, and even internal conflicts resulting from discordant beliefs (i.e., strong religious convictions against homosexuality and a conscious awareness of same-gender sexual attraction) (DiPlacido, 1998; Malyon, 1982; Shidlo, 1994). This distinction has been extremely helpful in clarifying the nature, sources, and diversity of stressors. Indeed, recent research has been more limited in scope, generally focusing on the specific health effects of experiences of discrimination and/or violence (D'Augelli, 1998; Rosario, Rotherham-Borus, & Reid, 1996; Russell et al., 2001; Savin-Williams, 1994). This general framework, though, further underlines the need to clarify other dimensions of minority stress in order to improve our understanding of the connection between the stigma of homosexuality and the health of g/l/b people. Here, we examine the affect that youth associate with their identity as a g/l/b person because of the special importance social identities hold in developmental process (Stryker, 1980; Troiden, 1988).

A DEVELOPMENTAL VIEW OF SEXUAL IDENTITY DISTRESS, SOCIAL SUPPORT, AND THE HEALTH OF GAY, LESBIAN, AND BISEXUAL YOUTH

While researchers interested in the health of g/l/b youth draw liberally on the theoretical importance of the stigma of homosexuality, most studies neglect the broader social context of g/l/b youth's psychosexual development. Virtually all of the theoretical models of homosexual identity development postulate or implicitly hypothesize that negative self-related feelings about being g/l/b will diminish–to varying degrees–over the course of the "coming out" process (Cass, 1979; Rosario et al., 1996; Savin-Williams, 1990; Savin-Williams, 1998; Troiden, 1988). During the early and middle stages of the coming out process, the developmental challenges for g/l/b youth are two-fold: (1) to define, clarify, and adapt emotionally to their self-identity as g/l/b; and, (2) to establish and develop a social network which includes individuals–both gay and non-gay–who are supportive of their sexual identity (Cass, 1979; Hetrick & Martin, 1987; Pimental-Habib, 1999; Ryan & Futterman, 1998; Troiden, 1988). Research on this process indicates that during the early stages of the coming out process, what Troiden (1988) has termed "sensitization," early self-identity work emphasizes primarily the recognition and labeling of same-gender sexual feelings. After defining one's self as (potentially) g/l/b, most youth experience serious psychological cognitive dissonance because of the conflicts between their emerging self-identity and the stigmatized images of homosexuals in society. This latter stage is what Troiden (1988) has described as "identity confusion" and is the developmental stage during which internalized homophobia is likely to be most severe (Hetrick & Martin, 1987; Meyer, 1995; Ryan & Futterman, 1998).

In the middle or "identity assumption" phase, youth's sexual identity "becomes both a self-identity and a presented identity" (Troiden, 1988). That is, youth begin to self-disclose their emerging identity to others and to form social relationships with people around their new identity. These relationships, for the most part, are initially forged with other g/l/b people (Troiden, 1988). This set of initial relationships are critically important for understanding g/l/b youth's internalization of stigma (Cass, 1979; Troiden, 1988) and their health status and risk behaviors (Wright, Dye, Jiles, & Marcello, 1999). Both Cass (1979) and Troiden (1988) argue that if these initial relationships are negative, youth will have significantly greater difficulties in developing positive attitudes about their sexual identity. On the other hand, if these early relationships are positive and largely supportive, youth will be more likely to develop a positive self-concept as a homosexual and be more comfortable in establishing future relationships as an "openly" g/l/b person with other gay and non-gay people.

Through the process of self-disclosure and public sharing young people typically become increasingly comfortable with their sexual identity and develop more effective stigma coping skills. Indeed, mental health professionals, community folklore, and some research suggests that "coming out" to one's support network is one of the most effective strategies for reducing internalized homophobia and the stress of being g/l/b (Pimental-Habib, 1999; Troiden, 1988). While there has been a dramatic increase in the public and media visibility of g/l/b people, developing maintaining a social support system is a critical but often difficult developmental challenge (Cass, 1979; Hetrick & Martin, 1987; Troiden, 1988), primarily because of the anxiety of coming out to family and friends and/or because of the potential for negative reactions of some family and friends to learning that someone they know or love is g/l/b (Rotheram-Borus, Hunter, & Rosario, 1994; Ryan & Futterman, 1998; Strommen, 1993). Regardless of the quality of these support relationships, support networks are important because they (along with many other factors) influence the development of young people's self-concept and self-esteem. Among g/l/b youth, though, g/l/b people often have special developmental significance in that they are typically the individuals seen by youth as being most knowledgeable about being g/l/b and various role-related behaviors (Troiden, 1988; Wright & Connoley, 2002).

As g/l/b youth's support networks and connections to the g/l/b community increase, young people's awareness of the broader g/l/b community also will increase and so will their opportunities to experiment with romantic and sexual relationships. While the timing of sexual experimentation with members of the same sex varies significantly (Coleman, 1982; Savin-Williams, 1998), sexual experimentation constitutes an important element of the psychosexual development of most people's sexual identities, heterosexual or homosexual (Gagnon & Simon, 1973; Troiden, 1988). Further, because of the private, often secret, nature of the g/l/b "community," young people's efforts to develop social ties with other g/l/b people frequently target easily accessible and widely known gay "hang outs" such as the parking lots of g/l/b bars, restaurants or clubs, or major "cruising" areas.

These developmental processes suggest a dynamic relationship and interplay between a young person's feelings of *sexual identity distress* (i.e., the negative identity-related feelings associated with being g/l/b) and *the size and nature of his/her social support network*. Here, we argue that these forces have distinct effects on particular health risks that work together to shape the health status of g/l/b youth. Like most prior theories, we hypothesize that sexual identity distress is most pronounced during the early stages of sexual identity development and diminishes as young g/l/b people come out to more people in their support network and build a support system in which they can be open about their sexual identity. We further hypothesize, following Rotheram-Borus et al. (1995), that elevated levels of sexual identity distress are associated with higher levels of psychological distress and related mental health problems among g/l/b youth.

While being out in one's support network represents a vital developmental resource, we also hypothesize that having close social connections to other g/l/b people increases the likelihood that young people use alcohol and drugs frequently and/or engage in more risky sexual activities. Youth's health behavior decisions have been shown to be heavily influenced by peers (Fisher, Misovich, & Fisher, 1992). We believe that, in the case of g/l/b youth, social contact with other g/l/b is particularly influential because of the psychological salience of these social relationships in the sexual identity development process and because of tendency of g/l/b youth to find and forge ties with g/l/b in higher-risk social settings. Finally, many of these health behaviors have a strong social component in that they require or are more likely to occur with a peer partner (e.g., sex or drug use-behavior). Thus, we hypothesize that more social connections to other g/l/b people are associated with higher levels alcohol and drug use and sexual risk taking among g/l/b youth, especially during the early stages of the coming out process.

The close relationship between social networks and sexual identity formation suggests a dynamic process that will evolve and change over the course of adolescent development (see Hetrick & Martin, 1987 for a similar conclusion). The establishment of a more open and supportive network, we believe, contributes directly to a reduction in sexual identity distress over time, both because these networks provide affirmation for youth's sexual identities and because the support will help them develop their stigma-coping skills. As youth mature, however, so will their interpersonal and stigma coping skills. In this regard, they will become less psychologically distressed and will be more likely to possess the psychological resources to negotiate complex social relationships with peers and others. This expected change in the psychological health of youth should, in turn, influence how support networks affect their health behaviors. Of course, the type of influence will depend, in part, on the nature and quality of the network ties with whom a young person associates, but the potential for resisting negative social influence also will be enhanced.

As a first step in testing this theoretical perspective, this paper examines a series of health status indicators, including drug and alcohol use, psychological distress, and patterns of sexual activity in a cross-sectional sample of g/l/b youth early in the coming out process. We propose a new, more focused measure for assessing a young person's sexual identity distress and examine its relationship to a number of coming out-related indicators. We then examine the relative influence of sexual identity distress and social support on an array of health status and health behavior variables. Because our data are cross-sectional, we cannot fully describe the theoretical process described above. Our aim here is to establish the validity of focusing more narrowly on sexuality identity distress and to examine the distinctive contributions that sexual identity distress and social support have on the health status of youth early in the coming out process.

DATA AND METHODS

The data for this study come from a research project conducted as part of the Indiana Youth Access Project (IYAP), an HIV prevention services demonstration project conducted at the Indiana Youth Group, Inc. (IYG) in Indianapolis, Indiana. Founded in 1987, IYG is one of the oldest g/l/b youth serving agencies in the country. IYG is a youth development agency that offers both youth-directed programming (e.g., social activities, dances, peer-run community projects) and an array of professional support services (e.g., mental health counseling, information and referral, support groups, parent education, advocacy) (for more information visit: *www.indianayouthgroup.org*). The IYAP was developed to enhance programming around HIV prevention and identify effective strategies for helping g/l/b young people reduce their HIV risk. The demonstration was funded through a grant from the Health Resources and Services Administration's Special Projects of National Significance (SPNS) program (Wright et al., 1999; Wright, Gonzalez, Werner, Laughner, & Wallace, 1998). The grant provided funds to hire new staff and train existing staff to integrate HIV prevention interventions and services for HIV infected youth into existing IYG services and programming (Wright et al., 1998).

As part of the IYAP evaluation, in depth surveys were conducted with the young people participating in the program during the demonstration period (June, 1994 through May, 1998). Each young person was invited to participate in an interview within the first two months of entering the program. Respondents were informed initially in writing of the study during the intake process which typically involved a face-to-face meeting with an IYG staff member. Trained field workers who had no formal affiliation with the agency were responsible for actually recruiting potential participants into the study. Most recruitment occurred during IYG programs and activities which field workers attended regularly; however, in some cases, field staff contacted youth by phone or at their home, when this information and permission was provided by the youth. The face-to-face interviews were conducted by professionally trained field interviewers employed by the Principal Investigator. Interviews took, on average, approximately an hour and a half to complete. All subjects received ten dollars cash incentive upon completion of the interview to thank them for their time. The study was completely voluntary, and young people who did not wish to participate were allowed to access the full array of IYG programs and services. All procedures were reviewed and approved by the Institutional Review Board at Indiana University.

Sample

For these analyses, we focus on the 156 young people who completed an intake interview and who self-identified as g/l/b in response to a fixed multiple choice question (we included those who responded "other" when they used other synonyms indicating a homosexual sexual identity such as "queer" or "dyke"). An additional 15 youth actually completed an interview but self-identified as "questioning," "don't know," "straight," or refused to apply a traditional sexual identity label. Because of our theoretical interest is in sexual identity-related feelings, these youth are excluded from these analyses. The overall response rate for the study was 93.4% of the youth who consented during the intake processes to be contacted by the research staff about the study. The final sample represents approximately 55.7% of the all "new" clients served through the agency during the demonstration period (Wright et al., 1999). Because this suggested the possibility of a selection bias, we analyzed the demographic characteristics of the population served and the sample of youth who participated in the interviews. These analyses failed to identify any significant systematic statistical differences between the study sample and the cohort of new program clients (Wright et al., 1999).

Measures

The focus of this analysis is on sexual identity distress, social support, and the impact they have on the youth's health status and health-related behavior. *Sexual identity distress* was measured using a seven item scale developed for the IYAP project. Because a major focus of the program was on improving the young people's self-concepts as g/l/b, the first author developed this scale to assess the identity-related distress youth felt about their sexual orientation. The seven items were administered consistently across all respondents; however, interviewers were instructed to use the sexual identity label offered by the subject which was offered near the beginning of the interview. A detailed analysis of the items suggests that the scale is unidimensional, has high internal and test-retest reliability, and exhibits strong criterion validity (results available upon request). Using these seven items, a total SID score was computed by summing the individual items after reverse coding several items so that high scores indicated greater distress about being g/l/b. The range of the final scale was 7-35.

Social support was measured using the personal network data provided by the youth. Each respondent was asked to name and describe the people in their life right now that they talk to and depend on for help regarding important matters and health concerns. We developed three support variables. First, we computed the total size of their support network (i.e., the number of non-duplicate names listed in the personal network battery). Second, we computed the percent of people in their support network who the respondent indicated knew about their sexual identity. Finally, to assess the extent of a young person's social ties with other g/l/b people, we counted the total number of g/l/b people named in the young person's personal network battery.

Seven measures of *health status* are used in this analysis. Respondents were asked if they used any of 16 different drugs or drug types during the past 30 days. For each drug, they acknowledged using, they were asked a follow-up question regarding the number of days they had used each drug. We computed three drug measures reflecting drug use behaviors in the past 30 days: (a) number of different drugs; (b) number days used marijuana; and (c) number of days used all other drugs. Similarly, alcohol use was measured first by asking the young person if she/ he had used alcohol within the last 30 days and, if so, how many days within the past 30 days did they drink alcohol). In each case, non-users were recoded to "0" for each of the drug-use variables. Psychological distress was measured using the Global Severity Index (GSI) score from Symptom Checklist 90-Revised (Derogatis, 1991). Sexual behavior was measured through a series of nine questions about specific types of sexual activity (e.g., penile-vaginal intercourse, oral and anal sex with male/female) developed by an evaluator under contract for the funding agency. Respondents were asked to indicate the frequency they engaged in each type of sexual activity during the past six months by selecting one of four response categories: (1) 1-2 times, (2) 3-10 times,

(3) 11-25 times, and (4) 25 times or more. For each type of activity, the youth were asked if any of the contacts that had occurred in prior six months had occurred without a condom. Because our interest is in "risky" sexual behavior (i.e., sex acts which could transmit a sexually transmitted disease), we developed two measures. First, we estimated the number of "risky" sex acts as the average frequency measure across the nine sexual activity questions when the subject indicated that one or more of the acts had occurred without a condom or other latex protection. Prior to computing the average, we recoded "never" responses to 0 and each frequency category to the median value of the category ($1 = 1.5$, $2 = 6.5$, $3 = 18$, $4 = 25$) to provide a more descriptive estimate of the frequency of risky sexual acts across the nine sexual activity questions. In addition to sex acts, we also estimated the number of different partners the youth had had by averaging the number of reported different partners reported for each of the nine sex acts and collapsing them into four category ordinal measure: no partners; 1 partner; 2 partners; and 3 or more partners.

We also included a number of control variables in the multivariate analyses. Specifically, we included three demographic controls because of their associations with the health measures. The individual's gender and race were included as dummy variable controls (coded 1 if female; coded 1 if non-white). In addition, we computed the age of the young person at the time of the initial interview (in years). We also included a dummy variable to indicate if the respondent had ever left home. Because of the strong association between religious upbringing and religiosity and attitudes about homosexuality, we also included two measures to account for these background factors. Because of the heterogeneity in religious upbringings, we coded the religion the youth reported being raised in into a dummy variable based the relative "conservatism" of the religious doctrine espoused (Pescosolido & Georgianna, 1989), where 1 equals being raised in a conservative religion. In addition, respondents were asked to state how religious they are using a 5 point Likert scale ranging from "not religious" (1) to "very strong" (5). Individuals who indicated they were raised with no religion were assigned a religiosity code of 1. Finally, because many of the above measures have been suggested as being influenced by where they are in the coming out process, we also included a measure of the length of time each young person had been "out" to themselves. During the interview, each respondent was asked to state the age at which he/she first applied the g/l/b label to him/herself (Bell, Weinberg, & Hammersmith, 1981). The respondent's answer to this question was then subtracted from his/her current age to measure how long (in years) the respondent has been living with a g/l/b self-label.

Analysis

The analyses for this paper were conducted in three steps. First, we present descriptive statistics on the sample and the youth's sexual identity distress and their health status. Second, we explore the correlates and predictors of sexual identity distress. Finally, we examine the relationship between sexual identity distress, social support from g/l/b people, and our demographic, background, and demographic controls and our seven health status measures. Because our central dependent variables in the multivariate analyses were measured at the continuous or ordinal levels, we rely on standard ordinary least squares regression analytic techniques to model these relationships.

RESULTS

The demographic and background characteristics of the 156 subjects in this study are presented in Table 1. In terms of age, the youth ranged in ages from 13 to 21 (the maximum age youth are allowed to participate in IYG programming). The average age (and standard deviation) of youth in this sample is 18.19 (1.41). Like the surrounding area, the sample of youth was primarily Caucasian (N = 133, 85.3%). The largest groups of minority youth were Native American (N = 10, 6.4%) and African American (N = 8, 5.1%). The sample was almost equally split between young women (48.7%) and young men (51.3%). Almost two-thirds (59.0%) were in school at the time of the interview, although 64 (40.9%) reported having completed high school or a GED. Nearly three quarters of the youth were living at home (N = 112, 71.8%). Finally, early in the interview, the youth were asked to define their sexual orientation using a fixed choice response format. The majority (N = 109, 69.9%) selected "gay" or "lesbian" while the remainder self-identified as "bisexual" (N = 47, 30.1%). In terms of their support networks, the youth mentioned an average of 6.12 people (SD = 2.86), with no youth reporting no supports and only 1.3% (N = 2) indicating 1 supporter. The youth further indicated that they knew an average of 2.6 (SD = 1.93) people who were also g/l/b. In terms of being out to their support network, the youth reported that they were, on average, out to about 86% of the people in their support network, with three quarters of the sample

TABLE 1. Descriptive Characteristics of the Indiana Youth Access Project (IYAP) Sample (N = 156)

Characteristic	N	%
Age (Mean ± SD = 18.19 ± 1.41)		
15 or younger	12	7.7
16 to 17	54	34.6
18 to 19	72	46.2
20 or older	18	11.5
Race		
African American	8	5.1
Caucasian/White American	133	85.3
Native American	10	6.4
Other	5	3.2
Gender		
Female	76	48.7
Male	80	51.3
Last Grade of School Completed		
8 years or less	8	5.1
9 years	17	10.9
10 years	35	22.4
11 years	32	20.5
12 years or GED	37	23.7
Some College/Technical School	27	17.2
Lives with Family	112	71.8
Ever Left Home	58	37.4
Self-Defined Sexual Orientation		
Gay/Lesbian	109	69.9
Bisexual	47	30.1
Years Since First Self-Labeled as G/L/B (Mean ± SD = 3.09 ± 2.60)		
Less than a Year	34	21.8
1-1.99 Years	34	21.8
2-2.99 Years	22	14.1
3-4.99 Years	34	21.8
5 or More Years	32	20.5

Characteristic	N	%
Support Network Size (Mean ± SD = 6.12 ± 2.86)		
0	0	0.0
1	2	1.3
2	7	4.5
3	17	10.9
4	26	16.7
5	28	17.9
6 or more	76	48.7
Number of Gay, Lesbian, or Bisexual People in Support Network (Mean ± SD = 2.60 ± 1.93)		
0	15	9.6
1	37	23.7
2	33	21.2
3	30	19.2
4	18	11.5
5	10	6.4
6 or more	13	8.4
Percent of Support Network That Knows About the Young Person's Sexual Identity (Mean ± SD = 86.09 ± 24.29)		
0-25%	7	4.5
26%-50%	12	7.7
51%-75%	19	12.2
76%-100%	118	75.6
Family Religion		
Catholic	28	17.9
Liberal Protestant	30	19.2
Conservative Protestant	58	37.2
Other	5	3.2
None	35	22.4
Religiosity (Mean ± SD = 1.88 ± 1.06)		
Not Religious/No Religion (1)	79	50.6
Not So Strong (2)	32	20.5
Moderate (3)	31	19.9
Strong (4)	12	7.7
Very Strong (5)	2	1.3

stating that they were out to more than three quarters of their support network.

Table 2 presents the individual items and descriptive statistics for sexual identity distress scale. Higher scores on the scale indicate higher levels of distress. Overall, the average score on the sexual identity distress scale was 13.58 (SD = 4.49), below the absolute midpoint of the scale (21). The scale has an alpha reliability of .83. A factor analysis of these items suggests that the scale has a single dimension (Eigenvalue =

TABLE 2. Scale Items, Descriptive Statistics, and Factor Analysis Summary of the Sexual Identity Distress Scale (N = 156)[a]

Question[1]	Mean	SD	Factor Loading
1. I have a positive attitude about being (gay/lesbian/bisexual).	1.67	.78	.808
2. I feel uneasy around people who are very open in public about being (gay/lesbian/bisexual).*	3.77	1.04	.586
3. I often feel ashamed that I am (gay/lesbian/bisexual).*	4.24	.84	.760
4. For the most part, I enjoy being (gay/lesbian/bisexual).	1.75	.75	.803
5. I worry a lot about what others think about my being (gay/lesbian/bisexual).*	3.36	1.18	.519
6. I feel proud that I am (gay/lesbian/bisexual).	1.78	.82	.816
7. I wish I weren't attracted to the same sex.*	4.25	.85	.792
Total Sexual Identity Distress (Range: 7-35)	13.58	4.49	
Cronbach's Alpha			.83
Eigenvalue			3.78
Percent of Variance Explained			54.03

[a] Each statement was read verbatim to the respondent by the interviewer. In the item wording above, the phrase "(gay/lesbian/bisexual)" was used to instruct the interviewer to substitute the sexual identity label provided by the young person in response to a multiple choice sexual identity question posed earlier in the interview. Subjects could answer these questions using the following responses: "strongly agree" (1), "agree" (2), "mixed feelings" (3), "disagree" (4), and "strongly disagree" (5). Responses of "don't know" were recoded to the midpoint of the scale (3). Items marked with an asterisk (*) were recoded such that higher values indicated higher levels of internalized homophobia before computing the total score. The means and standard deviations for the individual items reported here reflect the mean response prior to recoding.

3.78) and explains the majority of the variance (54.03%). Additional analyses were conducted to establish criterion validity of the scale and suggest that it is related to a number of psychological characteristics (e.g., self-esteem, mastery) theorized to be related to internalized homophobia (details available upon request).

Table 3 presents the frequency distributions and descriptive statistics for the seven health indicators. Nearly two thirds of the youth (64.1%) indicated that they had not used any drug in the past 30 days. Looking across the different types of drugs, marijuana was the most frequently used drug (3.51 days on average) compared with the 15 other drugs we asked about. Just over half (51.3%) of the youth indicated that they had not drunk alcohol recently; however, about a third (34.0%) indicated having drunk alcohol 1-4 days in the past month. In terms of mental health status, subjects had an average GSI rating of .94 (SD = .65) which is somewhat higher than what is normally found in nonpatient adolescents (.76) (Derogatis, 1991). Finally, in terms of sexual risk taking, we found that 70 (44.9%) of the youth had no sexual partners in the past six months. In terms of their sexual behaviors, however, only about a third of their sex acts involved no risk for transmitting HIV or other sexually transmitted diseases.

Table 4 reports the regression analysis of the sexual identity distress scale. Among our control variables, the only significant effect is for age (B = .327, p ≤ .001) indicating that older youth in this sample were significantly more distressed about their sexual identity. Somewhat unexpectedly, race, years since self-labeling g/l/b, religion, and religiosity are not related to sexual identity distress levels. More interesting, the extent that a youth is out to their support network, however, is associated with lower levels of sexual identity distress (B = −.211, p ≤ .01) while the number of g/l/b people in a youth's support network is not (B = −.138, p = NS).

Table 5 presents the regression analyses of the seven health status/ behavior measures. Across the seven health models, there are several important demographic and background effects. Being non-white is associated with more alcohol use (B = .292, p ≤ .001). Older youth are more likely to report using alcohol (B = .223, p ≤ .01) and engaging in more risky sex acts (B = .281, p ≤ .001). Having left home, however, is the most important of the background characteristics assessed, increasing the number of drugs used recently (B = .312, p ≤ .001), the number days they used marijuana (B = .211, p ≤ .01) or other drugs (B = .218, p ≤ .01), their overall psychological distress (B = .230, p ≤ .01), and the number of risky sex acts they report having participated in during the

TABLE 3. Frequency Distributions and Descriptive Statistics of the Health Risk Indicators, Indiana Youth Access Project (N = 156)

Health Risk Indicator		N	%	Mean	SD
Number of Different Drugs Used in Past 30 Days[a]				.65	1.13
	None	100	64.1		
	1	33	21.2		
	2-3	17	10.9		
	4-6	6	3.8		
Number of Days Used Marijuana in Past 30 Days				3.51	7.62
	None	107	68.6		
	1-4 Days	14	9.0		
	5-9 Days	12	7.7		
	10 Days or More	23	14.7		
Average Number of Days Used Other Drugs in Past 30 Days				1.25	4.14
	None	128	82.1		
	1-4 Days	14	9.0		
	5-9 Days	7	4.5		
	10 Days or More	7	4.5		
Average Number of Days Drank Alcohol in Past 30 Days				2.22	4.42
	None	80	51.3		
	1-4 Days	53	34.0		
	5-9 Days	9	5.8		
	10 Days or More	14	9.0		
Psychological Distress (SCL 90-Revised GSI Score, Range: 0-2.90)				.94	.65
Individuals Scoring 1 SD Above Adolescent Non-Patient Norm (Mean ± SD =.76 ± .54)		37	23.7		
Number of Risky Sex Acts in Past 6 Months				15.75	21.66
	None	52	33.3		
	1-9 Risky Sex Acts	33	21.2		
	10-24 Risky Sex Acts	33	21.2		
	25-49 Risky Sex Acts	27	17.3		
	50 or More Risky Sex Acts	11	7.1		

Health Risk Indicator		N	%	Mean	SD
Number of Sex Partners in Past 6 Months				--	--
	None	70	44.9		
	1 Partner	50	32.1		
	2 Partners	9	5.8		
	Three or More Partners	27	17.3		

[a]Respondents were asked about 13 drugs or drug types: (1) marijuana, hashish, (2) crack, (3) cocaine, (4) heroin by itself; (5) heroin & cocaine or heroin & speed mixed together; (6) amphetamines, (7) poppers (8) inhalants; (9) mushrooms; (10) MDMA; (11) Ecstasy; (12) acid; and (13) other (Respondents were allowed to specify only 1 "other drug").

TABLE 4. Regression Analysis of Sexual Identity Distress, Indiana Youth Access Project (N = 156)[a]

	B (S.E.)
Gender (Female)	−.117 (.717)
Race (Nonwhite)	.041 (.978)
Age (in Years)	.327*** (.255)
Left Home (Yes)	−.029 (.712)
Religion (Conservative)	.093 (.692)
Religiosity	−.096 (.325)
Years "Out" to Self About Sexual Identity	−.120 (.136)
Size of Support Network	.087 (.172)
Percent of Support Network Who Know About R's Sexual Identity	−.211** (.015)
Number of Gay/Lesbian/Bisexual People in Network	−.138 (.265)
F	3.680***
S.E.E.	4.150
R^2	.204

$+ = p \leq .10$; $* = p \leq .05$; $** = p \leq .01$; $*** \leq .001$
[a]Standardized regression coefficients (B) and standard errors (in parentheses) are reported.

TABLE 5. Regression Analysis of the Health Status Indicators, Indiana Youth Access Project (N = 156)[a]

	Number of Drugs Used in Past 30 Days	Number of Days Used Marijuana in Past 30 Days	Number of Days Used Other Drugs in Past 30 Days	Number of Days Drank Alcohol in Past 30 Days	Psychological Distress (GSI)	Risky Sexual Acts in Past 6 Months	Number of Sex Partners in Past 6 Months
	B (S.E.)	B (S.E.)	B (S.E.)	B (S.E.)	B (S.E.)	B (S.E.)	B (S.E.)
Gender (Female)	.003 (.183)	.061 (.189)	-.154+ (.128)	.100 (.727)	.142+ (.109)	-.004 (.212)	-.278*** (.178)
Race (Nonwhite)	.132 (.255)	.130 (.264)	.051 (.179)	.292*** (1.014)	-.038 (.151)	-.027 (.291)	.021 (.248)
Age (in Years)	-.038 (.067)	.017 (.069)	-.116 (.047)	.223* (.266)	-.144+ (.040)	.281*** (.078)	.093 (.065)
Left Home (Yes)	.312*** (.181)	.211** (.187)	.218** (.126)	.087 (.718)	.230** (.107)	.164* (.211)	.019 (.176)
Years "Out" to Self About Sexual Identity	-.001 (.035)	-.058 (.036)	.088 (.024)	.074 (.138)	.076 (.021)	-.069 (.041)	-.044 (.034)
Size of Support Network	.054 (.044)	-.092 (.045)	-.069 (.030)	.143 (.173)	.069 (.026)	-.159 (.051)	-.104 (.042)
Percent of Support Network Who Know About R's Sexual Identity	.001 (.004)	-.011 (.004)	-.011 (.003)	.044 (.015)	.068 (.002)	-.007 (.005)	.020 (.004)

	Number of Drugs Used in Past 30 Days	Number of Days Used Marijuana in Past 30 Days	Number of Days Used Other Drugs in Past 30 Days	Number of Days Drank Alcohol in Past 30 Days	Psychological Distress (GSI)	Risky Sexual Acts in Past 6 Months	Number of Sex Partners in Past 6 Months
	B (S.E.)	B (S.E.)	B (S.E.)	B (S.E.)	B (S.E.)	B (S.E.)	B (S.E.)
Number of Gay/Lesbian/Bisexual People in Network	.076 (.068)	.180 (.070)	.215+ (.047)	−.111 (.269)	−.041 (.040)	.250* (.079)	.335** (.066)
Sexual Identity Distress	−.170* (.021)	−.161+ (.022)	−.012 (.015)	−.171* (.084)	.293*** (.012)	.009 (.025)	−.112 (.020)
F	3.310***	2.126*	2.167*	2.917**	2.538**	3.020***	3.254***
S.E.E.	1.056	1.092	.738	4.190	.626	1.233	1.026
R^2	.179	.117	.119	.154	.137	.158	.169

+ = $p \leq .10$; * = $p \leq .05$; ** = $p \leq .01$; *** = $p \leq .001$

[a]Standardized regression coefficients (B) and standard errors (in parentheses) are reported.

past six months (B = .164, p ≤ .001). Religion and religiosity had no effect on any of our health status or health behavior indicators (details available upon request); consequently, they are not included in the final models presented in Table 5.

Some additional interesting patterns are apparent when we examine the effects of time since self-labeling as g/l/b, support from g/l/b people, and sexual identity distress. Across all seven models, we find no significant effect of time since self-labeling (B's range from −.001 to .088, p ≤ NS). Knowing more g/l/b, however, is associated with engaging in more risky sex acts (B = .250, p ≤ .05) and having more sexual partners in the past six months (B = .335, p ≤ .01). More frequent use of other drugs is also found to be associated with having more g/l/b people in youth's social support networks (B = .215), although only at the .10 level. In contrast to our hypothesis, there is no significant relationship between having social ties to g/l/b people on these young people's patterns of alcohol use (B = −.111, p ≤ NS).

Most interesting, our measure of sexual identity distress has significant effects on the number of drugs used (B = −.170, p ≤ .05), alcohol use (B = −.171, p ≤ .05), and, possibly, on the number of days the youth used marijuana (B = −.161, p ≤ .10). This effect, however, is consistently negative suggesting that higher levels of sexual identity distress reduce the frequency that g/l/b youth engage in these health risk behaviors. As hypothesized, higher levels of sexual identity distress, however, increase psychological distress among the youth (B = .293, p ≤ .01),

DISCUSSION

Like prior theory and research, our findings indicate that sexual identity distress, a theoretical sub-dimension of internalized homophobia, is an important factor in shaping the health status of g/l/b youth. Specifically, we find that sexual identity distress is strongly related to general psychological distress. That is, when youth feel more negative affect about their sexual orientation they are more likely to report significant mental health problems, an issue that appears to be especially problematic among the older youth in our sample. Our analyses also highlight that the more open a young person is about their sexual identity with members of their support network, the less likely he/she is to experience high levels of sexual identity distress.

Our results regarding the health status and health-related behavior of g/l/b youth, however, are more complicated. We find, perhaps not surprisingly, that youth who have left home one or more times are more likely to engage in poly substance use and do so more frequently than youth who have not. These youth also report higher levels of psychological distress and more risky sex acts over the past 6 months. The young women in our study tend to report fewer sex partners in the past six months than the young men. Minority youth drink alcohol more frequently than the white youth. Older youth, not surprisingly, indicate that they drink alcohol more frequently and engage in more risky sexual acts than younger youth.

With regard to our central theoretical variables, the size of our youth's support network and the extent that they are out to them had very little effect on their health behavior. However, our findings do suggest that having more g/l/b people in one's network is associated with having more frequent risky sexual activity, having more sexual partners, and, possibly, more frequent use of drugs other than marijuana. Sexual identity distress, in contrast, is associated with using fewer drugs and less frequent alcohol use. In sum, sexual identity distress and social support from g/l/b people have distinct and significant consequences for g/l/b youth's health.

At a more general level, the pattern of findings from our study challenge current theoretical thinking regarding the link between internalized homophobia and the health of g/l/b people (French et al., 1996; Rosario et al., 1997; Rotheram-Borus et al., 1995; Savin-Williams, 1990; Savin-Williams & Lenhart, 1990; Winters et al., 1996). As noted above, it is frequently theorized that internalized homophobia diminishes the capacity of g/l/b young people's abilities to make healthy decisions regarding risky behaviors and may even motivate them to engage in self-destructive behavior. Our results, however, suggest that this process is more complex and reflects a fundamental developmental tension between sexual identity distress and the support networks of g/l/b people that young people form.

On the one hand, sexual identity distress appears to have a significant, but specific, negative affect on the mental health status of youth. At the same time, it is associated with lower levels of some risk behavior, in particular the use of drugs and alcohol. This suggests that sexual identity distress may decrease the willingness and/or opportunities young people have to experiment in more peer-group-based risk behaviors common during adolescence and early adulthood. While it is not possible to specify the precise nature of this effect with the data available, we believe our findings reflect the social isolation that g/l/b youth often feel when they are first coming out and when they are most likely to feel sexual identity distress. That is, we believe that sexual identity distress reduces young people's use of drugs and alcohol, in part, because it isolates them socially and psychologically from traditional peer-groups where these behaviors are likely to occur (e.g., non-g/l/b youth at school).

At the same time, the current g/l/b social network context in which young people are located also impacts their health status. Being out to one's support network seems to reduce the young people's sexual identity distress, probably because this type of support relieves the internal and external stress associated with maintaining a concealed identity (DiPlacido, 1998). Our data, however, do indicate that having more supporters who are g/l/b is associated with engaging in more frequent risky sexual behavior and having more sex partners. We do not believe these results indicate that all g/l/b support is "bad" for g/l/b youth's health. Indeed, contact with g/l/b people is probably developmentally very important in helping young people learn about the g/l/b role and community (Troiden, 1988; Wright & Connoley, 2002). Rather, we believe that the observed effect probably reflects the fact that social ties to g/l/b people often create new opportunities for sexual behavior while also providing other types of informational and emotional support. While it is not possible to explain what is behind this effect, it underscores the need to devote more theoretical and empirical attention to the roles that g/l/b people play in the socialization of g/l/b youth (Wright & Connoley, 2002).

While the cross-sectional data make it impossible to specify the precise nature of the complex causal dynamics, prior theoretical models, described above, suggest that confronting sexual identity distress, in the very early phases of the coming out process, may be largely an individual, psychological process (Cass, 1979; Cass, 1984; Troiden, 1988). Coming out to others and developing ties with other g/l/b people are typically experiences that come somewhat later once a young person has been at least somewhat successful in challenging their internalized feelings of homophobia. The empirical relationships among being out, contact with other g/l/b people, and sexual identity distress clearly reflect complex social and developmental processes that need further longitudinal empirical exploration. The youth we surveyed, while clearly early in the coming out process, were contacted because they were reaching out to an agency that provides support services to g/l/b youth implying that they had already begun the process of becoming integrated into the g/l/b community. This fact, in particular, limits our ability to disentangle the causal inter-connections between social support and sexual identity distress.

When considered within a psychosexual developmental framework, however, our findings underline both the potentialities and risks associated with early social integration into the g/l/b community. Developmentally, having ties to other g/l/b people are critical for challenging stereotypes and learning about the g/l/b role (Troiden, 1988). At the same time, the types of relationships a young person establishes during this period will shape the types of socialization opportunities they have. When these relationships are with individuals who engage in risk behavior, they may encourage young people to engage in risky behavior and even establish risky behavior patterns. On the other hand, if these contacts are with youth or adults who promote or support lower risk behavior, the impact these networks have will likely be more positive (Fisher, 1988; Fisher et al., 1992; McKusick, Coates, Morin, Pollack, & Hoff, 1990; McKusick, Horstman, & Coates, 1985). Our data, however, suggest a correlation between having more g/l/b supports and more frequent risk sexual contacts and more sexual partners and point to the need to explore this dynamic process in future studies.

Finally, the findings of this study further underscore the social nature of g/l/b youth's health status. At the most basic level, it affirms the social sources of youth's distress about their sexual identities and the importance that having a supportive network of others has on these feelings. This study also hints that adults and peers can play important roles in the lives of g/l/b youth as health promoters. Early in the HIV/AIDS epidemic, adult gay men and lesbians identified both the political and community importance of trying to change their culture to be more supportive of reducing risky behaviors, and many of their efforts have been fairly successful (Fisher, 1988; McKusick et al., 1990). Because g/l/b youth's connections and understanding of the adult g/l/b culture are often more tenuous and experienced through their relationships with other youth, they have been relatively immune from the cultural changes in the adult community. In this regard, the growing media visibility of g/l/b people (or characters) may be an additional mechanism through which to influence g/l/b youth's health behavior, especially since shows like MTV's *Real World* or Showtime's *Queer as Folk* have been extremely successful in presenting open and frank depictions of growing up g/l/b, the challenges youth encounter, and various ways youth have resolved these dilemmas. In short, researchers, youth advocates, clinicians, and g/l/b community leaders need to focus more attention on understanding and developing community interventions to help youth become integrated into g/l/b communities in ways that support and encourage health.

Both the cross-sectional nature of our study and our reliance on a sample of youth early in the coming out process pose important limitations on the interpretations one can draw from this study, particular with regard to how these patterns may or may not persist over time. Indeed, we theorize that the early effect of sexual identity distress is specific to people in the early phases of coming out and may have different effects at different ages or in later phases of psychosocial sexual development. However, our data do not permit us to examine changes in sexual identity distress over the course of sexual identity development. At the same time, the fact that all of the youth were recruited following their initial contact with a g/l/b youth-serving agency suggests that they probably are not representative of the experiences of youth who do not have access to such support services. Further research is needed to determine the generalizability of these findings and to extend this analysis into a truly developmental framework that examines patterns of risk behavior, sexual identity distress, and social support over an extended period of time.

CONCLUSIONS

This research examined the impact of sexual identity distress and social support on the health of g/l/b youth. The findings indicate that being out to one's support network is an important predictor of lower levels of sexual identity distress. Support from g/l/b people, however, is associated with more frequent sexual risk taking. At the most general level, these findings suggest the need to think about the social and psychological dimensions of the developmental processes associated with coming out. Previous research and theory has emphasized the importance of reducing youth's feelings of sexual identity distress, commonly described as internalized homophobia, as a risk behavior prevention strategy. The present investigation suggests that this may oversimplify a much more complex developmental process.

REFERENCES

Allen, D. J., & Oleson, T. (1999). Shame and Internalized Homophobia in Gay Men. *Journal of Homosexuality, 37*(3), 33-43.

Barranti, J. (1998). Social Work Practice with Gay Male Couples. G. P. Mallon. Binghamton, NY: Haworth Press.

Bell, A. P., Weinberg, M. S., & Hammersmith, S. K. (1981). *Sexual Preference: Its Development in Men and Women.* Bloomington, IN: Indiana University Press.

Cass, V. C. (1979). Homosexual Identity Formation: A Theoretical Model. *Journal of Homosexuality, 4*(3), 219-35.

Cass, V. C. (1984). Homosexual Identity Formation: Testing a Theoretical Model. *Journal of Sex Research, 20*(2), 143-67.

Coleman, E. (1982). Developmental Stages of the Coming-Out Process. W. Paul, J. D. Weinrich, J. C. Gonsiorek, & M. E. Hotvedt (pp. 149-58). Beverly Hills, CA: Sage Publications.

D'Augelli, A. R. (1998). Developmental Implications of Victimization of Lesbian, Gay, and Bisexual Youth. G. M. Herek (Editor), *Stigma and Sexual Orientation: Understanding Prejudice Against Lesbians, Gay Men, and Bisexuals* (pp. 187-210). Thousand Oaks, CA: Sage Publications.

Derogatis, L. R. (1991). *SCL-90_R: Symptom Checklist-90-R: Administration, Scoring and Procedures Manual, Third Edition.*

DiPlacido, J. (1998). Minority Stress Among Lesbians, Gay Men, and Bisexuals: A Consequence of Heterosexism, Homophobia, and Stigmatization. G. M. Herek (Editor), *Stigma and Sexual Orientation: Understanding Prejudice Against Lesbians, Gay Men, and Bisexuals* (pp. 138-59). Thousand Oaks, CA: Sage Publications.

Fisher, J. D. (1988). Possible Effects of Reference Group-Based Social Influence on AIDS-Risk Behavior and AIDS Prevention. *American Psychologist, 43*(11), 914-20.

Fisher, J. D., Misovich, S. J., & Fisher, W. A. (1992). Impact of Perceived Social Norms on Adolescents' AIDS-Risk Behavior and Prevention. R. J. DiClementi (pp. 117-36). Newbury Park, CA: Sage.

Frabel, D. E. S., Wortman, C., & Joseph, J. (1997). Predicting Self-Esteem, Well-Being, and Distress in a Cohort of Gay Men: The Importance of Cultural Stigma, Personal Visibility, Community Networks, and Positive Identity. *Journal of Personality, 65*(3), 598-624.

French, S. A., Story, M., Remafedi, G., Resnick, M. D., & Blum, R. W. (1996). Sexual Orientation and Prevalence of Body Dissatisfaction and Eating Disordered Behaviors: A Population Based Study of Adolescents. *International Journal of Eating Disorders, 19*(2), 119-26.

Gagnon, J., & Simon, W. (1973). *Sexual Conduct: The Social Sources of Human Sexuality.* Chicago, IL: Aldine.

Gay and Lesbian Medical Association and LGBT Health Experts. (2001). *Healthy People 2010 Companion Document for Lesbian, Gay, Bisexual, and Transgender (LGBT) Health.* San Francisco, CA: Gay and Lesbian Medical Association.

Gibson, P. (1989). *Gay Male and Lesbian Youth Suicide* (Report of the Secretary's Task Force on Youth Suicide. Washington, D.C.: Alcohol Drug Abuse and Mental Health Administration (ADAMHA) Department of Health and Human Services (DHHS).

Gonsiorek, J. (1982). The Use of Diagnositic Concepts in Working with Gay and Lesbian Populations. *Journal of Homosexuality, 7*(2/3), 9-20.

Grossman, A., & Kerner, M. S. (1998). Self-Esteem and Supportiveness as Predictors of Emotional Distress in Gay Male and Lesbian Youth. *Journal of Homosexuality, 35*(2), 25-39.

Hardin, K. N. (1999). *The Gay and Lesbian Self-Esteem Book: A Guide to Loving Our-selves.* Oakland, CA: New Harbinger Publications.

Hetrick, E. S., & Martin, A. D. (1987). Developmental Issues and Their Resolution for Gay and Lesbian Adolescents. *Journal of Homosexuality, 14,* 25-43.

Malyon, A. K. (1982). Psychotherapeutic Implications of Internalized Homophobia in Gay Men. *Journal of Homosexuality, 7*(2/3), 59-69.

Mays, V. M., & Cochran, S. D. (1988). Issues in the Perception of AIDS Risk and Risk Reduction Activities by Black and Hispanic/Latina Women. *American Psychologist, 43*(11), 949-957.

McKusick, L., Coates, T. J., Morin, S. F., Pollack, L., & Hoff, C. (1990). Longitudinal Predictors of Reductions in Unprotected Anal Intercourse among Gay Men in San Francisco: The AIDS Behavioral Research Project. *American Journal of Public Health, 80*(8), 978-83.

McKusick, L., Horstman, W., & Coates, T. J. (1985). AIDS and Sexual Behavior Reported by Gay Men in San Francisco. *American Journal of Public Health, 75*(5), 493-96.

Meyer, I., & Dean, L. (1998). Internalized Homophobia, Intimacy, and Sexual Behavior Among Gay and Bisexual Men. G. M. Herek (Editor), *Stigma and Sexual Orientation* (pp. 160-86). Newbury Park, CA: Sage Publications.

Meyer, I. H. (1995). Minority Stress and Mental Health in Gay Men. *Journal of Health and Social Behavior, 36*(March), 38-56.

Miranda, J., & Storms, M. (1989). Psychological Adjustment of Lesbians and Gay Men. *Journal of Counseling & Development, 68,* 41-45.

Nungesser, L. G. (1983). *Homosexual Acts, Actors, and Identities.* New York, NY: Praeger.

Pescosolido, B. A., & Georgianna, S. (1989). Durkheim, Suicide, and Religion: Toward a Network Theory of Suicide. *American Sociological Review, 54,* 33-48.

Pimental-Habib, R. L. (1999). *Empowering the Tribe: A Positive Guide to Gay and Lesbian Self-Esteem.* New York, NY: Kensington Books.

Remafedi, G. (1994a). Cognitive and Behavioral Adaptations to HIV/AIDS Among Gay and Bisexual Adolescents. *Journal of Adolescent Health, 15,* 142-148.

Remafedi, G. (1994b). Predictors of Unprotected Intercourse Among Gay and Bisexual Youth: Knowledge, Beliefs and Behavior. *Pediatrics, 94,* 163-168.

Remafedi, G., Farrow, J., & Deisher, R. (1991). Risk factors for attempted suicide in gay and bisexual youth. *Pediatrics, 87,* 869-75.

Rosario, M., Hunter, J., & Gwadz, M. (1997). Exploration of Substance Use Among Lesbian, Gay, and Bisexual Youth: Prevalence and Correlates. *Journal of Adolescent Research, 12*(4), 454-76.

Rosario, M., Meyer-Bahlburg, H. F. L., Hunter, J., Exner, T., Gwadz, M., & Keller, A. M. (1996). The Psychosexual Development of Urban Lesbian, Gay, and Bisexual Youths. *Journal of Sex Research, 33*(2), 113-126.

Rosario, M., Rotherham-Borus, M. J., & Reid, H. (1996). Gay Related Stress and Its Correlates Among Gay and Bisexual Male Adolescents of Predominantly Black and Hispanic Background. *Journal of Community Psychology, 24,* 136-59.

Rotheram-Borus, M. J., Hunter, J., & Rosario, M. (1994). Suicidal Behavior and Gay-Related Stress Among Gay and Bisexual Males. *Journal of Adolescent Research, 9*(4), 498-508.

Rotheram-Borus, M. J., & Koopman, C. (1991). Sexual Risk Behaviors, AIDS Knowledge, and Beliefs about AIDS Among Predominantly Minority Gay and Bisexual Male Adolescents. *American Journal of Public Health, 81*, 208-210.

Rotheram-Borus, M. J., Rosario, M., Reid, H., & Koopman, C. (1995). Predicting Patterns of Sexual Acts Among Homosexual and Bisexual Youths. *American Journal of Psychiatry, 152*(4), 588-95.

Russell, S. T., Franz, B. T., & Driscoll, A. K. (2001). Same-Sex Romantic Attraction and Experiences of Violence in Adolescence. *American Journal of Public Health, 91*(June), 903-906.

Ryan, C., & Futterman, D. (1998). *Lesbian and Gay Youth: Care and Counseling.* New York, NY: Columbia University Press.

Savin-Williams, R. C. (1990). *Gay and Lesbian Youth: Expressions of Identity.* New York: Hemisphere Publishing Corporation.

Savin-Williams, R. C. (1994). Verbal and Physical Abuse as Stressors in the Lives of Lesbian, Gay Male, and Bisexual Youths: Associations with School Problems, Running Away, Substance Abuse, Prostitution, and Suicide. *Journal of Consulting and Clinical Psychology, 62*, 261.

Savin-Williams, R. C. (1998). *And Then I Became Gay: Young Men's Stories.* New York, NY: Routledge.

Savin-Williams, R. C., & Lenhart, R. E. (1990). AIDS Prevention among Gay and Lesbian Youth: Psychosocial Stress and Health Care Intervention Guidelines. D. G. Ostrow (pp. 75-99). New York, NY: Plenum Press.

Shidlo, A. (1994). Internalized Homophobia: Conceptual and Empirical Issues in Measurement. B. Greene, & G. M. Herek (pp. 176-205). Thousand Oaks, CA: Sage.

Strommen, E. F. (1993). "You're a What?": Family Member Reactions to the Disclosure of Homosexuality. L. D. Garnets, & D. C. Kimmel (Editors), *Psychological Perspectives on Lesbian and Gay Male Experiences* (pp. 248-266). New York, NY: Columbia University Press.

Stryker, S. (1980). *Symbolic Interactionism: A Social Structural Version.* Menlo Park, CA: Benjamin/Cummings Publishing.

Troiden, R. R. (1988). *Gay and Lesbian Identity: A Sociological Analysis.* Dix Hills, NY: General-Hall.

Wagner, G., Brondolo, E., & Rabkin, J. (1996). Internalized Homophobia in a Sample of HIV+ Gay Men, and Its Relationship to Psychological Distress, Coping, and Illness Progression. *Journal of Homosexuality, 32*(2), 91-106.

Walters, K. L., & Simoni, J. M. (1993). Lesbian and Gay Male Group Identity Attitudes and Self-Esteem: Implications for Counseling. *Journal of Counseling Psychology, 40*(1), 94-99.

Weinberg, M. S., & Williams, C. J. (1974). *Male Homosexuals: Their Problems and Adaptations.* New York, NY: Oxford University Press.

Winters, K. C., Remafedi, G., & Chan, B. Y. (1996). Assessing Drug Abuse Among Gay-Bisexual Young Men. *Psychology of Addictive Behaviors, 10*(4), 228-36.

Wright, E. R., & Connoley, R. E. (2002). Empowering Forces: Professional Careworkers in the Support Networks of Gay, Lesbian, and Bisexual Youth. F. Cancian, D. Kurz, A. London, R. Reviere, & M. Tuominen (Editors), *Carework for Children and Youth* (pp. 159-173). Boston: Routledge-Kegan Paul.

Wright, E. R., Dye, J. D., Jiles, M. E., & Marcello, M. K. (1999). *Empowering Gay, Lesbian, and Bisexual Youth: Findings From the Indiana Youth Access Project.*

Wright, E. R., Gonzalez, C., Werner, J. N., Laughner, S. T., & Wallace, M. (1998). The Indiana Youth Access Project (IYAP): Responding to the HIV Risk of Gay, Lesbian, and Bisexual Youth in the Heartland. *Journal of Adolescent Health, 23*(Supplement), 83-95.

Transgender Youth:
Invisible and Vulnerable

Arnold H. Grossman, PhD

New York University

Anthony R. D'Augelli, PhD

The Pennsylvania State University

SUMMARY. This study used three focus groups to explore factors that affect the experiences of youth (ages 15 to 21) who identify as transgender. The focus groups were designed to probe transgender youths' experiences of vulnerability in the areas of health and mental health. This involved their exposure to risks, discrimination, marginalization, and their access to supportive resources. Three themes emerged from an analysis of the groups' conversations. The themes centered on gender identity and gender presentation, sexuality and sexual orientation, and vulnerability and health issues. Most youth reported feeling they were transgender at puberty, and they experienced negative reactions to their gender atypical behaviors, as well as confusion between their gender

Arnold H. Grossman is Professor of Applied Psychology, The Steinhardt School of Education at New York University. Anthony R. D'Augelli is Professor of Human Development, Department of Human Development and Family Studies, The Pennsylvania State University. Correspondence may be addressed: Arnold H. Grossman, Department of Applied Psychology, New York University, 35 West 4th Street–Suite 1200, New York, NY 10012 (E-mail: arnold.grossman@nyu.edu). The New York University Research Challenge Fund funded this research.

[Haworth co-indexing entry note]: "Transgender Youth: Invisible and Vulnerable." Grossman, Arnold H., and Anthony R. D'Augelli. Co-published simultaneously in *Journal of Homosexuality* (Harrington Park Press, an imprint of The Haworth Press, Inc.) Vol. 51, No. 1, 2006, pp. 111-128; and: *Current Issues in Lesbian, Gay, Bisexual, and Transgender Health* (ed: Jay Harcourt) Harrington Park Press, an imprint of The Haworth Press, Inc., 2006, pp. 111-128. Single or multiple copies of this article are available for a fee from The Haworth Document Delivery Service [1-800-HAWORTH, 9:00 a.m. - 5:00 p.m. (EST). E-mail address: docdelivery@haworthpress.com].

identity and sexual orientation. Youth noted four problems related to their vulnerability in health-related areas: the lack of safe environments, poor access to physical health services, inadequate resources to address their mental health concerns, and a lack of continuity of caregiving by their families and communities. *[Article copies available for a fee from The Haworth Document Delivery Service: 1-800-HAWORTH. E-mail address: <docdelivery@haworthpress.com> Website: <http://www.HaworthPress.com>* © *2006 by The Haworth Press, Inc. All rights reserved.]*

KEYWORDS. Transgender, youth, gender, lesbian, gay, bisexual, sexual orientation, vulnerability, health

INTRODUCTION

Transgender youth are invisible in most Western cultures because social structures assume a binary classification of gender. Individuals are expected to assume the gender of their biological sex as well as the gender expectations and roles associated with it. As nearly all people are classified as male or female, those who express characteristics ordinarily attributed to the other gender are stigmatized and seen often as social deviants. Inconsistency in the presentation between biological sex and gender expression is usually not tolerated by others (Gagne & Tewksbury, 1996). Because these individuals violate conventional gender expectations, they become targeted for discrimination and victimization. Thus they become members of a marginalized and vulnerable population that experiences more psychosocial and health problems than other social groups (Lombardi, 2001).

Transgender is a term used to describe individuals who exhibit gender-nonconforming identities and behaviors, or in other words, those who transcend typical gender paradigms (Ryan & Futterman, 1997). This broad category of people includes transsexuals (i.e., those who have made the transition to living in the gender other than the one originally assigned to them), cross-dressers (e.g., transvestites, drag queens, drag kings), and gender benders/blenders (i.e., those who purposefully present an ambiguous gender expression). Although most transgender people are heterosexual, they may also be lesbian, gay, bisexual or asexual (Davenport, 1986; Ryan & Futterman, 1997). However, as sexual orientation is based on the gender of one's erotic object of choice, sexual orientation and gender are often confused (Bornstein, 1994). But gender is a combination of one's birth sex, gender role and gender identity, whereas sexual orientation encompasses sexual attraction, sexual identity and sexual behavior.

Many transgender individuals, however, seek services from gay-sensitive service providers. As Ryan and Futterman (1997) indicate, and as these providers have come to learn, transgender people are generally more stigmatized than lesbians and gay males in contemporary society and require more support and services. This situation is even more difficult if the person is an adolescent or young adult.

Exhibiting gender-atypical behavior makes transgender youth an especially vulnerable population. Flaskerud (1999) describes vulnerable populations as "social groups who experience relatively more illness, premature death, and diminished quality of life than comparable groups" (p. xv). She relates vulnerability to a lack of resources and increased risk associated with discrimination, marginalization and disenfranchisement. Facing significant prejudice and discrimination in school, employment opportunities, housing, and access to health care, many transgender youth live outside mainstream society (Burgess, 1999; Mallon, 1999b). As gender-atypical behavior is much less accepted in boys than girls, biological males who are transgender are most often the targets of verbal and physical abuse. Without resources and support, these youth often drop out of school, run away, and end up on the streets, where they may engage in survival sex and become at risk for HIV and other sexually transmitted infections (Klein, 1999).

BACKGROUND

Developing and integrating a positive identity is a developmental task for all adolescents. For transgender youth, however, there is the additional challenge of integrating a complex gender identity with their cultural and ethnic backgrounds, personal characteristics, and family circumstances. They are faced not only with the task of developing a sexual identity, but also with reconciling their gender identity with the traditional gender expectations associated with their biological sex. As Woodhouse (1989) observed in her study of transvestites, the appearance of femininity denoting female sex and masculinity denoting male sex is so ingrained in society that we take it for granted; and "all we have to go on is appearance" (p. 3).

Not much systematic, empirically based information is available about transgender individuals. Likewise, there is very limited knowledge about transgender youth. Indeed, Mallon (1999b, p. 9) noted, "If the research on gay and lesbians persons is slim, the research on transgendered persons is almost non-existent." In a comprehensive review of the needs of lesbian and gay youth in *Adolescent Medicine*, Ryan and Futterman (1997) devoted only two pages (out of more than 340) to transgender youth. They noted that most information has been obtained from transsexuals who have sought counseling or services from gender identity clinics (see Lewins, 1995). Other information has been provided in retrospective anecdotal reports by transgender individuals or their family members (e.g., Boenke, 1999; Bornstein, 1994; Evelyn, 1998). Lewins (1995) deduced that four themes emerge from these accounts: (1) a long history of tension between the person's biological sex and his or her preferred gender, (2) an awareness and experience of being different as a child, accompanied by bullying and teasing at school, (3) a current internal struggle to reconcile the conflict between psychosexual identity and biological sex, and (4) the need for continued coping with the negative social responses to the disclosure of these feelings. Many of the transgender individuals described in the literature have health problems, including high rates of substance abuse, attempted suicide, childhood abuse, past sexual abuse/assault, and psychiatric disorders (Cole, O'Boyle, Emory, & Meyer, 1997; Cosentino, Meyer-Bahlburg, Alpert, & Gaines, 1993; Devor, 1994, 1997; Rottnek, 1999; Ryan & Futterman, 1997). Some (e.g., Burgess, 1999) have suggested that the descriptions based on the self-selected transgender people who seek treatment have led to a pathologizing stereotype of these people. Additionally, many who have used hormones to develop desired female or male secondary sex characteristics, have obtained these hormones on the street, fearing negative reactions from health care providers. The improper use and abuse of sex hormones has led to serious health problems and may have impacted their pubertal growth. Furthermore, obtaining hormones on the streets has put transgender youth at risk for HIV infection due to contaminated needles. Therefore, hormonal therapy and informed, non-judgmental counseling may be lifesaving for transgender teens (Ryan & Futterman, 1997).

Other information about transgender individuals can be found in fiction (e.g., Feinberg, 1993) and in calls to action written by activists (e.g., Feinberg, 1998; MacKenzie, 1994; Wilchins, 1997). In a recent edited volume (Rottnek, 1999), some gay, lesbian and transgender individuals explored their lives as "sissies" and "tomboys," and others examined how their cross-gender behavior and identification led to their being classified as mentally ill, i.e., having Gender Identity Disorder (GID). The major criteria for a diagnosis of GID include a strong and persistent cross-gender identification, as well as discomfort with one's anatomical gender (American Psychiatric Association, 1994). Rather than "curing" or changing transgender youth, advocates call on providers to offer counseling, support, and access to appropriate resources that would enable adolescents to clarify identity confusion, resolve conflicts, and determine whether treatment (e.g., hormonal therapy following the growth spurt and/or future consideration of sex reassignment surgery) may be appropriate (Mallon, 1999c).

A number of empirical studies have been conducted to examine the relationship of sexual orientation to various gender-related characteristics. In a longitudinal study of 66 feminine boys and a control group of 56 nonfeminine boys (average age of 7 years), Green (1987) found upon reinterview (at an average age of 19 years) that three-quarters of the feminine boys who provided follow-up data had bisexual or homosexual fantasy scores (on a Kinsey rating scale), while none of the control boys did. Of the boys who had had interpersonal sexual experiences, 80% of the feminine boys had engaged in sexual activities with their same sex or both sexes, compared to 4% of the control group. Green concluded that highly feminine boys are more likely to become gay or bisexual adults than other boys. This study was initiated over two decades ago, and a replication is necessary to determine if similar findings would emerge today in a society that allows a wider range of gender behaviors.

Doorn, Poortinga, and Verschoor (1994) found that the development of a feminine gender identity system was present at an early age for male transsexuals, although the individual may not be aware of this identity until later in life. Zuger (1984) conducted a prospective study of 55 feminine boys. The boys were first seen at an average age of 9 years, and a follow-up study of 48 boys was conducted when they were at an average of 20 years. Similar to Green's findings, Zuger found that 73% were judged to have homosexual or bisexual orientations, 6% were judged to have heterosexual orientations, and 21% could not be determined because of lack of information. Tsoi (1990) conducted a study of the sexual development of male transsexuals. Findings indicated a distinct sexual developmental pattern. This pattern included the prepubescent appearance of effeminate traits, the development of homosexual feelings during puberty, a cross-dressing phase during the mid-to-late teen years, and a transsexual phase characterized by surgery and the adoption of living life as a woman. In a comprehensive analysis, Bailey and Zucker (1995) reviewed 32 studies in which both gay men and heterosexual men were asked retrospectively about behaviors related to childhood and gender identity. On all measures, gay men's scores reflected more traditionally feminine characteristics.

Unfortunately there are no prospective studies regarding gender-atypical females ("tomboys") becoming lesbians; however, retrospective studies have indicated that such an association exists. These studies suggested that, on average, lesbians were more traditionally masculine as children than heterosexual women. However, findings have indicated that masculine childhood gender identity in females is less predictive of adult same-sex sexual orientation than feminine childhood gender identity is for males (Bailey & Zucker, 1995).

Although there has been a growing number of empirical studies examining various developmental and adjustment issues of gay, lesbian and bisexual adolescents during the last decade (see Anhalt & Morris, 1998, and D'Augelli & Patterson, 2001, for reviews), these studies have not reported on gender atypicality. A recent report by D'Augelli, Pilkington, and Hershberger (2002) is an exception. They examined the victimization experiences of 350 lesbian, gay and bisexual high school and college age youth. Among the significant predictors of anti-lesbian-gay-and-bisexual victimization was childhood gender atypicality as well as parental rejection of this atypicality. In a qualitative study of lesbian and gay youth, Mallon (1998) found that not only was gender atypical behavior not acceptable to relatives and family members, but these distressed family members acted to discourage the expression of gender nonconforming ideas. Cooper (1999) has noted the serious challenges to families that transgender adolescents pose; the redefinition of a youth's gender may well be more difficult than the challenges faced following a youth's coming out as lesbian, gay, or bisexual.

STUDY DESIGN

The purpose of this study was to determine factors that affect the experiences of youth, ages 15 to 21, who either identify as transgender or describe their gender expression as atypical. Focus groups were used to examine the youths' social and emotional experiences. Focus groups, conducted in a nonthreatening environment, have been recommended as a research tool especially when working with people who have limited power and influence (Morgan & Krueger, 1993). The groups that comprised this study provided qualitative data on topics of interest and enabled the participants to present their own viewpoints, stimulated by the presence of group interaction to the researchers' questions (Morgan &

Krueger). In addition to examining the youths' experiences related to gender identity, gender presentation, and sexual orientation, the focus groups explored the transgender youths' vulnerability related to health, including exposure to risks (e.g., emotional, physical, sexual), discrimination, marginalization, and access to health resources. The focus groups were conducted in June and July 2000.

Transgender youth from the New York City metropolitan area were invited to participate in the focus groups. Announcements requesting volunteers were made to youth attending social, educational and recreational programs for lesbian, gay, bisexual, and transgender youths. It is estimated that transgender individuals comprise 3% to 10% of the United States population (Ettner, 1999). At the agencies from which the youth were recruited, they were estimated to be 10% of the population, as these agencies provided some of the safest spaces for gender nonconforming youth in the city. As transgender youth are a hidden population, it was decided that recruitment would take place at venues likely to yield a sufficient number of youths at one time so that a focus group could be conducted. A master's-level certified social worker with considerable professional experience working with lesbian, gay, bisexual, transgender and questioning youth facilitated the focus groups.

Each group contained eight individuals. This size allowed the members to explore issues in depth, gaining the benefits of small group interaction without splitting into subgroups. The groups lasted approximately two hours, in addition to time needed for explaining the purposes of the study, reading and signing consent forms, completing demographic questionnaires, and agreeing on ground rules (e.g., safe space, not "putting anyone down," speaking one's own thoughts and feelings). The sessions were conducted in private rooms of agencies providing services to lesbian, gay, bisexual, and transgender youth, and they were audio taped with youths' permission. In addition to providing consent, the youth could use their own names or pseudonyms during the group sessions. Each youth received $30.00 for participation.

The focus groups were conducted informally to simulate "rap sessions" that youths commonly have when they discuss topics with friends. They started with wide-ranging areas such as their experiences in childhood and early/middle adolescence (including feelings of being different), discovering their sexual and gender identities, their educational histories, types of support networks, access to resources, and their understanding of the notions of sex and gender. As the groups progressed, the facilitator was guided by a list of additional factors related to the youths' views of their vulnerability and health-related concerns.

The primary and secondary questions and probes used by the facilitator in leading the groups had been decided upon by a Planning and Evaluation Group convened for the project. That group consisted of the two investigators, the facilitator, and four consultants, i.e., three transgender youth and one adult transsexual. After the three focus groups were conducted, a three-member data analysis team individually listened to the audiotapes from each session and recorded themes that emerged from the group sessions. The team then met to compare and contrast the thematic points of the interviews and to ensure that the analyses were systematic and verifiable (Krueger, 1993). Findings from the data analysis team were presented to the Planning and Evaluation Group, which reviewed the themes for accuracy and categorized them in three major areas: gender identity and gender presentation, sexuality and sexual orientation, and vulnerability and health.

Before presenting the results, several important limitations to the study should be acknowledged. A main limitation was the use of convenience samples drawn from particular sites. This was necessary because there was no economically feasible method for selecting a random sample of transgender youth. Additionally, the participants had to self-identify as "trans" or "transgender" youth, make themselves visible to organizations providing social, educational and recreational services, and volunteer to participate in a group discussion. Therefore, the participants may have been more cooperative and sociable than other transgender youths. Furthermore, the focus groups met only once, and the sexual and gender identities of the youth may have been in transition. Thus, the findings may not be generalizable to all transgender youth. However, based on the professional and personal experiences of the members of the Planning and Evaluation Group, the authors believe that many of the participating youths' experiences were common among transgender youth.

RESULTS

Participants

The mean age of the 24 participants was 16.5 (range 15 to 20), and their average grade was the 11th (range 9th to 12th), with some youth returning to school for equivalency high school diplomas after having dropped out. Ninety percent of the youth lived in a major metropolitan area, and 95% were youth of color. Fifty percent of the youth lived with parents or other relatives, 29% lived in a group home, and the remainder had "other" living arrangements. A large majority of the youth (87%) had two or more siblings of both biological sexes; only 2.5% (3 youth) were only children. Half of the youth estimated their parents' or guardians' yearly family income to be less than $25,000, while the other half indicated that it ranged from $26,000 to over $100,000.

A large majority (83%) of the participants identified their anatomical gender as biologically male, while 17% identified as biologically female. When asked about their preferred gender, 54% indicated that it was male-to-female (M-to-F), 17% said female-to-male (F-to-M), and 29% expressed a preference of male-to-male. Members of this third group saw themselves as having a feminine gender expression, but would have preferred a masculine one. Because gender identity and sexual orientation are often conflated, the youth were asked how they would identify (if they would) their sexual orientation. All of the youth responded to this question, with 50% of the biological males identifying as gay, 35% as heterosexual, and 15% as "uncertain." Of the females, 75% labeled their sexual orientation as bisexual, and 25% as lesbian. The biological males indicated that they were moderately or very sexually attracted to other males, while the biological females were sexually attracted to both females and males.

Approximately two thirds of the youth (69%) indicated that they acted and dressed in the gender opposite their birth sex and, therefore, have started the processes of transitioning. Some of these individuals planned on taking hormones as part of their transitioning process, while a much smaller percentage (14%) were already taking hormones. More than three fourth of the male-to-female youth planned on having sex re-assignment (confirming) surgery.

In addition to determining the experiences of the transgender youth through the focus groups, the investigators wanted to learn about the social context of these youths' lives. Therefore, on the demographic questionnaire the investigators also asked such questions as: to whom they have disclosed their gender identity, how many people in their families were transgender, if they attended groups for transgender people, and the percentage of people who were aware of their transgender identities. The responses to these questions form the next section of the findings.

Since we were interested in comparing and contrasting their developmental trajectories to those of lesbian, gay, and bisexual youth, the demographic questionnaire also included questions about the milestones in these youths' sexual orientation development in these youths' lives. Questions ranged from the age they first became aware that their gender identity did not correspond to their biological sex to the age when they first demonstrated visible signs of their transgender identity. Their responses to these questions comprise the third section of the findings.

The fourth section of the findings describes the three major themes that emerged from the groups: gender identity and gender presentation, sexuality and sexual orientation, and vulnerability and health. The Planning and Evaluation Group thought that these three themes best summarized the conversations that occurred.

The Context of the Experiences

When asked who knew of their gender identity or gender expression, two-thirds (66%) indicated that their parents, brothers and sisters knew, 50% said that their grandparents knew, and 63% had disclosed their gender identity to their aunts or uncles. The two largest groups to which the youth had disclosed their gender identity were friends and teachers, 83% and 75%, respectively; these larger percentages are inflated by those who were living in a group home or attended an equivalency high school educational program. About one-quarter (22%) of the youth reported that they knew of relatives who were also transgender.

To determine the frequency of youths' interactions with others who describe themselves as transgender, the youth were asked how often they spent time with other transgender people and how many groups for transgender people they belonged. Half (54%) indicated that they spent time daily with other transgender people, while 44% spent time weekly, but not daily. Only one youth indicated never spending time with other transgender people. Additionally, 42% said that they belonged to groups for transgender people, with 33% of those attending the groups on a regular basis. Finally, the youth were asked to indicate the percentage of people who were currently aware of their transgender identity. Of the 21 youth who responded to this question, 19% indicated "less than 25%," while 24% said between "25% and 50%," and 9% indicated between "51% and 75%." Almost half (48%) indicated that "more than 75%" of the people that they knew were aware of their transgender identity.

Developmental Milestones

The youth indicated that they were, on the average, 10.4 years old (range 6 to 15) when they first became aware that their gender identity or gender expression did not correspond to their biological sex (even though they might not have labeled their feelings). At a mean age of 13.5 (range 7 to 16), the youth first realized that other people labeled them transgender. It was approximately a year later, at the mean age of 14.3 (range 7 to 18), that they first labeled themselves transgender, and that they disclosed their gender identity to someone else (mean age of 14.5, with a range of 8 to 18). At the same time (mean age of 14.1, range 10 to 18), they first made their transgender identity known to others, either by cross-dressing or by seeking hormones to change their physical appearance.

Of the 22 youth who responded to a question about their sexual activity, 95% of the males (19), and 75% of the females (3) had sexual experiences with biological males. Eighty-five percent of the males had their first sexual activity with a good friend or boyfriend, while three (15%) reported having anonymous sex. The mean age (13.3, range 9 to 17) of their first sexual partners was similar to their own. Four percent of the males also reported having biologically female sexual partners, whom they described as girlfriends of similar ages (mean age = 13, range 10 to 15). All three of the biological females reported having had sexual experiences with both biological males and females; all of these partners were described as friends or girls similar in age. Because of the small numbers involved, a mean age will not be reported; however, the range was from 9 to 17.

The mean ages of the developmental milestones reported in this study are similar to those given in recent studies for lesbian gay, and bisexual youth (e.g., D'Augelli & Hershberger, 1993; Rosario et al., 1996). While developmental averages for lesbian, gay, bisexual and transgender youth gives us a picture that highlights awareness and experiences that appear to be concurrent with pubescence, the age ranges remind us of the diversity of the life paths within these groups.

Theme #1: Gender Identity and Gender Presentation

Although for most youth, the awareness that their gender identity did not correspond to their birth sex occurred around puberty, but, for a few, it was at an earlier age. As one youth (M to F) said, "I used to play baseball and hangout with the boys, but I always felt like a girl." Another youth stated, "I knew that I was biologically a girl, but ever since I was little, I always wanted to be a man so bad. Other people said I want to be a lawyer, a doctor, and I said I want to be a man." A third youth (M to F) said, "Since I can remember, I always thought I was a girl. I used to do things as a girl, sit on the toilet. I wouldn't stand up. I never liked using urinals. I never liked boy things. I didn't like boys' stuff, I always liked girls' stuff." This awareness of difference later evolved to gender atypical behavior, i.e., wearing the clothes of the other sex, playing with an individual of the other sex whom they emulated, or presenting themselves as their preferred gender during adolescence. In the words of one youth (F to M), "Since I was young, and I would see people getting married, I always pictured myself in the groom's place instead of the bride's." Another youth (M to F) said, "I thought people would beat me up because I looked like a man in girls' clothes, but then people said I wiggle like a girl."

Reactions of others to their gender atypical behavior were mostly negative. The reactions ranged from physical assault by family members and neighbors to having their gender and sexual identity questioned. Attending school was reported to be the most traumatic aspect of growing up. As one youth (M to F) said, "At school there was a lot of harassment. I could walk around minding my business, and someone would throw something at me, would call me faggot, spit at me, do this do that." Verbal harassment and assault were not the only negative reactions. There were other things, such as regularly being propositioned for sex and being called by one's birth name after indicating that a chosen name was preferable. "Teachers don't realize," as one youth (F to M) said, "that when they call me by my 'government name,' everyone is going to call me that it's going to cause a fight. Because, if they don't stop, I'm going to fight." However, many of the youth found that some peers, transgender friends, lovers, teachers, and extended family members supported their gender identity and presentation. They reported that they had less access to knowledge about transgender individuals than about lesbian, gay, and bisexual people. Most indicated that they gained knowledge about the existence of transgender people either from the media, from transgender adults in their neighborhoods, or when they moved to New York City. Most whose gender identity was static began to identify as transgender or to live in their preferred gender role between ages 11 and 18, and told others (if anyone) between 11 and 18.

Theme #2: Sexual Orientation

For the large majority of the youth, awareness about their sexual orientation occurred between ages 4 and 9 or between 13 and 15. Physical attraction to others of the same sex informed this awareness. When they discovered this same-sex attraction, their reactions ranged from sadness and withdrawal to happiness. This same-sex attraction and their display of atypical social and sexual behaviors in childhood led to much confusion between their sexual orientation and gender identity. Two youths (M to F) stated it clearly, "I was really confused as to who I am. I looked at boys and I looked at girls, until I would identify as transgender when I was 17." As teenagers, most came to view their "gender" as about gender self-identification and gender expression, and they saw "sex" as their biological or birth sex.

They talked about their experiences of verbal harassment and physical assault by family members, neighbors, strangers and classmates because of their assumed or disclosed sexual orientation. As one youth (M to F) said, "The kids would say, 'That's just the faggot of the school.' I was the town's faggot and they would taunt me." Attending school, particularly high school, was a painful event for many of the youths. An example provided by one youth (M to F) was: "When I was in gym with another feminine boy and I had my pen in my mouth, there was this teacher; and he asked me if I wanted something else in my mouth. He grabbed me and said, 'This time I have you.'" Some youth transferred to high schools for lesbian, gay, bisexual and transgender youth (two of which exist in the New York City area), or to public high schools known to have large sexual minority populations. Some found support for their sexual orientation either from lesbian, gay or bisexual relatives, their friends, parents of those friends, or group home peers. Access to knowledge about their being lesbian, gay, or bisexual came from people in their neighborhoods or schools, family members who were lesbian, gay, bisexual or transgender, or youth who belonged to organizations that provided social and recreational services to sexual minority youth.

Theme #3: Vulnerability and Health Issues

Almost all of the youth talked about four major issues related to their vulnerability in health-related areas: the absence or lack of safe environments, lack of access to health services, few resources for their mental health concerns, and a lack of continuity of caregiving by their families and communities. The clear exception to the dismal picture of how others were not meeting their needs concerned organizations specifically dedicated to services for sexual minority youth.

The most important of the youths' concerns was safety issues related to being potential victims of violence on their disclosure of their transgender status or that information being disclosed by others. One youth (M to F) stated it directly, "I have no comfort or safety zones, and that puts me at risk for suicide." They also expressed fear that the constant verbal harassment and discrimination they faced might escalate into physical violence and sexual abuse, as they found themselves being continually objectified sexually. One youth (F to M) stated, "Men keep saying to me, 'I can turn you straight.'" They also expressed resentment for being seen only for their gender and sexuality and not for their other personal qualities.

Their primary concerns about the lack of access to health services related to two areas. First, they were concerned about sexually transmitted infections, including HIV. Sexual partners often do not perceive the male-to-female transgender youth as health risks because they cannot become pregnant; they are also thought of as sexually less inhibited because they are transgender. Consequently, others expect unprotected sexual activity, and resisting the expectation can lead to sexual abuse. Not only did they express concern about their lack of access to health care services for counseling and testing regarding sexually transmitted diseases, but they also feared discrimination by health care providers. A second concern was the lack of access to ongoing health care services to obtain hormones to change their secondary sexual characteristics to correspond to their preferred gender.

Lack of resources related to their mental health needs was strongly voiced by the youth. They realized that nondisclosure of their gender and sexual identities hide their selfhood and uniqueness; however, the negative reactions they receive on disclosure often has a severe negative effect on their self-esteem. Although they have come to rely on avoidance coping skills and to seek supportive others as their main coping mechanisms, the lack of competent mental health services to assist them reflects, in their views, their marginality and unimportance to society. Some consider themselves as having a high risk of self-harm because of their religious backgrounds and the pressures their families and communities put on them to conform to traditional gender behaviors. In the words of one youth (M to F), "If you come out, you may want to kill yourself if you come from a Catholic background, or Christian, or a very religious background. You love your parents so much you will try to kill yourself to keep them from misery."

Experiencing rejection and inconsistent caring from most of their parents, schoolmates, teachers, and communities, transgender youth have to constantly fight feelings of shame and unworthiness. As one youth said, "Throughout my whole life, I was abused physically and mentally by relatives in my family. I have marks on my body. I have things that I remember happened to me." Some of the youth have distanced themselves from their parents, while others have been forced to leave their homes, which can be an extremely traumatic experience. One youth told the following anecdote: "When my mother, who is a PhD, found out what I was (i.e., transgender), she used to hurt me with things. She hit me on the head with an iron once, and I had five staples. Finally, she disowned me." The lack of housing was frequently accompanied by an absence of financial support that forced a few of the youth into prostitution. (This may have been underreported, as engaging in survival sex is not something that youth readily talk about in public settings.) Some also experienced rejection in the lesbian, gay and bisexual community because of discrimination based on their racial or ethnic background as well as their gender identity. With the lack of support at home and the routine stigmatization at school, many had experienced serious academic difficulties, and dropped out of school. Some thought that they were very fortunate to attend an alternative high school for lesbian, gay, bisexual and transgender youth. But at the same time, they found themselves at risk for social isolation, as a result of being alone in a big city, and for substance abuse, as a way of coping with the others' negative reactions (e.g., peers, teachers, parents). As a number of youth said at the end of the focus groups, "There is nothing for transgender youth. Please help us."

CHALLENGES, IMPLICATIONS, AND RECOMMENDATIONS

It is unlikely that adequate health and other services for transgender youth will be provided until more is learned about this population and their needs. Consequently, research that recruits youth from various groups within the transgender community (e.g., male-to-female, female-to-male, cross-dressers, drag kings, drag queens, tranny fags, tranny dykes) need to be conducted. Additionally, studies of transgender youth must include youth from diverse socioeconomic and racial/ethnic backgrounds. It is especially important that our knowledge base not be built only on information gathered from youth who seek health or mental health services, or who attend support groups. Future investigations must develop inclusion and exclusion criteria regarding static and fluid gender identities and sexual orientation, and common operational definitions for key variables, such as gender, sex, gender identity, and sexual orientation, must be established (see Mallon, 1999a).

To reduce the harm currently experienced by transgender youth, a number of key actions are required. First, health and social service providers must acknowledge that transgender youth exist and that atypical gender expression is an acceptable way of behaving. Second, providers must intervene to reduce the risks experienced by transgender youth because of discrimination and marginalization, not only on an individual or group basis but also through the use of advocacy and public health education. Third, steps must be undertaken to reduce the vulnerability of these youth by providing them access to resources that meet their specific needs, including sensitive and effective physical health care, mental health services, schooling, employment and housing. Fourth, programs have to be established to assist families and communities to create culturally safe environments for transgender youth and to provide a continuity of caregiving when youth come out as transgender. Fifth, specialized programs should be established to assist transgender youth in developing plans to attain their preferred gender identity, including the steps to reduce the harm that some experience by taking "street hormones," or by being forced into prostitution. Sixth, education about transgender people should be included in the professional preparation and in-service training programs of all health care and social service providers. Finally, youth who identify as transgender must be educated about society's gender constructs and how these contribute to their vulnerability and devalue their health status. Strategies to enhance emotional, social and physical development must be established to assist transgender youth in building the resiliency they need to live in a culture that tenaciously maintains a binary concept of gender.

REFERENCES

American Psychiatric Association. (1994). *Diagnostic and statistical manual of mental disorders, 4th ed.* Washington, DC: American Psychiatric Association.

Anhalt, K., & Morris, T.L. (1998). Development and adjustment issues of gay, lesbian, and bisexual adolescents: A review of the empirical literature. *Clinical Child and Family Psychology Review, 4*(1), 215-230.

Bailey, J.M., & Zucker, K.J. (1995). Childhood sex-typed behavior and sexual orientation: A conceptual analysis and quantitative review. *Developmental Psychology, 31*, 43-55.

Boenke, M. (Ed.). (1999). *Transforming families: Real stories about transgender loved ones.* Imperial Beach, CA: Walter Trook Publishing.

Bornstein, K. (1994). *Gender outlaw: On men, women, and rest of us.* New York: Vintage.

Burgess, C. (1999). Internal and external stress factors associated with the identity development of transgendered youth. *Journal of Gay & Lesbian Social Services, 10 (3/4)*, 35-47.

Cole, C., O'Boyle, M., Emory, L., & Meyer, W. (1997). Comorbidity of gender dysphoria and other major psychiatric diagnoses. *Archives of Sexual Behavior,* *26*(1), 13-26.

Cooper, K. (1999). Practice with transgendered youth and their families. *Journal of Gay & Lesbian Social Services, 10 (3/4),* 111-129.

Cosentino, C., Meyer-Bahlburg, M., Alpert, J., & Gaines, R. (1993). Cross-gender behavior and gender conflict in sexually abused girls. *Journal of the American Academy of Child and Adolescent Psychiatry, 32*(5), 940-947.

D'Augelli, A. R., Pilkington, N. W., & Hershberger, S. L. (2002). Incidence and mental health impact of sexual orientation victimization of lesbian, gay, and bisexual youths in high school. *School Psychology Quarterly, 17,* 148-167.

D'Augelli, A. R., & Patterson, C. J. (Eds.) (2001). *Lesbian, gay, and bisexual identities and youth: Psychological perspectives.* New York: Oxford University Press.

Davenport, C. (1986). A follow-up study of ten feminine boys. *Archives of Sexual Behavior, 15*(6), 511-517.

Devor, H. (1994). Transsexualism, dissociation, and child abuse: An initial discussion based on nonclinical data. *Journal of Psychology and Human Sexuality, 6*(3), 49-72.

Devor, H. (1997). *FTM: Female-to-male transsexuals in society.* Bloomington: Indiana University Press.

Doorn, C.D., Poortinga, J., & Verschoor, A.M. (1994). Cross-gender identity in transvestites and male transsexuals. *Archives of Sexual Behavior, 23*(2), 185-201.

Ettner, R. (1999). *Gender loving care: A guide to counseling gender-variant clients.* NY: W.W. Norton.

Evelyn, J. (1998). *Mom, I just need to be a girl.* Imperial Beach, CA: Walter Trook Publishing.

Feinberg, L. (1993). *Stone butch blues.* New York: Firebrand Books.

Feinberg, L. (1998). *Trans liberation: Beyond pink and blue.* Boston: Beacon Press.

Flaskerud, J.H. (Ed.). (1999). Preface. Emerging nursing care of vulnerable populations. *Nursing Clinics of North America, 34*(2).

Gagne, P., & Tewksbury, R. (1996). Hide in plain sight: Conformist pressures and the transgender community. Paper presented at the annual meetings of the Society for the Study of Social Problems, New York, NY.

Green, R. (1987). *The "sissy boy syndrome" and the development of homosexuality.* New Haven: Yale University Press.

Klein, R. (1999). Group work practice with transgendered male to female sex workers. *Journal of Gay & Lesbian Social Services, 10 (3/4),* 95-109.

Krueger, R.A. (1993). Quality control in focus group research. In Morgan, D.L. (Ed.), *Successful focus groups: Advancing the state of the art* (pp. 65-85). Newbury Park, CA: Sage.

Lewins, F. (1995). *Transsexualism in society: A sociology of male-to-female transsexuals.* South Melbourne, Australia: Macmillan Education Australia.

Lombardi, E. (2001). Enhancing transgender health care. *American Journal of Public Health, 91,* 869-872.

MacKenzie, G. (1994). *Transgender nation.* Bowling Green, OH: Bowling Green State University Press.

Mallon, G.P. (1998). *We don't exactly get the welcome wagon: The experiences of gay and lesbian adolescents in child welfare systems.* New York: Columbia University Press.

Mallon, G. P. (1999a). Appendix: A glossary of transgendered definitions. *Journal of Gay & Lesbian Social Services, 10 (3/4)*, 143-145.

Mallon, G. P. (1999b). Knowledge for practice with transgendered persons. *Journal of Gay & Lesbian Social Services, 10 (3/4)*, 1-18.

Mallon, G. P. (1999c). Practice with transgendered children. *Journal of Gay & Lesbian Social Services, 10 (3/4), 49-64.*

Morgan, D.L., & Krueger, R.A. When to use focus groups and why. In Morgan, D.L. (Ed.), *Successful focus groups: Advancing the state of the art* (pp. 3-19). Newbury Park, CA: Sage.

Rosario, M., Meyer-Bahlburg, H.F.L., Hunter, J., Exner, T.M., Gwadz, M., & Keller, A.M. (1996). The psychosexual development of lesbian, gay, and bisexual youths. *The Journal of Sex Research, 39*(2), 113-126.

Rottnek, M. (Ed.). (1999). *Sissies and tomboys: Gender nonconformity and homosexual childhood.* New York: New York University Press.

Ryan, C., & Futterman, D. (1997). Lesbian and gay youth: Care and counseling [Special issue]. *Adolescent Medicine, 8*(2).

Tsoi, W.F. (1990). Developmental profile of 200 male and 100 female transsexuals in Singapore. *Archives of Sexual Behavior, 19*(6), 595-605.

Wilchins, R.A. (1997). *Read my lips: Sexual subversion and the end of gender.* New York: Firebrand Books.

Woodhouse, A. (1989). *Fantastic women: Sex, gender and transvestism.* London: Macmillan.

Zuger, B. (1984). Early effeminate behavior in boys: Outcome and significance for homosexuality. *Journal of Nervous and Mental Diseases, 172*, 90-97.

Slivers of the Journey:
The Use of Photovoice and Storytelling
to Examine Female to Male Transsexuals'
Experience of Health Care Access

Wendy Hussey, MPH

Oakland, California

SUMMARY. The purpose of this research project was to examine female to male transsexuals' (FTMs) experiences of accessing health care. This was accomplished by documenting and recording the experiences of five FTMs through the use of photography and interviews. It was hoped that such an inquiry would provide a starting point for future research about the health care needs of the transgender community, and document some of the health care needs of the FTM community that would lead to recommendations for policy changes and educating providers. *[Article copies available for a fee from The Haworth Document Delivery Service: 1-800-HAWORTH. E-mail address: <docdelivery@haworthpress.com> Website: <http://www.HaworthPress.com> © 2006 by The Haworth Press, Inc. All rights reserved.]*

Wendy Hussey received her MPH from San Jose State University in 2001. She is currently Project Director at UCSF's Center for AIDS Prevention Studies. She has an extensive background in grassroots community organizing and is passionate about using participant-driven methods like Photovoice and storytelling in qualitative research (E-mail: whussey@psg.ucsf.edu).

[Haworth co-indexing entry note]: "Slivers of the Journey: The Use of Photovoice and Storytelling to Examine Female to Male Transsexuals' Experience of Health Care Access." Hussey, Wendy. Co-published simultaneously in *Journal of Homosexuality* (Harrington Park Press, an imprint of The Haworth Press, Inc.) Vol. 51, No. 1, 2006, pp. 129-158; and: *Current Issues in Lesbian, Gay, Bisexual, and Transgender Health* (ed: Jay Harcourt) Harrington Park Press, an imprint of The Haworth Press, Inc., 2006, pp. 129-158. Single or multiple copies of this article are available for a fee from The Haworth Document Delivery Service [1-800-HAWORTH, 9:00 a.m. - 5:00 p.m. (EST). E-mail address: docdelivery@haworthpress.com].

Available online at http://www.haworthpress.com/web/JH
© 2006 by The Haworth Press, Inc. All rights reserved.
doi:10.1300/J082v51n01_07

KEYWORDS. Female to male transsexual, health care access, Photovoice

INTRODUCTION

Seeking health care can be a challenging and alienating experience for many people. Several factors contribute to the vast disparities in health care access. The most widely documented disparities are related to the key variables of race, ethnicity, socioeconomic status, and geography (HHS News, January 25, 2000). Disparities also exist for people of varying sexual orientations, and physical and mental abilities.

Female to male transsexuals (FTMs) have remained absent from mainstream discussions of health disparities for many reasons. An article published for FTMs on the Internet cites providers' lack of knowledge and understanding, as well as insensitivity to FTMs and their health care needs, as the main factors preventing FTMs from seeking health care (Morton, Hans & Lewis, 1997). The lack of understanding about FTMs and their specific health care needs may also be placing FTMs at greater morbidity risk (Morton, Lewis & Hans, 1997).

Gynecological health care is one specific health need that is seldom addressed for FTMs. FTMs who are taking testosterone carry an increased risk for endometrial hyperplasia, and subsequent endometrial carcinoma (Lee, 2000). Furthermore, FTMs who use hormones but decide not to undergo a hysterectomy continue to be at risk for endometrial cancer, just as male to female transsexuals (MTFs) taking estrogen remain at risk for prostate cancer (Lee, 2000). The need for sex specific (biological sex at birth) health care does not change with one's gender identity.

Another serious gynecological health risk to FTMs is ovarian cancer. Ovarian cancer is the fifth most common cause of cancer-related death, and the most common fatal gynecologic malignancy (Hage, Dekker, Karim, Verheijen & Bloemena, 2000). Hage et al. suggested that long term exposure to increased levels of androgens (male hormones) pose an increased risk of ovarian cancer to FTMs. Among women in general, an ovarian cancer diagnosis is often delayed due to the lack of an effective screening test. For FTMs, this delay in diagnosis may be exacerbated due to their reluctance to seek regular gynecological check-ups (Hage et al., 2000).

Little in the way of scholarly research addresses the health care needs of the FTM community. The prevalence of transsexuality in the US, as estimated by the *American Psychological Association's Diagnostic and*

Statistical Manual IV, is 1/30,000 (born) males and 1/100,000 (born) females (1994, pp. 536-537). Most studies about FTMs have been conducted outside of the US in places such as the Netherlands, the Czech Republic, Germany and Canada, where the standards and quality of care for transsexuals are more complete. These studies examined specific health risks, such as long-term exposure to cross sex hormones, and the links with ovarian cancer (Hage et al., 2000). Much of the current literature links testosterone use with ovarian and endometrial cancer for FTMs who retained their ovaries and uterus (Hage et al., 2000). While these studies provided some insight into the specific health care issues of transsexuals, none addressed the issue of health care access.

One of the first transgender health studies was conducted in 1997 by the San Francisco Department of Public Health. The Transgender Community Health Project (TCHP) was a quantitative study designed to assess HIV risk among male to female transsexuals (MTFs) and female to male transsexuals (FTMs) in San Francisco (Clements, Katz, Marx, 1999). The study, which included 392 MTFs and 123 FTMs, consisted of an anonymous survey and HIV test. The study also included a confidential standardized face to face interview that addressed the following: (1) socio-demographics, (2) medical history and health status, (3) HIV prevention service access, (4) sexual behaviors, (5) drug use behaviors, and (6) psychosocial factors. The findings of the study suggested an urgent need for effective HIV prevention interventions that targeted MTFs, as 35% of the MTF participants were infected with HIV. The FTM participants' HIV prevalence was low, less than 2%, and their HIV-related risk behaviors were infrequent, yet a history of unprotected receptive anal intercourse was reported in 28% of the FTM sample. Among those who reported a history of injection drug use (18% of the sample), 91% of that group had shared syringes. Based on the results of this study, it was recommended that HIV prevention interventions be provided specifically targeting FTMs who have sex with men, and those that inject street drugs (Clements et al., 1999).

The Transgender Community Health Project also indicated that FTMs might be at risk for other Sexually Transmitted Diseases (STDs), such as Human Papilloma Virus (HPV), a precursor to cervical cancer. Thirty-one percent of the sample of FTMs had been diagnosed with an STD at some point in their life, 64% had engaged in receptive vaginal intercourse without a condom, and 59% had experiences of forced sex or rape (Clements et al., 1999).

A series of focus groups were also conducted as a part of the study, which yielded qualitative data about other aspects of transgender lives and illuminated some of their experiences of accessing health care. The results of these focus groups indicated that transgender people have a difficult time accessing competent and respectful health care. This finding suggests a need for further inquiry into the experiences of transgender access to health care, and transsexuals' overall experience of health (Clements et al., 1999). Much of the information gained from the San Francisco focus groups (Clements et al., 1999) mirrored the results of four focus groups that were conducted in Boston in July 2000 (JSI Research and Training Institute, 2000). The results of the Boston groups suggested that transgender people often encounter providers who will deny them treatment or provide sub-standard care as a result of lack of knowledge about transgender specific health concerns. The focus groups found that insensitivity, ignorance and discrimination are the norm for this community when its members try to seek health care (JSI Research and Training Institute, 2000).

Transgender individuals are often likely to experience some form of discrimination or violence in their lifetimes (Lombardi, 2001). The fear of discrimination and stigma often keeps transgender people from seeking health care for themselves, and when they do, this fear keeps them from disclosing relevant personal information to the provider with whom they are receiving care (Clark, Landers, Linde, & Sperber, 2001). Often times a transgender person is reluctant to access care due to the insensitivity of the provider (Lombardi, 2001). Furthermore, this lack of sensitivity by providers may keep transgender people from returning for follow-up treatment if it is needed (Lombardi, 2001). Transgender individuals' access to health care is affected by the lack of provider knowledge about transgender people and their specific health care needs (JSI Research and Training Institute, 2000). The results of a series of focus groups conducted with transgender adults and youth in Massachusetts suggested that many providers lack the knowledge to treat routine health care issues having to do with transgender people. These health care issues included hormone use and monitoring, HIV prevention, and preventive gynecological care (JSI Research and Training Institute, 2000). The lack of understanding of transgender patients points to the need for health professionals to be educated and made aware of the lives and health care issues of their transgender patients (Bockting, Robinson, and Rosser, 1998).

METHODOLOGY

The conceptual framework used to guide this project came from Freirian Popular Education. Paulo Freire's problem-posing education is based on the understanding that education starts with the issues that are central to people's lives, the things they see. By examining the themes that emerge from everyday life, people can begin to question and start talking about the things that challenge them in their environment, and look at the forces that keep those challenging conditions in place (Freire, 1970).

Participants

The participants in this project were five self-identified female-to-male transgender individuals in the San Francisco Bay Area who were born with and still had at least one of the following female sexual organs: breasts, clitoris, cervix, vagina, ovaries and/or uterus. The participants were 18 years of age and older. In order to participate in the project, individuals must have had experiences of gaining access to, or trying to access health care as an FTM. The five men varied in age from 33 to 52 years of age. Four of the men self-identified as Caucasian, one self-identified as Latino. Two of the participants identified their sexual orientation as straight, and the other three participants identified their sexual orientation as queer. Three of the participants (60%) had private medical insurance. Of the two (40%) that were uninsured, one received regular health care from a city clinic and the other rarely accessed healthcare.

Participants were recruited by distributing flyers and discussing the study within the FTM community in the San Francisco Bay Area. Three of the participants were recruited from an FTM support and advocacy group called FTM International. The other two participants heard about the project from colleagues or peers and contacted the facilitator to enroll in the study.

Photovoice

This research project used a data gathering method called Photovoice. Photovoice is a process by which people can identify, represent and enhance their community through photographs, and their related dialogue. Dr. Caroline Wang from the University of Michigan developed the Photovoice technique, which provides people with cameras to photograph their perceived health and work realities. The meanings of the photographs are then discussed and analyzed with the people who took them in an effort to provide insight into their lived experiences (Wang & Cash, 2000). Through Photovoice, participants act as recorders and potential catalysts for change. Photovoice uses the photographs taken by participants to create an opportunity for sharing the experiences and expertise of the community members (Wang & Burris, 1997). Photovoice has three main goals: (1) to enable people to record and reflect their community's strengths and concerns, (2) to promote critical dialogue and knowledge about important issues through large and small group discussion of photographs, and (3) to reach policy makers (Wang & Burris, 1997).

Data Collection

Each participant in this study was given a point-and-shoot camera, four rolls of color film, and one practice roll. This allowed each participant to take up to 120 pictures. Participants were asked to tell the story of their experiences of gaining access to health care by taking pictures. The assignment was kept broad so that the participants could decide what kind of story they wished to tell through the photos. The participants had seven weeks to collect their photographs.

The participants were asked to select the ten photos that best illustrated their story. The project facilitator then met with each participant to hear the stories behind their photos. Freirian problem-posing questioning was used to debrief the stories. This debriefing technique used pointed questions to elicit information about the content of each photograph. Participants were asked each question associated with each letter in the PHOTO acronym for each of their ten selected photographs.

- Describe your picture.
- What is happening in your picture?
- Why did you take a picture of this?
- What does this picture tell us about your life?
- How can this picture provide opportunities for us to improve life *with regard to healthcare*? (phrase in italics added by project facilitator to adapt specifically to this project.)

This questioning technique provided a way to focus on the specific experiences and stories portrayed in the photographs. After discussing each photo in this way, they were asked if they would like to say anything else about the photograph that might not have been captured by the five questions. The sessions were audio-recorded and the interviews were then transcribed for analysis. The photos and transcripts were examined for common themes. Participants were invited to be advisors during the analysis of the project, to ensure that the identified themes represented their experiences accurately and respectfully.

RESULTS

Six themes emerged consistently from the data: (1) The Health Care System, ("The System") (2) Provider Competence, (3) Vulnerability, (4) Invisibility, (5) Perseverance, and (6) Activism. These themes represent common topics discussed by all or a majority of participants when telling their stories.

"The System"

This is a hallway in a hospital, and it is leading straight down into a black hole. And here on the side is a gurney, and it's all ready there with a nice white sheet and it's just lonely. It's scary to me. It is not comforting or reassuring at all. {What's happening in this picture?} It's the system sitting out there waiting, and heaven forbid you end up on that gurney wheeled down into that black hole, because it is lonely and scary.

FIGURE 1. Gurney in Hospital

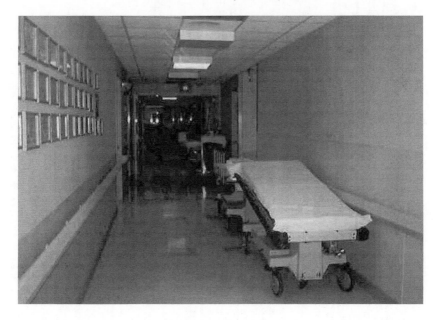

"The System" was the phrase most often used by participants to describe the medical industry, the health care industry, or the public health system where they went for care. Some of the words used by participants to describe how they felt about accessing and navigating "The System" were: "humiliating," "daunting," "imposing," "lonesome," "dark, a black hole," "prejudiced," "ignorant," "scary," and "cold and inhuman." Most participants described numerous experiences of inhumane treatment when attempting to access the Health Care System. One participant described the inhumanity of the system in a broad sense with this image of the entrance to a hospital:

FIGURE 2. Hospital Entrance

The health care system is so imposing and it is so daunting. It is not me looking in someone's eyes and having them understand that I have a problem that they have the expertise to help me, but it is in fact me out here off to the side terrified that the first person that I see is going to do something to shame me or embarrass me or cause me to be ridiculed in front of other people.

"The System" included the insurance companies, to which each participant made numerous references. All of the participants' told stories about dealing with, or the fear of dealing with insurance regardless of whether or not they had health insurance. One participant took a photograph depicting what he termed his "house of cards":

My little house of cards is what I call it. I got these five cards in the space of three months from the same insurance company. First, they said that I didn't have insurance, then they said that I did have insurance but it was with this primary care physician. Then they said 'no it's a different primary care physician and you have a

FIGURE 3. House of Cards

different subscriber number, we can no longer use your social security number because that is someone else's social security number.' I tried to explain to them, 'it is still mine, I'm not changing it, and I am just changing my name and gender on all of my documentation.' So they decided to give me a new number altogether, but they didn't bother to tell me or anyone else that. So when I would go to seek services I would be denied because they would say 'who are you? You're not this person. This is not the right social security number from this name . . .' etc. We went back and forth on this. I finally got documentation from them stating that I did indeed have insurance, and then three days later got a bill from [the hospital] saying 'you don't have insurance; you have to pay this bill.'

Another participant chose to avoid health insurance altogether, stating that the fear of navigating the health insurance system was too overwhelming:

I don't even consider insurance when I think about accessing the health care system, particularly for gynecological care and things like that. I would pay out of pocket before I would try to get an insurance company to cover me. It is just too overwhelming enough to think of trying to access a gynecological clinic when I am an FTM; to try to involve an HMO in the process . . . I just won't do it.

Several of the participants shared stories of being treated poorly when they tried to access the health care system. These experiences varied in range from fear that service providers would be rude, to actual poor treatment as a result of the participant's gender identity. One participant shared a story about poor treatment that he received at a city-funded public pharmacy. To illustrate his story he used the image of the outpatient registration offices at a hospital where he was required to go before getting his testosterone prescriptions filled. In this story, he had just returned to the pharmacy with his paperwork completed from outpatient registration:

While [the pharmacists] were handling our stuff they were smirking at each other and laughing and elbowing each other because they knew what we were there for, and they thought it was hilarious–and they were not even hiding it. They were one inch away from us, and they were acting like we were not even there . . . Any-

FIGURE 4. Outpatient Registration Area

way when they hand us our vials of testosterone and bags of syringes, my friend wanted to know how he was supposed to store it.
'Do I keep it refrigerated or do anything special to it?' Because no-
body tells us anything; they just hand you stuff and expect us to
know what to do with it. They laughed at him. They openly
mocked him for asking a question like that. My friend just stood
there and endured it so that he could get the information.

As participants discussed their experiences of inhumane treatment
and of navigating the insurance maze within the health care system,
they also began to reveal stories about their experiences with individual
providers. Provider competence emerged as its own theme.

Provider Competence

This theme reflected the ways participants described the ability of
their individual health care practitioners to provide adequate medical
care and to address their specific health care needs as transgender patients. Participants reported on both interpersonal relationships with
providers, and the providers' willingness and ability to address participants' transgender-specific health care needs.

Three participants identified language as a powerful marker of provider competence. For example, they described their reactions to providers' use of gender pronouns when referring to them. Participants stated that they noticed and appreciated when providers used the proper (i.e., male) pronoun. One participant spoke of the positive impact of providers' awareness and proper pronoun use when referring to him:

> The thing that I really appreciate about the clinic is that they are very aware of the little things that make a transgender person's experience at the doctors go smoother–like they always use the right pronouns. They use language that lets me know that they don't think of me as a freak or an oddity.

Some of the participants expressed frustration and feelings of identity invalidation when providers did not use the proper pronoun:

> I had two hours of being Ms. X even to my continual objection . . . and because the technician had said 'Ms. X' the doctor started saying 'Ms. X' even when she looked at the file and recognized that it said 'Mr. X' . . . I don't want someone to come up and say I thought you said you were . . . or not even give me that much . . . just go away and come back and change pronouns, change their demeanor toward me, as if a woman should be treated differently than a man when seeking health care.

Another aspect of provider competence was their ability or willingness to treat transsexual patients with respect, dignity, and compassion. One participant talked about how providers could be more compassionate to their patients in the following statement:

> [It is important] to have doctors that have the ability to look past you as a patient and ask what is it that you really need . . . to see what are your trigger points that are going to make you hurt more emotionally or physically, and how they can *not* hit those spots.

Another participant expressed the need for medical professionals to behave respectfully when treating transgender people:

> When a transsexual person comes into a doctor's office and is requiring care, that medical professional needs to be *professional*. They absolutely need to be medical, but they also need to be pro-

fessional. They need to not ask questions that are irrelevant. They need to not ask questions that if asked of them, would put them on edge. They need to remember that they have got someone's life in their hands.

Participants also photographed and/or shared stories of receiving good health care. All of the participants who had a primary care provider reported receiving good health care from that provider. One participant photographed himself receiving good health care and described his experiences at the Tom Waddell clinic:

FIGURE 5. Receiving Good Health Care

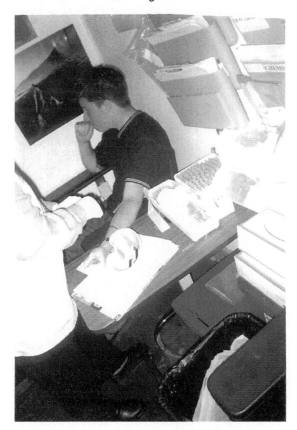

> I wanted to have an image of a nice experience of health care . . .
> The staff [at the clinic] are really sweet and very caring and very
> professional. Even though they are overworked and always in a
> rush, they are always warm and caring, even my doctor . . .

Vulnerability

All the participants discussed feeling vulnerable at some point in
their contact with health care providers or the health care system. Participants' expressed vulnerability when they had to remove their clothing,
or "come out" (the process of telling their health care providers that they
were transgender). Participants' vulnerability occurred in three distinct social contexts: (1) when accessing emergency or specialty care, (2) when
putting on "the gown," or having to disrobe for a physical examination,
and (3) when in "the waiting room," the experience of waiting amongst
the general public for specific types of health care, such as gynecological
care.

While all the participants with a primary care provider reported receiving good care from that provider (as described above), they all
expressed fear when they required emergency or specialist care
from a new provider. Each visit to the emergency room or to a specialist required "coming out," telling the providers that they were
transsexual. Participants explained their vulnerability as the fear of exposure to unknown providers and potentially negative reactions from
those providers–reactions that could affect the provision of adequate
medical response. One participant's image of the emergency room entrance was described with this comment:

> The emergency thing is so traumatic for so many of us, and having
> had a number of experiences with emergency rooms myself, both
> accompanying other people and being the patient myself, I just
> know how important that little portal is . . . I want to talk about how
> important and how frightening the emergency room is. It's impor-
> tant for everyone. It's absolutely terrifying for transsexuals.

Many of the participants talked about feeling vulnerable when they
had to disrobe for a physical examination, stating that disrobing made
them extremely vulnerable because they were unable to hide that their
sex organs were incongruent with their gender appearance. Participants
stated that they feared being ridiculed or having their gender identity
questioned, denied or ignored by health care providers, despite their re-

FIGURE 6. Emergency Room Entrance

quests to the contrary. One participant photographed the gown itself and shared the following:

> I don't know what they are actually called: the dressing gown that you have to wear when you are getting tests done in the hospital. I wanted to represent that this is what I have to wear when I am going to have testing done, and it makes me very uncomfortable. I am very vulnerable . . . I was in this gown with nothing else on which is the first thing that puts a transsexual at a great disadvantage, and feeling very uneasy . . . So again, I can be who I am as long as I don't have to take my clothes off, and I don't have to be examined.

Participants expressed feeling vulnerable when sitting in waiting rooms prior to seeing their health care provider. The type of waiting room that caused the most anxiety was the gynecologist's waiting room. One participant stated that his waiting room anxiety and feeling of vulnerability were so intense that it kept him from seeking gynecological

FIGURE 7. The Gown

health care. He depicted his feelings through a series of photographs taken in a hospital waiting room:

> The thing that came to my mind was that I need to take a picture of myself in the waiting room, because that is where I would feel the most anxiety . . . This is actually where it would be the hardest, sitting here knowing that these women probably think that I am here waiting for my wife or girlfriend who's in there having an exam, and that she is going to come out and we are going to leave. What's going to happen when the receptionist calls out my name and I stand up and go in to the room?

Invisibility

> This is my collection of transgender health information . . . this is all that I had to work with when I was making my decision about whether to take hormones or not . . . that is not a lot of information

FIGURE 8. In the Waiting Room

and all of it has disclaimers in the front . . . [This picture says] that transgender health information is sparse and a lot of it is conflicting . . . This picture tells you that I have to make my health care decisions based on folklore information from people I talk to who are not experts . . . I would like to get more information from people who have more training but I don't know where they are.

Participants described feeling invisible on many levels, from not having their gender identity acknowledged by individual providers, to the absence of transgender-specific health information. Participants noted that it was particularly difficult to find accurate or relevant information about transgender health care, and stated that this limited the ability to understand their own health care needs. This was expressed by one participants' photograph of gynecological information taken from the Internet:

This is a conclusion people could come to about gynecological health care and FTMs. It is a very dangerous conclusion, because

FIGURE 9. Collection of Transgender Health Information

FIGURE 10. Photo of Text

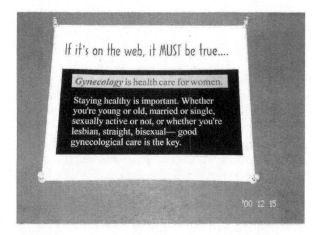

biologically I am still female and I haven't had a hysterectomy, I haven't had any lower surgery whatsoever. So from that point of view I very much need gynecological health care, particularly in light of the fact that I do take testosterone and I believe, see I don't even know myself, I believe from what I have heard that puts me at higher risk for cervical cancer. I don't even know that for sure. It is something that I have heard from other FTMs, but not all of them have said the same things. We don't know that much about our own health care needs, which is another component of being invisible.

According to all of the participants, providers lacked knowledge regarding transgender health and often relied upon patients to educate them about their relevant health care needs.

I can't get answers because I have to educate them about transgender stuff . . . I think training needs to be in medical school. They need to know about us; they need to know how to deal with us.

Perseverance

All participants framed their path through the world as a "struggle," and discussed feeling alone. Each described ways in which they had persevered against all odds, finding ways to cope with the difficulties they faced. Participants described ways in which they had learned to take care of themselves within a health care system that they perceived was ill equipped to handle their needs. They explained how a sense of optimism helped them to cope with the painful experiences of living as a transgender person in the world. They all spoke of trying to maintain a positive attitude, and believing that "things would get better" if they persevered. One participant related how optimism helped to counter painful feelings about his gender expression:

Luckily, I have this eternal optimism. I can distract myself about pain I am feeling. I figured eventually I will figure this out, but there is nothing that I can do about it right now . . .

Some participants shared stories about reaching a point of crisis, where they no longer felt they could cope with the obstacles before them. One described such a crisis as a juncture, at which point he faced a choice between persevering or giving up on himself (and on his life).

This is exemplified by a photo in which he is holding a gun to his head. *(Note: the participant was not in distress when this photograph was taken; he staged the photograph to illustrate that previous time in his life.)* According to several of the participants, suicidal feelings are not uncommon for transgender individuals. When asked how they persevered through these crisis points, participants responded that they made a decision to choose life:

> This is literally a place I came from of making the decision to choose life [or death], and fortunately for me I chose life. This [suicide] became a very viable option for me at one time before my transition.

Participants emphasized the importance of transgender visibility, the visible presence of self-identified transgender people in the media and within health care environments, as a factor in their perseverance. For example, one participant created a montage of images of transgender people in the media, explaining how seeing those images validated his experience and allowed him to see himself mirrored in the world.

FIGURE 11. Montage of Images

Participants also described community as a key to their ability to persevere. One participant found community through a group called FTM International, as pictured in his photograph:

> This is actually the meeting space for FTMI which is Female to Male International . . . It's a very sweet home place for me . . . I went there for my first meeting and cried the entire time . . . 'oh my god, I found where I am supposed to be.'

Activism

Like perseverance, activism was a strategy used by all the participants in the face of adversity. Participants' stories each revealed some form of

FIGURE 12. FTMI Meeting Room

leadership or participation in activities that increased transgender visibility or awareness. Some accomplished this through volunteering for transgender organizations; others were leaders in national and international efforts to increase transgender awareness. Each described his activism as an effective, positive, and in some cases necessary means of moving through the world and through the health care system as a transgender individual.

Activism was described by participants as not only a means for coping with the "system" and lack of provider competence, but also as a path to creating change through their interactions with the system and with providers. One participant saw it as giving back some of what had been given to him:

> Right now I facilitate the support group meeting there [at FTMI]. So the room not only has meaning of that to me, it's also a way of me giving back for what I have received . . . It is a space of me giving back chunks of me . . .

Another participant described himself as a "pioneer":

> I do have a vision for a future where it won't always be as hard as it is now. I feel like a pioneer–very much so, like I am on the frontier.

Thus, participants described how their "pioneer" and activist efforts were "giving back" to people who had come before them, and "paving the way" for other FTMs who would come along in the future.

Participants told stories of acting as educators, advocates and supporters within and outside the FTM community and with their health care providers. Participants stated that they often needed to educate their own provider about transgender health issues. Some saw this as an opportunity to improve the quality of health care for all transgender people, one provider at a time. One participant shared a story of such a teachable moment with a medical student who was working with his gynecologist:

> [My provider asked] 'If it's O.K. with you I'd like for you to come sit in the chair and I'd like to do an exam. We have a student here today who has never worked with Trans-people and I'd like her to be able to talk with you. You can say no.' I said, 'I think it's important for students to get to know us, to get comfortable with us and what our medical needs are.' So this woman came into the room

FIGURE 13. Gynecologist's Office

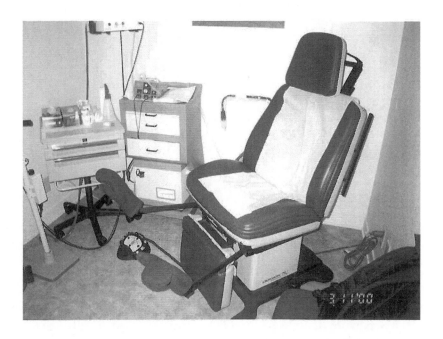

and helped to examine me. The doctor was explaining what to expect because of testosterone. The student was asking me about other surgeries, my health care, and was just generally concerned, asking me 'If I want to find out more about transgender people, where do I go? How do I talk to them?' We had a conversation about it. It made me feel a little bit more comfortable about the fact that I had to sit in that chair. It was good to know that a least a little bit of what I was doing was providing someone with some education so that when they see a transgender person later on, that person is going to get treated with respect. They're going to get treated with the medical care that they really need to be. They're not going to get asked inappropriate questions.

Participants shared about being educators in their own community. One participant talked about teaching other transgender men to inject hormones properly, and how to dispose of needles properly. Another explained how transgender people disseminate health information to each other via the Internet or at meetings:

> Transgender people are taking this task of providing information into their own hands. We do it ourselves. We collect information and share it with people in the only ways we know how. We spend our money photocopying stuff and handing flyers and brochures out at meetings. The Internet has also been an amazing help . . . We are taking things into our own hands. If the government and health care industry are not going to do it for us, then we are going to do it until they catch on and start doing it with us.

DISCUSSION AND RECOMMENDATIONS

The participants' photographs and stories confirmed that the FTM community is challenged to find competent and culturally respectful health care. The study also showed that FTM individuals are hesitant to seek regular preventive healthcare. This may be due to the fear and anxiety surrounding gynecological care for this population, as well as the lack of provider knowledge regarding gynecological needs of FTMs, and provider insensitivity towards FTMs when they do access preventive gynecological care.

Emerging Themes

The themes identified from the data illustrated that many of the causes of the current lack of competent health care services for transgender people are directly linked to one another. Thus, working to improve the quality of one aspect begins the process of change in other areas. An example of this can be seen with the connections between the themes of vulnerability and invisibility. These themes emerged separately, but are related to and influenced by one another. Participant stories reflected that the vulnerability they feel when seeing a specialist, getting emergency care, disrobing for an exam, or sitting in the waiting room is related to the invisibility they feel as transgender people (particularly FTMs) in society. In this study, invisibility was described as (1) inaccurate information, or complete lack of information about transgender-specific health care, (2) a general lack of understanding or acknowledgement about the existence of transgender people, and (3) the disbelief, shock, and other negative reactions on the part of practitioners–

including incorrect female pronoun use, despite the patient's insistence upon his male identity. In those moments of invisibility, participants also described feeling vulnerable. Because of their experience of being made to feel invisible by providers, and their ensuing sense of vulnerability, the FTMs in this study often felt reluctant to seek care. Those two themes of invisibility and vulnerability thus interact to create a barrier to gaining access to health care.

Coping Mechanisms

Perseverance and activism emerged as both themes and coping mechanisms for participants to overcome barriers to competent care. In addition, these coping mechanisms helped them to reduce invisibility and vulnerability, and served to create improvements in provider competence and in the health care system overall.

Participants attributed their perseverance to a variety of support systems (community, positive media images) as well as to the necessity of survival (the choice of persevering in order to survive, or "chose life"). In one story a participant explained how he first heard the words "female to male transsexual" and discovered the possibility of an FTM identity through a documentary film. This is an example of how media visibility can support an individual transsexual's identity. Seeing this film enabled him to attach a label to his identity, and begin making sense of his inner gender confusion:

> I was sitting there watching this movie with my girlfriend and crying 'cause . . . I had always thought, I feel like a guy, but I am not, so I'll deal with that, but I saw all these guys and they were telling their story, and it was my story, and I had never heard anyone tell my story before . . . and I thought oh my god I never had a word for it they are female to male transsexuals! FTM, that's what I am. I never had a word for it before.

In this example, the presence of visible transgender people was key to the participant's ability to persevere, giving him hope and lessening his feelings of isolation. The need for community was also discussed by several participants as a means of coping with invisibility and lack of competent health care. The search for community encompassed finding a place where participants did not feel judged, where they did not have to define or defend who they were. Within their communities, participants could let down their guard, be themselves, and feel respected.

The theme of activism emerged as a means for participants to overcome some of the barriers to health care, and thus was related to the themes of invisibility, vulnerability, and provider competence. Participants described their willingness to be visible in society and to act as agents of change (activists), particularly within the health care environment, as helping to remedy the invisibility perpetuated by the health care system. For example, the participant who allowed the medical student to take part in his gynecological examination stated that he was willing to be an educator in that instance in order to improve that provider's future ability to work with transgender patients. The participant also described his decision to educate his providers as a coping mechanism in the moment, helping alleviate some of the stress he felt during gynecological visits. The participant's response thus linked the theme of activism to other themes by reducing vulnerability and invisibility while increasing perseverance and provider competence.

Improving Provider Competence Through Perseverance and Activism

Provider competence, which includes direct contact and the administering of care to a patient, can thus be impacted by individual transgender people who are bold enough to act as agents of change (activism). Provider competence can be improved by informing providers about current transgender health trends and concerns, increasing transgender visibility, openly discussing life experiences that affect transgender health, and holding providers accountable for the quality of treatment that they are administering to their transgender patients.

The participant story about transgender people disseminating health information amongst themselves is another illustration of the advocacy component of activism, as the participant described how transgender people are "taking this task of providing information into their own hands" and thus advocating for themselves. This statement reflects the perseverance demonstrated by many transgender individuals, and the importance of FTMs educating one another about navigating the health care world as a transsexual. The education, advocacy and support roles in which the participants all found themselves reinforced their roles as pioneers and activists and as men who envisioned a better world for all people.

Thus, participants drew a connection between their own health care interactions and working towards a vision of equitable health care for all. Participants each saw their own lack of adequate health care treatment as a product of greater problems of a system in which transgender invisibility was only one aspect. Each in his own words described greater injustices in the "system" that impact underrepresented communities. Participants perceived that these systemic injustices played a role in some of the improper or disrespectful treatment they received as transsexuals. Likewise, participants with positive experiences of receiving care felt hopeful of greater possibilities for improving the health care system for many other marginalized populations.

Participants all extrapolated from their own experiences to envision greater possibilities for improving the health care system for many other marginalized populations. Their ideas included improved education and training, adequate compensation and optimal working conditions for people who work in health care, and broad-based solutions such as a national health care system. One participant's comment exemplifies a vision of a world in which all people could get their health needs met:

> We all deserve to have our health, and if there is anything that you can do as somebody who provides that or has the power to provide it, then do it! What is stopping you? There are people dying and being sick and leading miserable lives that don't have to. Why not make it a world where people can get what they need and deserve, instead of suffering? I don't see the point really. That's not the kind of world I want to live in.

Recommendations

Participants indicated that with provider training and a clearer understanding of transgender people, the level of vulnerability and invisibility that an FTM experiences trying to access health care may begin to diminish. As illustrated in this study, change begins to occur when (a) transgender people insist on their own visibility and act as agents of change (activists), advocating on their own behalf, and when (b) the health care system takes responsibility for educating its providers and practitioners to treat transgender patients with compassion, dignity and respect.

Furthermore, participants noted that they felt invisible when research studies and basic health care information did not include specific references to transgender health care. They felt the lack of transgender-inclusive research perpetuates the dearth of relevant and necessary transgender health information.

Therefore, recommendations for practice, as derived from participant comments, are summarized into three categories: training, service provision, and research. Training recommendations are those made for professional development among health care professionals, medical office staff, and emergency response workers. Service provision recommendations refer to guidelines for the delivery of health care to transgender patients. Research recommendations refer to further study needed in order to provide information on health risks, concerns, and needs of the FTM population.

Training. Increasing the knowledge of health care providers and health care staff is a crucial step in improving transgender access to care. Training that specifically addresses all aspects of working with transgender people in a health care setting is recommended: (1) at the provider level (including doctors, nurses, physician assistants, and nurse practitioners); (2) at the frontline staff level (including the office staff and receptionists who are the often the first to encounter a patient in an office setting); and (3) at the emergency and crisis intervention level (including, emergency medical technicians (EMTs), paramedics, police, and firefighters who may deal with transgender people in emergency situations). The training should be specific to the level of care that is being provided, and should be designed in consultation with transgender individuals.

Service provision. The results of this project made clear the need to create health education and health support systems that are specifically designed for, and inclusive of, transgender people. For example, transgender people would benefit greatly from gynecological services designed specifically for them. Such transgender specific programs would make these services more accessible and would increase the likelihood of transgender people seeking health care. Additionally, transgender focused support services would allow individuals seeking services to focus on their actual health care needs rather than spending their time combating others' discomfort, pushing for their own visibility, and educating their own health care providers about transgender identity.

Another area of focus for service provision to transgender people would be the creation of specific health support for people who are in the process of gender transition. FTMs who are transitioning may have questions and need vital information about basic health maintenance as their bodies go through tremendous chemical and physical change. Major concerns regarding testosterone injection might include dosage; self-administered injection; interaction of hormones with tobacco, alcohol, and other substances; long-term health risks of testosterone; side effects of and physical reactions to hormone injection; emotional and physical changes resulting from testosterone; and development of male secondary sex characteristics. Other relevant concerns might include sex reassignment surgery options and their health effects; interaction with the health care system for non transgender-related health concerns, and necessary elements of gynecological health maintenance during and after transition to male identity.

Finally, participants recommended clear guidelines for health care providers, medical office staff and emergency personnel on providing sensitive, quality care to transgender individuals.

Research. Overall, the lack of information about transgender specific health care issues inhibits providers' ability to deliver competent care. More research is needed to assess the health risks, preventive health needs, and health care needs of transgender individuals. Dissemination of such research results within the medical community has the potential to improve health care delivery to transgender individuals. Results of these studies should also be shared with the transgender community, so that FTM individuals can be educated about their own health care needs and can seek appropriate care.

CONCLUSION

This project used Photovoice as a way to gather information about a segment of the transgender population (female to male transsexuals) that has rarely been studied. While the small sample size of this project prohibits making generalizations about the experiences of all FTMs, the insights and information gathered from these men and their stories may to inform health care providers and researchers about the need for more inquiry into this segment of the transgender population.

This project started an important dialogue with FTMs about the issues of health care access, and provided insight into needed areas of future research inquiry related to the transgender community. Transgender people are the experts on their community; therefore, they should be included at the table when policymakers and practitioners are discussing research, training curricula, and standards of care related to transgender people and their communities.

The project participants were paving the way for others, their stories revealing individual and collective struggles navigating the health care system. From a system that disregards and discriminates against them, to providers who are unable to treat them adequately, participants each illustrated a great deal of hope and courage to persevere through all of these challenges. These men have not only persevered and overcome barriers to health care access, but have thrived and helped others like them to do so as well. The themes that emerged from the participants' stories provided a dynamic picture of individuals who have taken great risk in their lives in order to live in a way that is most true to their identity. Although the group of men came from many different walks of life, the themes that emerged from their stories reflect a commonality in their experiences of accessing health care.

REFERENCES

Bockting,W.O., Robinson, B.E., & Rosser, B.R.S. (1998). Transgender HIV Prevention: a qualitative needs assessment. *AIDS Care*, (4):505-25.

Clark, M.E., Landers, S., Linde, R., & Sperber, J. (2001). The GLBT Health Access Project: a state-funded effort to improve access to care. *American Journal of Public Health*, 91, 895-896.

Clements, K., Katz, M., Marx, R., (1999). The transgender community health project: Descriptive results. Unpublished raw data.

Freire, P. (1970). *Pedagogy of the oppressed.* New York: Seabury

Hage,J.J., Dekker, M. L., Karim, R. H., Verheijen, M., & Bloemena, E. (2000). Ovarian cancer in female-to-male transsexual: Report of two cases. *Gynecologic Oncology, 76*, 413-415.

Lee, R., (2000). Health care problems of lesbian, gay, bisexual and transgender patients. *Western Journal of Medicine, 172*, 403-408.

Lombardi, E., (2001). Enhancing Transgender Healthcare. *American Journal of Public Health*, 91: 869-872.

Morton, S., Lewis, Y., & Hans, A., (1997). Notes on Gender Transition: FTM 101–The invisible transsexuals. [47 paragraphs]. *FTM International Online Newsletter.* Available FTP: Hostname: FTMI. Org/newsletter

Wang, C., & Burris, M. (1997). Photovoice: concept, methodology, and use for participatory needs assessment. *Health Education and Behavior, 24*, 369-387.

Wang, C., Cash, J. L., & Powers, L. (2000). Who knows the streets as well as the homeless? Promoting personal and community action through Photovoice. *Health Promotion and Practice, 1*, 81-89.

Wang, C., Yuan, Y. L., & Feng, M. L. (1996). Photovoice as a tool for participatory evaluation: the community's view of process and impact. *Journal of Contemporary Health, 4*, 47-49.

Understanding the Experiences
of Lesbian, Bisexual and Trans Survivors
# of Domestic Violence:
A Qualitative Study

Danica R. Bornstein, MSW

The Northwest Network of Bisexual, Trans, Lesbian and Gay Survivors of Abuse

Jake Fawcett, BA

The Northwest Network of Bisexual, Trans, Lesbian and Gay Survivors of Abuse
University of Washington, School of Public Health and Community Medicine
Evans School of Public Affairs

Marianne Sullivan, MPH

Public Health-Seattle & King County

Kirsten D. Senturia, PhD

Public Health-Seattle & King County

Sharyne Shiu-Thornton, PhD

University of Washington, School of Public Health and Community Medicine

---

This research was supported by the U.S. Department of Justice Programs award numbers 98-WT-VX-0025 and 98-WE-VX-0028

[Haworth co-indexing entry note]: "Understanding the Experiences of Lesbian, Bisexual and Trans Survivors of Domestic Violence: A Qualitative Study." Bornstein, Danica R. et al. Co-published simultaneously in *Journal of Homosexuality* (Harrington Park Press, an imprint of The Haworth Press, Inc.) Vol. 51, No. 1, 2006, pp. 159-181; and: *Current Issues in Lesbian, Gay, Bisexual, and Transgender Health* (ed: Jay Harcourt) Harrington Park Press, an imprint of The Haworth Press, Inc., 2006, pp. 159-181. Single or multiple copies of this article are available for a fee from The Haworth Document Delivery Service [1-800-HAWORTH, 9:00 a.m. - 5:00 p.m. (EST). E-mail address: docdelivery@haworthpress.com].

159

SUMMARY. *Objectives:* Using a participatory approach, our objectives were to understand community perspectives on domestic violence (DV) in lesbian, bisexual and trans (LBT) communities, and to assess access to and cultural appropriateness of DV services for LBT survivors.

Methods: We used qualitative methods and conducted focus groups and semi-structured interviews with LBT survivors of DV.

Results: Nearly all participants reported that the level of awareness regarding DV in their communities was limited. Survivors reported difficulty identifying their partners' behavior as abusive. Isolation was described as central to experiences of abuse, and respondents discussed a variety of isolation tactics specific to LBT communities. Isolation also contributed to difficulty seeking help. Respondents reported that they often did not access mainstream DV services due to concerns about homophobia and transphobia. To address DV in LBT communities respondents pointed to the importance of friendship and community networks, sharing information about queer DV, and holding batterers accountable for their behavior.

Conclusions: LBT people face challenges identifying and responding to DV that are specific to their cultural context. Services for LBT DV survivors must be culturally appropriate and accessible. Community-based solutions for addressing and preventing DV should be encouraged. *[Article copies available for a fee from The Haworth Document Delivery Service: 1-800-HAWORTH. E-mail address: <docdelivery@haworthpress.com> Website: <http://www.HaworthPress.com> © 2006 by The Haworth Press, Inc. All rights reserved.]*

KEYWORDS. Lesbian, bisexual, trans people, domestic violence, participatory research, qualitative methods, community-based

Domestic violence (DV) is widely recognized as a leading public health issue with significant consequences for women's health (Satzman & Johnson, 1996). It has been documented in diverse populations and settings, suggesting it is a pervasive problem affecting all cultural and economic groups worldwide, including lesbian, bisexual and trans (LBT) populations (Fischbach & Herbert, 1997; Wilt & Olson, 1996; Renzetti, 1992). The term "trans" refers to a wide range of people whose gender identity or expression varies from the cultural norm for their birth sex (Feinberg, 1998).

Existing literature on DV in LBT communities falls into three main categories: (a) writing by survivors and activists that describes personal experiences of DV, and lays the theoretical groundwork for addressing

DV in LBT relationships; (b) estimates of the prevalence of violence in LBT relationships; and (c) descriptions of barriers LBT victims face in accessing support services.

In early analysis of lesbian DV, activists in the battered women's movement recognized that dynamics of DV in lesbian relationships are similar to those in heterosexual relationships, but that homophobia is an important factor in shaping the particular experience of DV in same sex relationships (Lobel, 1986). The prevailing model of heterosexual DV defines DV as an attempt by batterers to gain power and control over their partners (Pence & Paymar, 1993). In the groundbreaking anthology *Naming the Violence,* published by the National Coalition Against Domestic Violence Lesbian Task Force, Barbara Hart defined DV in lesbian relationships in similar terms. Hart writes, "Lesbian battering is that pattern of violent and coercive behaviors whereby a lesbian seeks to control the thoughts, beliefs or conduct of her intimate partner or to punish the intimate for resisting the perpetrator's control over her. Individual acts of physical violence, by this definition, do not constitute lesbian battering. Physical violence is not battering unless it results in the enhanced control of the batterer over the recipient" (1986).

Also in this anthology, Suzanne Pharr explicitly identifies the political context of homophobia and heterosexism as essential to understanding the experience of battered lesbians: "There is an important difference between the battered lesbian and the battered non-lesbian: the battered non-lesbian experiences violence within the context of a misogynist world; the lesbian experiences violence within the context of a world that is not only woman-hating but is also homophobic. And that is a great difference" (1986). Elsewhere, Pharr outlines the consequences of homophobia and internalized homophobia that shape lesbians' experience of DV including isolation and the risk of losing employment, housing or family (1997).

With respect to quantitative studies of LBT DV, several surveys have estimated the incidence and prevalence of DV in LBT communities based on self-reported incidents of violence or abuse (Brand & Kidd, 1986; Lie, Schilit, Bush, Montagne & Reyes, 1991; Loulan, 1987; Scherzer 1998; Waldner-Haugrud, Gratch & Magruder, 1997). Prevalence estimates in these surveys vary widely (Waldner-Haugrud et al., 1997)–reported rates range from 17 (Loulan, 1987) to 75 percent (Lie et al., 1991). Reasons for this variation include the use of non-representative samples and the lack of a standard definition of DV across surveys (Renzetti, 1992; Waldner-Haugrud et al., 1997). National and statewide prevalence studies, while based on representative samples, often do not report victimization rates for LBT people (Centers for Disease Control and Prevention, 2000; Schafer, Caetano & Clark, 1998). Recently, the National Violence Against Women Survey (NVAW) (Tjaden & Thoennes, 2000) reported rates of DV both for women with female intimate partners and for women with male intimate partners. Lifetime prevalence of rape and physical assault by female intimate partners was 11.4% compared to 20.3% by male intimate partners. The NVAW was unable to report rates by sexual orientation or gender identity (e.g., lesbian, bisexual, trans) and the authors noted that further research is needed to confirm the finding of lower rates of DV among same-sex couples. We are aware of only one study that estimated DV rates for trans people (Courvant & Cook-Daniels, 1998): 50% of respondents reported being raped or assaulted by an intimate partner, and 31% identified themselves as survivors of DV (Courvant & Cook-Daniels, 1998).

In addition to estimating prevalence, literature on DV in LBT communities is largely focused on barriers and access to victim services (National Coalition of Anti-Violence Programs, 2000; National Coalition of Anti-Violence Programs, 2001; National Coalition of Anti-Violence Programs, 2002). Previous reports have suggested that for lesbians, barriers to seeking help may include commitment to the abusive partner (Renzetti, 1992), homophobia on the part of police and DV service providers (Allen & Leventhal, 1999; Renzetti, 1992), concerns about confidentiality (Renzetti, 1992), and a perception that DV services are only for heterosexual women (Renzetti, 1992).

For trans survivors, expectations of indifference and/or violence from police and service providers and fear of exposure of trans status may be obstacles to seeking help (Courvant & Cook-Daniels, 1998). The shame and self-doubt often experienced by survivors may be compounded by the stigma of mental illness attached to the diagnosis of "gender identity disorder" (Courvant & Cook-Daniels, 1998). Finally, the gender segregation of most DV services makes them inaccessible to some trans survivors (Courvant & Cook-Daniels, 1998).

Although bisexual women have no doubt been included in previous studies of both "heterosexual" and "lesbian" domestic violence, we are not aware of any research that specifically describes bisexual women's experiences with domestic violence.

Published research on DV in LBT communities has emphasized quantitative studies over contextual qualitative research. While quantitative approaches are useful for understanding the extent of the problem, qualitative methods help to improve understanding of issues such as the cultural context of DV in LBT communities, factors that influence survivors' response and community perspectives on preventing DV. Qualitative reports about the experiences of LBT survivors consist mostly of individual accounts from survivors and case studies by therapists. Our study makes a significant contribution by focusing on respondents who have been identified as survivors of domestic violence, and by using interviews and focus groups to examine both the individual and community experiences of and responses to DV.

METHODS

Because little is known about the issues that LBT people face in accessing DV services, a qualitative approach that seeks to understand these issues inductively is appropriate. Qualitative methods are useful for gaining depth of knowledge and illuminating the context of a problem (Morgan & Krueger, 1998). In qualitative open-ended interviewing, response categories are not proscribed, allowing informants flexibility to describe their experiences in rich detail. Additionally, qualitative interviewing emphasizes non-judgmental understanding of individual experiences in their cultural context (Rubin & Rubin, 1995), an important consideration in this study.

Participatory Action Research

Participatory Action Research (PAR) (Frankish, George, Daniel & Doyle-Waters, 1996; Whyte, Greenwood & Lazes, 1991) provides the over-arching framework under which the project was carried out. PAR is an approach to research that values participation by those affected by the study both throughout the research process and for putting research findings into action (Whyte et al., 1991). Ideally, through PAR, participants in the research project benefit both from participating and from the results. In order for such benefits to occur, community partners must be involved in the earliest stages of conceiving and shaping the research project as well as carrying out the research, analyzing findings, and making recommendations for action.

This research was part of a larger collaborative study conducted by Public Health-Seattle and King County, the University of Washington, and five Seattle community-based DV agencies serving LBT people, refugee and immigrant women and other women of color. The research focused on nine communities (LBT, African American, Cambodian, Ethiopian, Filipina, Latina, Russian-speaking, Urban Indian, and Vietnamese), to understand experiences of non-majority DV victims/survivors both within their communities and in seeking services for DV, in order to contribute to a more culturally competent response to DV. A full report of our methods and findings is available elsewhere (Senturia, Sullivan, Shiu-Thornton & Ciske, 2001). This report is concerned only with findings from the LBT community.

Consistent with a PAR approach, the research team was composed of three professional researchers and nine additional team members representing each of the nine cultural groups being studied. Each of the nine members was employed as a victim's advocate at one of the five DV service agency partners. Level of involvement varied from some members collaborating only on design and data collection to others participating through the duration of the project. In the case of the LBT community, the team member was a DV advocate at the Northwest Network (a DV agency serving the LBT community) who self-identified as bisexual and a survivor of domestic violence. She participated through all stages of the research including analysis and writing findings.

Data Collection

The specific data collection techniques used were focus groups and semi-structured interviews. Each technique has strengths and limitations; combining techniques, or triangulating, therefore, allows the researcher to address the limitations of one strategy with the detail offered by the other (Denzin & Lincoln, 1994). Focus groups have the potential to yield rich data as participants interact and compare their experiences. This process of interaction helps to elucidate the range of opinions among participants. Focus groups can also be useful for exploring complex social phenomena that may be difficult for an individual to explore in isolation but more easily clarified in group discussion (Morgan & Krueger, 1993). In this project, focus groups help describe *community* definitions and responses to DV.

Data from semi-structured interviews complement information gained through focus groups by providing in-depth individual accounts of people's experiences. Since in-depth sharing can be limited in a focus group setting, individual interviews were an important additional data source. The use of both focus groups and interviews allows for validation of findings across methods (Miles & Huberman, 1994). Additionally, since we used both focus groups and interviews, participants had the choice of talking about their experiences in a group setting or one-on-one.

Focus group facilitators and interviewers self-identified as lesbian or bisexual. The facilitators/interviewers were non-researchers with backgrounds in DV and sexual assault. The researchers trained them in interviewing and facilitation techniques. Attention to the safety of participants and a culturally appropriate approach were key factors in this research. Facilitators and interviewers provided information on DV resources to participants who requested it as a result of participating in this project.

We obtained approval for the study from the Institutional Review Board of the University of Washington. Each participant gave informed consent prior to participating in the study. We have taken care to protect the identities of the participants in presenting these findings.

Instrument Development

The focus group/interview guide was designed in close collaboration with community partners and adapted for in-depth interviews. The steps to developing the guide included:

1. Initial topics prepared by research staff.
2. Review and brainstorming for additional topics by entire research team, including partners.
3. First draft of language prepared by research staff.
4. Review, editing and approval by research team.

The general, open-ended questions we used provided a framework for participants to share their experiences that is in alignment with our overall research questions but also allowed for significant flexibility in shaping responses.

Sampling and Recruitment

Respondents self-identified as lesbian, bisexual and/or trans and were currently experiencing or had formerly experienced abuse by an intimate partner. Purposive sampling (Bernard, 1995) was used to recruit participants who had and had not used DV services. Since we were working closely with a community-based provider of DV services to LBT people, this was a significant source of referral of participants. We also attempted to recruit participants from other community settings, posting flyers at LBT-oriented community clinics, cafes, gyms, salons, and a community center in the neighborhood identified with LBT communities. Additionally, we placed an ad in the local lesbian oriented newspaper. While we received several phone calls in response to ads and flyers, few participants were recruited in this way. Recruitment by a trusted provider proved to be much more effective. It is likely that concerns about confidentiality due to small community size had an effect on recruitment. Respondents participated in either 1-2 person interviews or 4 person focus groups. In total, 22 LBT people participated in 3 focus groups and 6 interviews. Our original intent was to conduct focus groups of 6 to 10 people. However, due to recruitment challenges we modified our strategy to accommodate respondents' confidentiality and safety concerns.

Screening interviews with potential participants determined eligibility for the study. People determined to be at risk of violence due to their participation in the project were not included. The advocate from the LBT community DV agency used a screening tool specifically developed to accurately differentiate victims from perpetrators in same-sex relationships. This screening tool has been described elsewhere (Goddard & Hardy, 1999). Participants were screened for whether an intimate partner had used physical, sexual, or emotional abuse to establish power and control. Careful screening of participants was particularly important to ensure that batterers were not included in focus groups with survivors.

Participants in focus groups and interviews were compensated for their time ($35.00) and were provided with food, childcare and transportation.

Data Management and Analysis

With permission of participants, all focus group and interviews were audio-taped and then transcribed. The first step in data analysis was to develop a codebook to structure the analysis. The researchers developed the first draft of the codebook by intensively reviewing the transcripts to identify main themes. The second step in developing the codebook was for the advocates on the research team to each review several transcripts and expand or revise the codebook. Each addition and change to the codebook was discussed among the full research team until we came to consensus on which codes should be added, modified or retained. With this preliminary codebook, each team member coded two transcripts (the same two for each coder). Then, the team reconvened, discussed the coding for these two transcripts and revised the codebook as appropriate. After finalizing the codebook, each team member was given a set of transcripts to code. Periodically all team members coded the same transcript to check for consistency. Any discrepancies in perspective were discussed until the group came to consensus on how particular text should be coded.

In order to organize and retrieve coded data, transcripts were entered into NUΔIST (Qualtitative Solutions and Research Pty Ltd., 1996), a software package for analyzing text-based data. NUΔIST assists the researcher in organizing, searching, and retrieving text-based data and is indispensable for analyzing the large amounts of data generated by this type of project. All entry of codes into NUΔIST was done by the researchers, who reviewed all coding done by the team members and made adjustments as necessary. NUΔIST output was generated for each of the codes. Review of the output provided the basis for writing the findings. Since this was a participatory research project, community partners on the research team also participated in writing and interpreting the findings. Separate reports were written for each cultural group, following the same outline. In the case of the LBT group, the findings were written by the LBT DV advocate. Throughout, quotes are used to illustrate typical ways in which respondents talked about main themes.

RESULTS

Table 1 shows select demographic characteristics of LBT participants, based on self-report. The LBT focus groups included survivors with a wide range of gender and sexual identities, who sometimes used the word "queer" to refer to themselves and the communities with which they identify. While not all LBT people identify as "queer," many prefer it as an empowering term inclusive of a diverse community.

Lack of Community Awareness About LBT Domestic Violence

Nearly all participants reported that awareness of DV in their communities was limited. Many noted that people in their communities lacked the language to describe abusive relationships in terms of DV or abuse. Participants offered several explanations for this limited awareness, including a general lack of available information about queer relationships and a specific lack of information about DV among LBT people.

I think my friends really tried to understand the personal distress that I was in, but they didn't consider it domestic violence at all.

They considered it an incident that needed to be taken care of, and then moved away from.

Everybody, straight and gay, said, "We had no idea the statistics were that high. Are you sure? Where did you get your information?"

TABLE 1

Characteristics of Respondents	
Age	Years
Mean	34
Range	21-62
Time Since Abuse	Years
Mean	3.5
Range	.2-20
Sexual Orientation*	%
Lesbian	69.2%
Bisexual	30.7%
Gender Identity*	%
Female	76.9%
Trans	23%
Income	%
% under $10,000	23.8
% under $20,000	47.6
Services**	%
Used DV services	81.8
Had not used DV services	18.1
Abuser's Relationship to Survivor***	%
Girlfriend	68.1
Partner or Lover (gender not specified)	31.8
Race/Ethnicity	%
White	81.8
Chicana	4.5
Native American	13.6
Total Number of Respondents	22

*Questions about sexual identity and gender identity were added to the short survey that was administered to focus group and interview participants after data collection was in progress. Percentages in these categories are based on the responses of 13 participants.

**Services include the range of services available to victims/survivors. Types of services used included community-based advocacy and support, protection orders, and counseling.

***While most of the participants in the study reported that their abuser was female, some did not report the gender of their abuser. For the purposes of this study, it is the sexual identity of the survivor that is most salient since the focus is on the experiences of survivors who identify as LBT and the community context in which they experience and respond to DV.

Participants also attributed the lack of community discussion about DV in queer relationships to a minimization of the seriousness of women's use of violence and a reluctance to draw negative attention to relationships that are already unsupported by a homophobic and transphobic culture.

> *I think that people are very afraid to add to [the stigma of being queer] by saying . . . not only are we queer, but we also have violence in our relationships and in our community.*

> *[Gay people] just don't want to hear [about the abuse]. They want me to shut up as soon as possible.*

Difficulty in Identifying Abuse

Several participants reported that this lack of information about DV in queer relationships left them unprepared to handle abuse when it occurred, and increased their sense of isolation. Many noted that the fact that the available information about DV referred almost exclusively to heterosexual relationships contributed to a tremendous degree of difficulty in identifying abuse. For example, if survivors believed that an abusive partner must be male, or physically bigger, they may have had difficulty identifying their partner's abusive tactics.

> *Yeah, because they're gay and women don't really hit each other: women don't hit women.*

In addition, survivors noted that their partners' tactics of emotional control were elusive enough to confuse them; for example, one participant reported being controlled by a constant fear that her partner would commit suicide, but had difficulty identifying her partner's suicide threats as a mechanism of control. Several noted they were confused about who was the abuser in the relationship, and, in fact, initially believed themselves to be abusive.

> *She would attack me, and I would fend her off, and she would end up with scratches or something, and [she] would be like, "See! She's abusing me."*

> *Size, sex . . . it's really hard to figure out what power dynamic is at work.*

Abuse Experiences: Isolation and Community Connections

Participants described a wide range of criminal abuse experiences, including physical and sexual violence, threats of homicide, stalking, and destruction of property. Although these experiences were shared by many, most participants focused the majority of their attention on describing (and, in focus groups, comparing notes about) emotional abuse, which encompasses a wide range of abusive tactics.

Participants gave particular attention to the topic of isolation. Isolation was almost universally identified as central to participants' experiences of abuse, and a variety of isolation tactics were described. Survivors reported that abusive partners used threats and intimidation to prevent them from making connections within the community.

Some observed that because their abusive partner was female, she could access all of the supports and resources the survivor could. This made it difficult for survivors to have any community contacts that did not involve their partners. Many also noted that their abusers were well-liked by friends, and were able to take advantage of the small size of the community and the fact that both knew the same people to cut survivors off from their friends.

> *If it was a guy you wouldn't have access to all of the places that she was able to have access to. There was just no shaking her.*

> *I know that if I were to tell any of the friends of my abuser they would not believe me. They would say she's such a great person and she's so outgoing and she's so charming and she's so gorgeous and so funny and so capable and she's told them things about me, that I'm crazy, and they wouldn't believe me.*

Many participants reported a shared experience of abusers questioning or challenging the survivors' queer identities as a tactic of control. For example, many participants reported that they were accused of being straight, or not "good enough" at their chosen gender identity. Challenges to authenticity or "realness" were reported across a variety of sexual and gender identities, and served to make survivors feel unsure of themselves or "inauthentic." Participants reported that such challenges served as a means of coercion, sometimes connected to sexual abuse; for example, several survivors reported being pressured into sex in order to prove they were "really a lesbian." These challenges both supported and were reinforced by isolation, which made it difficult to get information about identity issues from sources outside the relationship.

> *It got to the point where I would go out . . . and I would stare at the ground because I didn't feel like I should make eye contact with men . . . It just became such . . . an attack of not just my bisexuality, but just my freedom.*

> *With my case it was trans stuff. Like, "Oh, this person's more trans [than you] . . ." Pressure that way.*

> *"Well, why don't you want to have sex? Hello, you must not really be a lesbian if you don't want to have sex or this kind of sex. Well, why do you want that kind of sex, do you really want a penis?"*

Isolation served to keep survivors in abusive relationships. For example, participants overwhelmingly reported needing support in identifying their relationships as abusive. They needed to be believed about their experience–and their isolation made this very difficult. Participants also reported that they needed social interactions, and friends to help them feel safe in community settings with an abusive ex-partner. In addition, survivors reported that because they had been cut off from many of their friendships and supports, they needed help with housing, planning for safety in a small community, and relief from loneliness.

> *I didn't have any gay friends who weren't friends of my partner, so I didn't have anybody to turn to.*

> *[It would be helpful to] have five friends who would say, "If you want to go dancing tonight, I'm there with you, and if she comes up to me, I'll stand in front of her and tell her she's not welcome here." You know, I would have felt a lot safer cause . . . there's people sticking up for me.*

Many participants reported that their experience of abuse was affected by not having information about healthy, non-violent queer relationships. They said their abusers benefited from the silence around queer relationships and the lack of visible models because survivors did not have other examples against which to compare their experiences. This enabled abusive partners to set the tone for their relationships. This was particularly difficult for people in their first same-sex relationship, when they had little information to counter what their partners said.

> *I just thought relationships were like that . . . You don't really get to see, like on TV and the movies . . . especially if you grew up really homophobic like I did, you really don't get to see what [a queer relationship] would look like if it was ugly or what it would look like if it were healthy. So when she went around saying things I just thought, "Well, I guess that's what people do in relationships."*

Experiences with Seeking Support

Many participants reported getting support from the specialized LBT community DV service provider who participated in the research project; this was undoubtedly connected with this agency's role in recruiting participants. Nearly all reported that the agency's services were extremely helpful in dealing with abuse, and many noted that they would not have sought support from a program that was not queer- specific.

> *And when I went and I sat in the first group, it was the most amazing feeling to sit in a room full of women who knew exactly what I was feeling, and who . . . may as well have taken the words out of my mouth.*

> *I would never have gone any other way . . . Even if my choice was straight people or straight people, I would have chosen none.*

Very few people reported using protection orders or law enforcement. Participants reported that they believed authorities would not treat them respectfully, believe them, or offer them protection. Some felt that, even though they needed help to escape abuse, they did not want to subject their partner to potentially discriminatory or dangerous interactions with police.

> *You were lovers with this person. You're a lesbian. It's basically relationship or date rape, and very little is done . . . So [I thought,] don't bother to put yourself through that process, because it's just going to be hideous.*

No one in the study reported using DV shelters. Many said that they did not consider seeking support at DV shelters because coming out and possibly facing violent and discriminatory reactions created insurmountable barriers. Participants also mentioned doubts about the capacity of shelters to keep them safe by screening out their abusers. Several noted that though they had contacted a shelter, there was no space available when they needed it.

> *It wouldn't cross my mind... I've heard about lesbians going to shelters–the homophobia, having to hide the violence. It's usually never the staff, because usually the staff are queer, but the other residents are very homophobic and there's a lot of violence and trashing.*

Many participants reported getting support from therapists and couples counselors during and after the relationship, and most reported negative experiences working with these providers. They said that therapists and couples counselors failed to recognize abusive tactics, minimized violence, or made survivors feel responsible for the abuse. A few, however, reported positive experiences with therapists who helped identify abuse in the relationship.

> *My therapist at the time was a lesbian and ... she never gave me the impression that I might be in an abusive relationship ... She implied that I was to blame by saying that she felt that I had one of those relationships that we brought out the worst in each other.*

Community Solutions for Domestic Violence

While participants suggested a wide range of solutions for supporting LBT survivors of abuse and ending DV, they focused the greatest attention on solutions that involved community organizing and community building. Participants identified a wide range of ways queer communities might work together to support survivors, hold batterers accountable for abuse, and eliminate the conditions that allow violence to occur.

They emphasized the importance of friendships in helping survivors identify abuse. Survivors described the potential of friendship and community networks to support and challenge one another, share information about queer DV, hold batterers accountable for their behavior, and help each other understand and identify the complexities of emotional abuse. They suggested sharing information within communities about what healthy queer relationships could look like, particularly for people who are new to queer relationships. In addition, participants suggested that communities create the expectation that intimate partnerships should support connections with the community, not undermine them. Some participants described interventions that occurred within their communities, from holding batterers accountable to helping survivors escape from danger.

> *The entire group intervened. They kept her away from me, they took me to a movie or something and then others took her to the house that we lived in together to get all of her stuff out, and then they brought me home. And they kept her away from me and gave me some support . . .*

> [There should be a value that] *it's not cool to fall off the face of the earth. You should have . . . friends that are your own, she should have friends that are her own, you should have some common friends . . . And not just throw it away . . . or assume that you are not going to hear from [your friend] for the next six months because they're in a brand new relationship.*

> *I think if I had seen a poster I wouldn't have come [to seek services] . . . I had to be able to see healthy, queer relationships. I had to be able to identify unhealthy queer relationships and I think it would have had to come through friends.*

Many called for the creation of new sites where community members could break isolation, learn from each other's relationships, and get support and information about their own queer identities. These sites were described as places where survivors could get support, but that would also work to eliminate the conditions that make DV possible.

> *Making more space for queer people . . . to be supported in different queer identities . . . A huge thing for people I know that contributes to isolation is coming out about gender stuff and dealing with gender and being trans . . . not having support around that, or all kinds of other queer identities, keeps people in relationships if that is their only link to that kind of thing.*

> *The goal would be that wherever you are . . . if you're just talking about your life, if you're at the barbershop or wherever and you're talking about your life, there will be somebody that could say, "Well, that sounds like this is what's going on for you," and get some support about that.*

DISCUSSION

In examining these findings, it is important to consider the limitations of the research. The findings presented are based on fewer responses than would have been ideal to reach saturation. This limitation suggests the need for further research to confirm and expand our findings. Possible reasons for the difficulty in recruiting from LBT communities may include the short time frame for recruitment (approximately 3 months), community norms which may have inhibited open discussion of DV, and concerns about confidentiality due to small community size. Additionally, our sample is weighted towards those who have accessed DV services. Those who have accessed services may be more likely to have had immediate needs for support and safety met. This may contribute to the emphasis on community-wide intervention among the participants. Further, the sample size is not large enough to discern differences among lesbians, bisexual women and trans people who experience DV. Further research could help elucidate similarities and differences among these sub-groups.

This research provides important contextual information about the experience of and response to DV in LBT communities. Based on a shared political experience, LBT people form a cultural group whose history, family structures, community institutions, and cultural values are distinct from straight populations (Allen & Leventhal, 1999). Some of the elements of LBT culture that have implications for survivors' experience of DV include the illegal or extra-legal nature of LBT people's experiences and relationships, a history of police and state violence against LBT people, the existence of small and interconnected communities, a cultural value of chosen families, and a political and social context of homophobia, heterosexism, biphobia, and transphobia. Although the dynamics of DV in queer relationships are similar to those in heterosexual relationships (Hart, 1986), the cultural context of LBT communities significantly shapes the experience of abuse (Allen & Leventhal, 1999).

Consistent with previous analysis of DV (Allen & Leventhal, 1999; Renzetti, 1992), isolation from community and family was a significant part of the experience of DV for these participants. Isolation increases survivors' dependence on abusive partners and cuts them off from support and resources. LBT people are often estranged to some extent from family support and may not have access to institutional supports that are available to heterosexual couples through churches, workplaces and schools. This isolation from the larger community, along with the small and interconnected nature of LBT communities, creates a context of intense vulnerability for LBT survivors. Within a very limited arena of LBT affirming spaces, survivors and their abusive partners are likely to have the same friends and community connections. For example, if every friendship network a survivor has access to includes one person who also knows her batterer, the survivor's isolation may be intensified significantly.

Historically, the lives and experiences of LBT people have either been overtly criminalized, or have existed in contexts outside what is recognized by the law (Allen & Leventhal, 1999). This shared cultural and historical experience, together with the context of police and state violence, may account for the fact that focus group participants did not identify police, protection orders and the legal system as significant supports. By contrast, the cultural significance of chosen family and friendship networks may help to explain why participants focused so much of their attention on the role of community networks as key resources.

Homophobia, biphobia and transphobia render LBT people and their experiences invisible. This invisibility of LBT lives and relationships may impede survivors' ability to distinguish abusive behavior from "normal" relationship dynamics. Specifically, the lack of positive, public role models for healthy queer relationships and the prevailing model of DV in which men are perpetrators, women are victims, and sexism alone (to the exclusion of other systems of oppression) is the underlying cause, contribute to the difficulty of defining a partner's abusive behavior as DV.

Bisexual and trans people's experiences are often marginalized within LBT communities as well as in the broader social context (Armstrong, 1995; Califia, 1997; Dahir, 1999; Rust, 1995). Abusive partners can use the marginalized position of these identities to isolate, pressure and coerce their partners. For example, one participant reported being made to feel not "good enough" at being trans; another was accused of flirting with men because she identified as bisexual. These experiences highlight that in order to effectively address DV in LBT communities, these internal community dynamics must be addressed and challenged. Community-based interventions must be shaped by the experiences of bisexual and trans people if they are to avoid replicating this marginalization.

Participants reported expectations of encountering indifference, harassment or violence, when accessing mainstream services including shelters and police. For many, this was a considerable barrier to using these services. Notably, many participants sought support from therapists and couples counselors rather than DV shelters and advocates. Previous reports indicate that, although survivors are more likely to seek help from therapists than other sources (Lie & Gentlewarrier, 1991; Renzetti, 1992), the effectiveness of counseling is limited by therapists' lack of information about same-sex DV (Farley, 1992; Renzetti, 1992). Most participants in our study found therapists unhelpful in identifying patterns of abuse.

It is clear that service providers of all kinds must be able to offer services that are appropriate to the cultural context of LBT survivors in order to meaningfully respond to abuse in LBT communities. However, participants did not focus on improving cultural competence of mainstream services as a primary strategy. Rather, they prioritized community-based solutions to addressing DV and its consequences over individual-level approaches such as victim services. Participants called for interventions that build and strengthen community connections and provide community members with the skills to support victims and hold batterers accountable for abusive behavior. Such strategies respond appropriately to the cultural context in which LBT people experience domestic violence, and challenge the systems of oppression that make silence around queer relationships the norm.

Our findings indicate that LBT community members can play a key role not only in offering creative solutions to DV, but also in defining the problems to be solved. The open-ended and participatory approach of this research allowed participants to articulate community priorities and direct researchers to concerns that may have been overlooked using a different methodological approach.

Consistent with the PAR model, community partners were integrally involved in analyzing the results and were committed to incorporating the findings into their work. Because of the consistent involvement of The Northwest Network in the research process, they were able to respond quickly to participants' call for interventions that would strengthen the community's ability to support survivors and address DV at a community level by developing the FAR Out (Friends Are Reaching Out) Project. This community organizing project convenes and facilitates discussions among existing friendship groups, helping community networks develop strategies for breaking isolation in order to build and sustain connections that can interrupt and outlast battering. Rather than developing strategies for short-term support based on agency services, this program builds connections within the community that persist over time. Since its inception in 2000, this innovative project has received national attention as a promising community-level intervention to increase the community's capacity to support survivors, hold batterers accountable, and undermine isolation.

The Northwest Network has also developed a Relationship Skills Class for bisexual, trans, lesbian and gay people and their partners and loved ones. This six-week course responds to the need for information about healthy queer relationships by exploring topics such as negotiation, communication, accountability, identifying the values that we bring to relationships, understanding the impact of oppression and privilege, and staying connected with friends and family. Community response to the class has been extraordinary.

The research findings have also prompted the Northwest Network to convene a Community Advisory/Action Team (CA/AT) of therapists and counselors in the Puget Sound area who work within LBT communities. The CA/AT is currently working to develop a training for therapists on DV in queer relationships. The purpose of this training is to increase therapists' capacity to recognize and respond to DV in queer relationships, inform therapists about LBT-specific DV services, and develop working relationships between DV advocates and therapists who work within LBT communities.

More research is needed to fully understand DV in LBT communities, the social and political context in which LBT relationships exist, and community based responses to DV. Questions regarding sexual orientation and gender identity should be incorporated into national prevalence surveys so those estimates can be developed for LBT people. Partnerships between researchers and community-based providers help ensure that research is culturally appropriate and relevant and findings will be implemented in community settings to address DV in queer communities.

AUTHOR NOTE

Danica Bornstein is a private practice therapist and an advocate at the Northwest Network of Bisexual, Trans, Lesbian and Gay Survivors of Abuse. Jake Fawcett is a volunteer at the Northwest Network of Bisexual, Trans, Lesbian and Gay Survivors of Abuse and an MPH/MPA candidate at the University of Washington. Marianne Sullivan is an epidemiologist with Public Health-Seattle & King County and a doctoral student at Columbia University. Kirsten D. Senturia is Research Anthropologist at Public Health-Seattle & King County, and affiliate Clinical Assistant Professor at the School of Public Health and Community Medicine, University of Washington. Sharyne Shiu-Thornton is a medical anthropologist and ethnic minority mental health specialist, and is a lecturer at the School of Public Health and Community Medicine, University of Washington. Correspondence may be addressed: Danica Bornstein, P.O. Box 95782, Seattle, WA 98145-2782.

REFERENCES

Allen, C., & Leventhal, B. (1999). History, culture, and identity. In B. Leventhal & S.E. Lundy (Eds.), *Same sex domestic violence: Strategies for change* (pp. 73-81). Thousand Oaks, CA: Sage Publications.

Armstrong, E. (1995). Traitors to the cause? Understanding the lesbian/gay "bisexuality debates." In N. Tucker (Ed.), *Bisexual politics: Theories, queries, and visions* (pp. 199-217). Binghamton, NY: The Haworth Press, Inc.

Bernard, H.R. (1995). *Research methods in anthropology: Qualitative and quantitative approaches.* Walnut Creek, CA: AltaMira Press.

Brand, P.A., & Kidd, A.H. (1986). Frequency of physical aggression in heterosexual and homosexual dyads. *Psychological Reports, 59,* 1307-1313.

Califia, P. (1997). The backlash: Transphobia in feminism. In *Sex changes: The politics of transgenderism.* San Francisco: Cleis Press, Inc.

Centers for Disease Control and Prevention. (2000). *Prevalence of intimate partner violence and injuries–Washington, 1998.* (Morbidity and Mortality Weekly Report No. 49). Washington, DC: U.S. Government Printing Office.

Courvant, D., & Cook-Daniels, L. (1998). Trans and intersex survivors of domestic violence: Defining terms, barriers, and responsibilities. In *National Coalition Against Domestic Violence 1998 conference handbook.* Denver, CO: NCADV.

Dahir, M. (1999, May). Whose movement is it? *The Advocate.* Retrieved from http://www.findarticles.com/cf_0/m1589/1999_May_25/54775067/p1/article.jhtml.

Denzin, N., & Lincoln, Y. (Eds.). (1994). *Handbook of qualitative research.* Thousand Oaks, CA: Sage Publications.

Farley, N. (1992). Same-sex domestic violence. In S.H. Dworkin & F.J. Gutierrez (Eds.) *Counseling gay men & lesbians: Journey to the end of the rainbow* (p. 231). Alexandria, VA: American Counseling Association.

Feinberg, L. (1998). *Trans liberation: Beyond pink or blue.* Boston: Beacon Press.

Fischbach, R.L., & Herbert, B. (1997). Domestic violence and mental health: Correlates and conundrums within and across cultures. *Social Science and Medicine, 45,* 1161-1176.

Frankish, C.J., George, A., Daniel, M., & Doyle-Waters, M. (1996). *Participatory health promotion research in Canada: A community guidebook.* Vancouver, BC: Consortium for Health Promotion Research.

Goddard, A.B., & Hardy, T. (1999). Assessing the lesbian victim. In: B. Leventhal & S.E. Lundy (Eds.), *Same-sex domestic violence: Strategies for change* (pp. 193-200). Thousand Oaks, CA: Sage Publications.

Hart, B. (1986). Lesbian battering: An examination. In: K. Lobel (Ed.), *Naming the violence: Speaking out about lesbian battering* (pp.173-189). Seattle, WA: Seal Press.

Lie, G.Y., & Gentlewarrier, S. (1991). Intimate violence in lesbian relationships: Discussion of survey findings and practice implications. *Journal of Social Service Research, 15,* 41-59.

Lie, G., Schilit, R., Bush, J., Montagne, M., & Reyes, L. (1991). Lesbians in currently aggressive relationships: How frequently do they report aggressive past relationships. *Violence and Victims, 6,* 121-135.

Lobel, K. (Ed.). (1986). *Naming the violence: Speaking out about lesbian battering.* Seattle, WA: Seal Press.

Loulan, J. (1987). *Lesbian passion: Loving ourselves and each other.* San Francisco: Spinsters/Aunt Lute.

Miles, M.B., & Huberman, A.M. (1994). *Qualitative data analysis: An expanded sourcebook.* Thousand Oaks, CA: Sage Publications.

Morgan, D.L. & Krueger, R.A. (1993). When to use focus groups and why. In D.L. Morgan (Ed.), *Successful focus groups: advancing the state of the art* (pp. 3-19). Newbury Park, CA: Sage Publications.

Morgan, D.L., & Krueger, R.A. (1998). *The focus group guidebook.* Thousand Oaks, CA: Sage Publications.

National Coalition of Anti-Violence Programs. (2000). Lesbian, *Gay, Bisexual and Transgender Domestic Violence in 1999.* New York: Author.

National Coalition of Anti-Violence Programs. (2001). *Lesbian, Gay, Bisexual and Transgender Domestic Violence in 2000.* New York: Author.

National Coalition of Anti-Violence Programs. (2002). *Lesbian, Gay, Bisexual and Transgender Domestic Violence in 2001.* New York: Author.

Pence, E., & Paymar, M. (1993). *Education groups for men who batter: The Duluth model.* New York: Springer Publishing.

Pharr, S. (1986). Two workshops on homophobia. In: K. Lobel (Ed.), *Naming the violence: Speaking out about lesbian battering* (pp. 202-222). Seattle, WA: Seal Press.

Pharr, S. (1997). *Homophobia: A Weapon of Sexism.* Berkley, CA: Chardon Press.

Qualitative Solutions and Research Pty Ltd (1996). *User's guide for QSR NUΔIST: Qualitative data analysis software for research professionals.* Victoria, Australia: Author.

Renzetti, C.M. (1992). *Violent betrayal: Partner abuse in lesbian relationships.* Newbury Park, CA: Sage Publications.

Rubin, H.J., & Rubin, I.S. (1995). *Qualitative interviewing.* Thousand Oaks, CA: Sage Publications.

Rust, C. (1995). Bisexuality and the challenge to lesbian politics: Sex, loyalty, and revolution. New York: New York University Press.

Satzman, L.E., Johnson, D. (1996). CDC's family and intimate violence prevention team: Basing programs on science. *Journal of the American Medical Women's Association*, 51, 83-86.

Schafer, J., Caetano, R., & Clark, C.L. (1998). Rates of intimate partner violence in the United States. *American Journal of Public Health*, 88, 1702-1704.

Scherzer, T. (1998). Domestic violence in lesbian relationships: Findings of the lesbian relationships research project. *Journal of Lesbian Studies*, 2, 29-47.

Senturia, K., Sullivan, M., Shiu-Thornton, S., & Ciske, S. (2001). Cultural issues affecting DV service utilization in ethnic and hard to reach populations. Seattle, WA: Public Health–Seattle & King County. Retrieved from http://www.metrokc.gov/health/dv/dvreport.htm.

Tjaden, P., & Thoennes, N. (2000). *Extent, nature, and consequences of intimate partner violence: Findings from the national violence against women survey.* Washington, DC and Atlanta, GA: National Institute of Justice, Centers for Disease Control and Prevention.

Waldner-Haugrud, L.K, Gratch, L.V., & Magruder B. (1997). Victimization and perpetration rates of violence in gay and lesbian relationships: Gender issues explored. *Violence and Victims*, 12, 173-184.

Whyte, W.F., Greenwood, D.J., & Lazes, P. (1991). Participatory action research, through practice to science in social research. In W.F. Whyte (Ed.), *Participatory Action Research* (pp. 19-55). Newbury Park, CA: Sage Publications.

Wilt, S., & Olson, S. (1996). Prevalence of domestic violence in the United States. *Journal of the American Medical Women's Association*, 51, 77-82.

Need for HIV/AIDS Education
and Intervention for MTF Transgenders:
Responding to the Challenge

Tooru Nemoto, PhD
Lydia A. Sausa, PhD, MSEd

University of California, San Francisco

Don Operario, PhD

University of Oxford

JoAnne Keatley, MSW

University of California, San Francisco

SUMMARY. The purpose of this paper is to report on the use of qualitative and quantitative research to develop an HIV/AIDS education intervention for MTF transgenders. Findings revealed that MTF transgenders

Tooru Nemoto, Lydia A. Sausa, and JoAnne Keatley are all affiliated with the Center for AIDS Prevention Studies, University of California, San Francisco. Don Operario is affiliated with the Department of Social Policy and Social Work, University of Oxford. Correspondence may be addressed: Dr. Tooru Nemoto, Center for AIDS Prevention Studies, 50 Beale Street, Suite 1300, San Francisco, CA 94105 (E-mail: tnemoto@psg.ucsf.edu).

The authors would like to thank everyone who assisted in the research study and the current implementation of the community intervention project, including the study participants, community collaborators, outreach workers, health educators, and health professionals who provide services to MTFs of color. The study was supported partially by the Substance Abuse and Mental Health Services Administration Grants H79-TI12592 and U97-SM53769.

[Haworth co-indexing entry note]: "Need for HIV/AIDS Education and Intervention for MTF Transgenders: Responding to the Challenge." Nemoto, Tooru et al. Co-published simultaneously in *Journal of Homosexuality* (Harrington Park Press, an imprint of The Haworth Press, Inc.) Vol. 51, No. 1, 2006, pp. 183-202; and: *Current Issues in Lesbian, Gay, Bisexual, and Transgender Health* (ed: Jay Harcourt) Harrington Park Press, an imprint of The Haworth Press, Inc., 2006, pp. 183-202. Single or multiple copies of this article are available for a fee from The Haworth Document Delivery Service [1-800-HAWORTH, 9:00 a.m. - 5:00 p.m. (EST). E-mail address: docdelivery@haworthpress.com].

have high prevalence of adverse health outcomes such as HIV, substance use, and psychological problems. MTF transgenders of color–African American, Latina, and Asian Pacific Islanders–experience heightened risk due to multiple stigmas associated with ethnicity and gender identity. Based on this evidence of need, we developed a series of transgender-specific HIV prevention, substance use and mental health treatment, and health education programs. Future health programs for stigmatized gender minorities, such as MTF transgenders, will benefit from conducting descriptive studies to identify the health needs of the community, and by linking research scientists, health providers, and community agencies to form a collaborative network for delivering evidence-based and community sensitive services. *[Article copies available for a fee from The Haworth Document Delivery Service: 1-800-HAWORTH. E-mail address: <docdelivery@haworthpress.com> Website: <http://www.HaworthPress.com> © 2006 by The Haworth Press, Inc. All rights reserved.]*

KEYWORDS. Transgenders, HIV/AIDS, intervention, health promotion

Male-to-female transgenders (MTFs) are individuals who reassign the sex and gender that were assigned to them at birth. Some MTFs may have body modifications to assist with their gender transition. Body modifications may include hormone therapy, various surgeries to restructure the physical body including genitalia and breasts, silicone injections to help shape the body, binding of genitalia, and other body feminizing techniques. Although several studies have documented health factors and medical procedures associated with the physical and anatomical aspects of transgenderism, focusing particularly on sexual reassignment surgery (see Israel & Tarver, 1997), relatively few studies have documented health education programs for MTFs related to the health vulnerabilities they may confront.

There is strong need for health education programs for MTFs focusing on their risk for HIV and co-occurring problems such as other STDs, substance use, and psychological issues (Lombardi, 2001). Studies in the US consistently report high prevalence rates of HIV infection among MTFs: 68% in Atlanta (Elifson et al., 1993), 40% in Miami (Bay, 1997), 32% in Washington DC (Xavier, 2000), and 26-48% in San Francisco (Clements, Katz, & Marx, 1999; Nemoto, Luke, Mamo, Ching, & Patria, 1999; Nemoto, Operario, Keatley, Han, & Soma, 2003). Despite these epidemiological findings, research indicates that MTFs have a low perceived risk of HIV and STD transmission, and continue to engage in high risk activities including unprotected sex, sex while under the influence of alcohol/drugs, and sharing needles (Bemis, Simon, Reback, & Gatson, 2000; Kenagy, 1998; Sykes, 1999). Kenagy found that 67% of HIV negative and 82% of HIV positive MTFs had engaged in unprotected sexual activities in the past year. Further, 57% of MTFs in Kenagy's (1998) study said their chances of getting HIV/ AIDS were none or low, though the majority of MTFs (70%) reported engaging in unprotected sexual practices in the past three months and reported they would engage in unprotected sexual practices in the future.

Substance use is also widely prevalent in studies with MTFs (Lombardi and van Servellen, 2000). A study of 392 MTFs [San Francisco Department of Public Health (SFDPH), 1999] found high lifetime prevalence use for marijuana (90%), cocaine (66%), speed (57%), LSD (52%), poppers (50%), crack (48%), and heroin (24%). The most common substances used during the past 6 months were marijuana (64%), speed (30%), and crack (21%). Clements-Nolle et al. (2001) reported 34% prevalence of lifetime injection drug use. Furthermore, 47% of the transgender IDU sample reported sharing syringes, 49% reported using someone else's syringe to load their own drugs, and 29% shared cookers with someone else during the past 6 months.

Psychosocial vulnerabilities have been shown to underlie HIV and substance use risk behaviors among MTFs. A study by Krammerer, Mason, Conners, and Durkee (2001) outlined three psychological factors contributing to high-risk behaviors: (1) social stigma and related negative self-image, (2) economic vulnerability and related sex work and substance abuse, and (3) the quest for a feminine body and the need for identity affirmation. Some research suggests that MTF transgenders are disproportionately prone to depression, feelings of alienation, and suicide (Gagne et al., 1997; Kreiss & Patterson, 1997).

The socioeconomic opportunities for the MTF community are also discouraging. Due to stigma and discrimination against transgender individuals, many MTFs experience difficulty obtaining or maintaining employment, housing, and basic social and health services (Bemis et al., 2000; Bockting, Robinson, & Rosser, 1998; Boles & Elifson, 1994). Kelly (1995) stated that the stigmatization and disenfranchisement often experienced by transgenders may result in isolation, shame, low self-esteem, anxiety, depression, and substance abuse that in turn are likely to add to HIV risk. Moreover, many MTFs must rely on sex work as a source of income (Sykes, 1999).

MTFs of color may confront additional biases and pressures above and beyond their transgender-related issues. Studies of gay men of color have documented how multiple levels of stigma associated with race/ethnicity and sexual orientation contribute to their disproportionate risk for HIV, substance use, and psychological problems (Diaz; 1998; Diaz, Ayala, Bein, Henne, & Marin, 2001; Nemoto, Operario, Soma, Bao, Crisostomo, & Vajrabukka, 2003; Stokes & Peterson, 1998). Similar dynamics may be at play for MTFs of color, for whom gender identity and race/ethnic issues are intimately interconnected and may collectively exacerbate their health risks. Research by Bay (1997) and Clements-Nolle et al. (2001) have shown that MTFs of color, in particular African-American and Latinas, are at highest risk for HIV infection (Bay, 1997; Clements et al., 1999). Bay (1997) also noted that 81% of African-American and Latina MTFs injected weekly doses of hormones, and 60% reported having silicone injections. A study of 75 Asian Pacific Islander (API) MTFs by Nemoto, Iwamoto, and Operario (2003) indicated alarming rates of substance use, unprotected sex, and sex while under the influence of alcohol and drugs. Furthermore, in a comprehensive review of HIV prevention studies for MSM of color, Darbes et al. (2001) concluded that interventions are most effective when they consider racial/ethnic issues that contribute to HIV risk. This simple principle of cultural sensitivity is likely to hold for MTFs of color.

There are few health and social services offered to transgender related to HIV/AIDS, substance use, and psychological issues (Lombardi, 2001). In some cases in which transgenders have accessed existing services, they have reported feelings of isolation and discrimination (Grimaldi & Jacobs, 1997). Krammerer et al. (2001) noted that MTFs struggled with disclosing their gender history to health care providers due to safety concerns and discrimination. Schilder et al. (2001) discovered that abuse by providers, unprofessional behavior, and a lack of transgender competence and sensitivity in existing health care agencies resulted in fractured care for the transgender population. Kenagy (1998) reported that 26% of trans individuals had been denied medical care specifically because they were transgenders, and 63% of MTFs had obtained hormones from a source other than a licensed physician. Furthermore, very little research has described the health service needs and experiences for MTFs of color, who are truly a minority group within a minority.

The purpose of this paper is to describe findings from a descriptive study of substance use, HIV risk, and psychosocial issues among MTFs of color in San Francisco. In addition to an overview of the major health-related behavior and psychosocial findings that emerged, we describe how two community-based health education and intervention projects and one substance abuse treatment program for MTFs were developed from research findings. Hence, this paper offers an important step toward linking descriptive research on MTFs with health intervention programs that can deliver community sensitive and appropriate services.

METHODS

Data were gathered in two phases. The first phase was a qualitative focus group study of and the second phase was a quantitative survey using a structured questionnaire instrument. The eligibility criteria for both research phases included self-identification as: (1) an MTF transgender (regardless of body modification or surgery status); (2) an African-American, Latina, or API; (3) a history of exchanging sex for money or drugs; and (4) be 18 years or older. Recruitment for both phases used snowball sampling methods and referrals from collaborating community based organizations (CBO's) that had transgender support programs.

Phase 1 was conducted between November 1999 and February 2000. Focus group methodology was used as a strategy for obtaining first-person narrative accounts of HIV-related social and behavioral risk factors among participants; preliminary findings from focus groups were also used to develop a transgender-sensitive quantitative survey instrument. Seven focus groups were conducted, facilitated by a MTF moderator who used a semi-structured discussion guide. A pilot focus group consisted of a multiethnic sample of MTFs who were recruited from transgender-related service programs at local CBOs. Then we conducted two focus groups for African American MTFs, two focus groups for Latina MTFs, and two focus groups for API MTFs. Latina focus groups were conducted in Spanish facilitated by an English-Spanish bilingual MTF moderator. All participants provided informed consent after reading the information sheet approved by the Committee for Human Research (CHR), UCSF. Discussions were tape recorded and transcribed verbatim; focus groups conducted in Spanish were transcribed into Spanish and subsequently translated into English and checked validity of translation by a Spanish-English bilingual project staff member. In total, 48 participants (16 African-American, 15 API, 12 Latina, and 5 mixed ethnicities) participated in the focus groups.

Phase 2 was conducted between November 2000 and July 2001. Based on findings from the focus groups, we finalized the social and cognitive factors included in the quantitative survey instrument, and conducted a pilot study of the survey with 40 MTFs of color to ensure its gender and cultural appropriateness, clarity, and ease of completion. Potential survey participants were approached and recruited by a member of our MTF interviewer team at local MTF communities venues (e.g., bars, clubs, beauty salons, apartment buildings, health clinics); about half were recruited at or referred by collaborating CBOs. MTFs who expressed interest in the study were scheduled for an interview at a private office where they were provided informed consent, interviewed by trained staff members using a structured questionnaire, and received cash reimbursement for participation. Both the survey instrument and the informed consent form were translated into Spanish, and staff members fluent in Spanish administered the questionnaire.

RESULTS

Four major themes emerged from both quantitative and qualitative data that crystallized the need for a community intervention: (1) High levels of HIV-related risk behaviors; (2) Inadequate knowledge about HIV transmission; (3) Persistent discrimination against MTFs of color in health services; and (4) Lack of sexuality education and health services for MTFs. An overview of descriptive results from the quantitative survey is presented (see Nemoto et al., 2003 for more detailed information on quantitative findings), followed by qualitative focus group data to highlight each of the four themes (see Nemoto et al., in press, for more on qualitative findings).

Behavioral and Psychosocial Risk Survey Findings

A high rate of HIV infection (26%) was reported among MTFs of color in the survey sample. African-American and Latina MTFs reported higher rates of HIV (41% and 23%, respectively) compared to APIs (13%). HIV risk behaviors were prevalent among participants, including sex work, sex under the influence of alcohol and illicit drugs, and unprotected sex. Among the participants, 36% had engaged in sex work in the past 7 days. African Americans and Latinas also reported higher frequency of risk behaviors compared to APIs, including sex under the influence of drugs, sex work, and receptive anal sex with all partner types: primary partners such as boyfriends or "husbands," casual partners such as one-night stands, and commercial sex partners (see Nemoto et al., 2003, in detail).

Substance use was common among the participants; overall the participants reported use of alcohol (56%), marijuana (38%), non-injection amphetamines (24%), crack (13%), ecstasy (9%) and non-injection cocaine (7%), in the past 30 days. Reported injection drug use during the past 30 days was low (7%) compared to non-injection drug use, though 23% had a history of injecting drugs. In addition, over 40% of the participants reported having sex under the influence of alcohol, and over 50% had sex under the influence of illicit drugs. Drug use in the past 30 days differed by ethnicity. African Americans reported the highest rate of using marijuana, crack, and IDU, and Latinas reported the highest rate of using cocaine and downers. APIs were most likely to report using methamphetamines (speed).

Participants reported sexual behaviors with primary partners, casual partners, and commercial sex partners. Primary partners were defined as people with whom participants had a relationship, such as boyfriends, spouses, partners, lovers, or significant others. Casual partners were defined as non-paying private partners such as one-night stands. Commercial sex partners were defined as customers who paid for sex. MTFs were more likely to engage in high risk sexual behavior with primary partners compared with casual and commercial sex partners. In the past 30 days, 47% of the participants reported unprotected receptive anal sex with primary partners, 26% with casual partners, and 12% with commercial sex work partners. African Americans were over four times more likely to engage in unprotected receptive anal sex with commercial sex partners compared to APIs.

Discrimination against MTFs of color was a significant issue. The most common experience (reported by 79% of participants) was being made fun of or called names as a child. Other common experiences were hearing that transgenders were not normal as a child (68%), hearing that transgenders were not normal as an adult (63%), being made fun of or called names as an adult (61%), and being harassed by police for being transgender (61%). Over one-third (37%) of the participants reported experiencing childhood physical abuse for being transgender, and 20% reported physical abuse as adults for being transgender. In general, Latinas reported the highest degrees of depression followed by African Americans; APIs reported the lowest levels.

Many MTF participants reported a lack of sexuality education and health care services; 59% reported a need for STD screening, 46% psychological counseling, 41% general medical care, 25% alternative health care, 21% emergency room care, 21% treatment for substance abuse, and 19% urgent care. Due to limited access to hormone therapy, 32% of participants reported acquiring hormones from friends, 21% from Mexico (where hormones are sold without required prescription), and 9% from another non-prescription source (usually from underground market). Among the participants who reported ever having silicone injections, 49% received injections by a non-medical person–often a vendor who sells silicone and regularly conducts silicone injections for MTFs. Silicone injections were conducted by medical professional in the United States (18%), by friends (18%), and by medical professional outside the United States (15%).

Qualitative Narratives on HIV-Related Risk

HIV risk behaviors. MTFs highlighted various HIV risk behaviors, including sex work, sex under the influence of alcohol and illicit drugs, and unprotected sex. Participants shared their experiences about the high incidence of sex work among MTFs:

> I'm going to state why most transgender girls prostitute–it's not because they really want to, it was just, it was a means of support. I would lose my job in the daytime . . . I still have to pay rent, I still have to pay light bill, I still have to buy hormones, which at the time hormones were very, very important to me.

> It was a way, a means of support. Because after a while I gave up, and prostitution was easy; it was easier than going out than dealing with society, it was easier than going out looking for a job and getting fired, and I was my own boss.

MTFs reported that sex work was a form of survival due to lack of employment opportunities, career training, and education. "For me, prostitution was a source of survival. And yeah, I had to eat, I had to do . . . you know have clothes, a roof over my head."

Many MTFs who engage in sex work did not use protection consistently because they had poor negotiation skills to address condom use and drug use with clients. One participant revealed, "Many times a client can give you more money for not using a condom or for doing drug[s] with them." Another supported this experience by reporting:

> Unfortunately in this business of sexual work there are days that you do very well; there are days that you don't do well. Then if a client comes and offers more money and you have to pay your hotel room if not they are going to kick you out then you don't do it [referring to condom use].

Participants also lacked self-efficacy and abilities to negotiate with clients due to their feelings of desperation. "To me one time they were giving me $20 if I took off the condom. My life is more than $20; I said $40." Another stated, "I think that sometimes we lose conscience because we are under drugs, we are drunk. Sometimes one forgets to have the condom or the other, but I think that always it is better to use it . . ." When asked about drug use with partners, one participant replied, "All the time with drugs being injected. I, with one of them, I used to do much cocaine." Another discussed sharing needles for drug use, "I never . . . inject myself [with] hormones. I have never shared. But we have shared other things, needles to inject drugs." And participants often reported not using protection when under the influence, "At first we didn't, you know we used rubbers, and then after that because it feels good so we didn't use, you know, and we're under influence too. Crystal and ecstasy."

Many MTFs reported unprotected sex not only with sex work clients, but also with primary sex partners. When asked about practicing safer sex with primary partners or husbands, a participant responded, "I was going with this guy and at that time I was not, you know, using IV drugs anymore, and I knew he was. And then when we would have sex I didn't use condoms with him, it varied." Others added:

> I should have just followed my biggest rule, because I did not have sex with nobody without a condom, didn't suck a dick, did not get fucked, didn't do nothing without a condom. And that was my rule. If you wanted to have sex with me, if you wanted to taste the forbidden fruit, you've got to use a condom, otherwise there's the door. But that one time, I had been with this person for 2 years and . . . we started off using condoms, and then we got married, and then we decided not to use condoms, and that's when I found out I was HIV positive, after we divorced.

> Love can really be devastating. You fall in love, you can fall in love but don't be stupid, cause love will take you there. It took me there . . . I too got mine [referring to contracting HIV] from my husband. We had sex and . . . he started messing around with other people, and I didn't know, cause I was at work, and he'd be home having affair[s].

Participants discussed how their emotional attachment to a primary partner overshadowed their knowledge of HIV transmission and prevention, because they viewed it as a mean of acquiring or sustaining love. "We're like emotionally attached, and we don't like safe sex, although I do it with tricks and customers, because with them I don't care. If it has something to do with emotions, or like a partner, we don't practice safe sex." Another participant revealed how low self-esteem can contribute to high risk behaviors with primary partners: "I just felt, well I deserve it, I'm not worth anything, so better to have a man that mess around with than no man at all, honey." MTFs are in need of HIV prevention education specifically aimed at sexual behaviors and relationships with primary partners. One woman summed this up by stating, "I have always said that when we are infected, almost 99% is because of our husbands, because with them none of us becomes to protect [use protection]."

HIV-Related Knowledge and Attitudes. Many myths and stereotypes about HIV transmission existed among the focus group participants. The qualitative data crystallized some of the more salient attitudes and current knowledge about HIV and condom usage. Below are quotes from participants regarding using more than one condom at a time and using "grease" as lubrication to assist with penetration; both practices can result in condom breakage or microscopic tears in condoms, therefore increasing the possibility of HIV and STD transmission. One participant explained, "So I even piggybacked condoms now. They'll say, 'oh you don't need two, I want to get that sensation baby.' I say, oh we need two, you know, if we're gonna have sex we would need two." Another participant stated the reason she uses multiple condoms is her fear of contracting STDs:

> About the condom, it is charged double. If I see it right next to me, I put it double because it rips. I swear to you, seriously. No matter how beautiful you are, but if you see him with some strange things, like that, like some little things, I put three.

> I have always put two because they rip, yes! It is safer, and they rip and I put a lot of grease so that they will slide well.

If the participant used "grease," or any oil-based lubricant, it may be the reason her condoms "rip" or break during sex.

Many participants discussed not practicing safer sex. A statement from one MTF participant highlighted myths about transmission, and the need for increased self-esteem and self-efficacy among MTFs:

> Well basically my sex is safe because I don't allow them to penetrate me fully. What oral sex is very low incidence but however there's still a chance of getting HIV from their pre-cum and stuff. But I feel I'm old enough, I'm ready to go anyway so why should I practice safe sex because I'm ready to go any minute now. It doesn't matter. (Participant was 51 years of age)

Though one participant was a health educator, even she did not use protection consistently:

> In my case since I am [a] health educator, I am very conscious of the methods of transmission and the methods of protection. I can say that for anal sex with receptive or insertive I always use condom[s]. For oral sex, I can say that 75% there are times that I do not use it and many times it works crooked, that is, there is not much protection.

Failure to use barriers to prevent HIV and STD transmission is echoed by another participant:

> Sometimes, sometimes we forget to use them also . . . we get so involved and then when we realize that of using the condom we already did it. Oh my God, but why did I forget.

Many MTFs in the study were in need of HIV and STD education to assist them in exploring their attitudes about protection; improve self-efficacy and intention to increase condom use with primary and casual partners and customers; and increase their knowledge about transmission and the correct way to use a condom, as well as what proper steps to take if a condom breaks, highlighted by one participant's comment, "One time, one time, I had a client and the condom ripped on me and I left home and I gave myself a Clorox bath."

Discrimination in health services. Focus group participants described barriers to accessing services because they provided inadequate and inappropriate services for MTFs. Many participants encountered discrimination and prejudice by insensitive or uneducated providers and staff.

> [In regards to health care services and programs] treatments, in San Francisco, for transgender women, especially African-American transgender women, is hell. Pure hell because they don't–they tell you it's gonna be safe, they tell you it's gonna be this, its gonna be that . . . most programs aren't prepared for dealing with a transgender female . . .

Another participant discussed her discrimination with San Francisco shelters:

> I've experienced some discrimination being in a shelter, living in the shelter. Because I lived in transitional housing in the shelter for 8 months and just being there is just . . . being treated like a third class citizen. It just I was never comfortable there, simply because of the fact being transgender. It was just very difficult . . . The staff was very, very callous. They weren't supportive at all. As a matter of fact, they were very discouraging and it only because I had a good relationship with God that I was able to make it through there.

Concerns for safety were expressed many times among the participants. One woman, who immigrated to the United States, explained her need for safety and community:

> Where I may feel safe that I am going and that it is a place for transgenders only . . . we come to this country to try to succeed, but since you are a transgender, many doors are closed and you find yourself in a loneliness because sometimes you do not have anybody in this country.

MTFs also reported problems with access to facilities such as bathrooms, "She went to use the women's bathroom, and the security guard threw her out of the building because she was transgender." Another participant elaborated:

> There is no specific place for transgender . . . if you send them to . . . the shelter, they are discriminated as well. For instance, in the use of the restrooms, the showers, the women have complained that

they do not want to share a restroom with a transgender . . . many times they cannot even take a bath or they have to bathe in the men's bathroom . . . but in the men's bathroom they bother you a lot.

Participants also reported insensitivity, discrimination, and abuse by health care providers. One person recalled, "Some of the doctors that we went to in order to get certain things; we used to have to have sex with them. It's real degrading when we have to do those things." Another stated:

They had me on six different psychotropic medications at one time, and the reality, all I needed was some Premarin® (a hormone used to assist in feminizing the body). You know what I mean? All I needed was Premarin® and some support.

Participants also shared concerns about the need for health care providers to be trained on how to address the health needs of MTFs, and understand the differences among transgender identities, including the fact that not everyone desires surgery.

Some of the challenges that a lot of MTFs face, going into treatment facilities, is when you go into a treatment facility everybody basically acts as if we all are transsexual, everybody is basically pushing you toward surgery, you know what I'm saying? It's like everybody thinks because your trans, you're going to have surgery, and you're going to have the sex change and one of the things is, for me, I feel like I have too many recovery issues that I need to work on . . . my friends have told me that they didn't feel comfortable going into facilities because, even though they were MTFs, they felt like they were made to feel bad because they still had their tool.

Yes, people who run the programs need to be educated more on what a transsexual is and what a transsexual is about. Like for instance, maybe they should have a program for transsexuals only . . . the girls would be more comfortable if they would have their own.

Lack of Sexuality Education and Health Services. The need for health care services was repeatedly expressed by participants throughout the study. Some health care programs and services may target lesbians, gay men, and bisexuals, though do not provide transgender specific services or staff that is knowledgeable and trained to meet the unique health needs of MTFs of color. One participant remarked, "We do not have services for transgender[s]." Another stated: "I'm 22 and there's a lot of young transgenders who want to know, you know, how they can start or where they can start to use hormones and is it right to do this everyday, or every week, how many dosage? We don't have information." Other MTFs discussed the need to improve services for MTFs of color and for those who are not fluent in English:

> Many times the places which provide services to the Latina transgender community do not have a person who speaks Spanish. Then, that prevents to do a good intervention or it prevents that the Latina obtains the services.

MTFs highlighted their need to access public health care and have services provided more than one evening a week, ". . . basically a public health care that you can go to like Tom Waddell [a community health clinic in San Francisco], but they only have it like what one, once a week." Many of the participants had suggestions and recommendations on how to improve health services. One woman suggested:

> . . . Create a system of outreach which is consistent and continuous which provides services exclusively to transgender, and that not only gives out condoms or lubricants, but create conscious to the people of what a transgender is, how to live as a transgender, how to accept oneself as a transgender, and how to protect oneself in terms of AIDS one, and how to protect the client.

Another participant highlighted the difference between research studies that report on trans people and projects which intend to create new services or improve conditions for the trans community. She emphasized a need to:

> . . . create services and programs designed for transgender, not that they may be just investigations that what we are going to prove. We already know that AIDS exists, that there is too much incidence and prevalence of AIDS in the transgender community we already know. We already know that the drug is a risk factor we already know all of that. We need to educate ourselves in our community.

Participants stated that health care providers not only needed to be trained in transgender health concerns, but also be MTFs themselves to reflect their community. "Your best teacher in transgenderism is another transgender," stated one participant, and another highlighted the importance of peer health educators and MTFs as health care professionals:

> . . . I think what transgender women need is to see more of [referring to a MTF in the focus group], you know, more of this girl here get where they've come from. You know she's got a job, she can show another transgender woman . . . I did the same thing you did, I done been the same little places you done been, I've been to jail and everything else, I've come aboard, you know. And I think a lot of girls can see that, that we can come up, you know, and do better . . .

Many MTFs highlighted the importance of transgender specific health services:

> I would like [services] targeted specifically to transgenders. I don't want to walk in the clinics and see gay men sitting there . . . [or] see lesbians sitting there, because our needs are different. A lesbian can rent an apartment. She's a woman . . . no one's going to kill a gay man if he finds a dick between his legs. . . . they will definitely put a knife though a tranny's throat if they see breasts and a dick. These are issues that need to be addressed. Transgender is transgender. It's not gay. It's not lesbian. It's just what it is. It is changing from what you were into something else, and that means that people around you, environments have to change and be sensitive to this.

HIV/AIDS Intervention for MTF Transgenders

In response to the research findings gathered by both phases of the investigation, a community intervention project consisting of three different health service programs were established and implemented: *Transgender Resources and Neighborhood Space* (TRANS), the *Transgender Recovery Program* (TRP), and the *Transgender Life Care* (TLC). These programs are collaborations between research scientists and community health care providers, and combine descriptive research with evidence-based service delivery strategies.

Transgender Resources and Neighborhood Space. The goal of TRANS is to create a socially accepting and supportive environment for MTFs most at risk of HIV infection. Through a grant funded by the Substance Abuse and Mental Health Services Administration (SAMHSA), TRANS provides a series of health education workshops and a community space which includes a living room lounge area with TV/VCR, shower facilities, a resource closet containing clothing, shoes, and accessories. TRANS is staffed by a trained, multicultural team of health educators, who are all MTFs of color.

Eighteen different health awareness workshops are conducted in English and in Spanish on a wide range of transgender specific health-related topics based on needs identified through focus group analysis. Participants are encouraged to complete 10 workshops, and they can select from three different programs consisting of six different workshops. Program A includes: (1) Introduction to AIDS knowledge and services; (2) Commercial sex and relationships with private partners; (3) Protection from violence; (4) Drug use and sex; (5) Culture, gender, and sex; and (6) Hormone use and other gender concerns. Program B includes: (1) Drug abuse assessment and treatment experiences; (2) Information about treatment programs; (3) Self-expression; (4) Self-presentation; (5) Self-esteem and coping skills; and (6) Life skills. Program C includes: (1) Immigration; (2) Meditation and relaxation; (3) Hormones and medications; (4) Transgender law 101; (5) Returning to work; and (6) Networking and empowerment. Facilitators use non-didactic education methods, including experiential exercises, art and writing, and small group discussions. Workshops are repeated every 6 weeks and provide participant incentives (including gift coupons, cash, and a certification of completion). Workshops are evaluated by comparing participants' substance abuse and sexual risk behaviors, as well as, psychosocial risk factors measured at baseline, post-test, and 6-month follow up.

Transgender Recovery Program. TRP was created in collaboration with a local substance abuse treatment agency (Walden House) to offer treatment and residential services specific to the substance abuse needs of MTFs clients. Both the Program Manager, a licensed social worker, and the Substance Abuse Counselor of TRP, are MTFs. In addition to providing transgender-specific clients therapy, educational workshops, and inpatient and outpatient recovery services, TRP provides sensitivity training about transgender health care needs for other clients, and for staff of the treatment program who are involved in intake, treatment, vocational development, or administrative work.

Transgender Life Care. The TLC program was created in collaboration with a community public primary care facility to provide transgender-specific mental health services including case management, HIV testing, and therapy and counseling services for all MTFs and FTMs. In addition, TLC offers mental health support groups for MTFs and FTMs in English and Spanish, facilitated by trained health professionals at the TRANS site.

CONCLUSION

The HIV/AIDS education intervention for MTFs of color described here, based upon findings from two phases of qualitative and quantitative research with 380 participants, has established three different health service programs which to date have provided services to more than 500 MTFs and conducted outreach to more than 3,000 transgender people. The intervention projects confirm the importance of research investigations providing the foundation for developing effective health education and intervention services, especially in hard-to-reach transgender communities that suffer multiple oppressions. Multidimensional intervention projects that are collaborations between research scientists, community health providers, and members of the community are effective modes of substance abuse and HIV prevention, as well as, health promotion. This project provided a successful mechanism for integrating research and health service interventions, and established a role model for future research and intervention endeavors.

REFERENCES

Bandura, A. (1986). *Social foundations of thought and action: A social cognitive theory.* Englewood Cliffs, NJ: Prentice-Hall.

Bay, J. A. (1997). Transsexual and transvestite sex workers: Sexuality, marginality and HIV risk in Miami (Doctoral dissertation, University of Florida, 1997). *Dissertation Abstracts International, 59* (02), 536. (AAT No. 9824022)

Belzer, M. & Radzik, M. (1997). High risk characteristics in a cohort of HIV infected and noninfected transgender youth. *Journal of Adolescent Health, 20* (2), 156.

Bemis, C. C., Simon, P. A., Reback, C. J., Gatson, B. (2000). *Relationship between self-assessed HIV risk, self-reported risk behavior, and HIV seroprevalence in a male-to-female transgender population.* Los Angeles, CA: Health Research Association, Health Assessment and Epidemiology, & Van Ness Recovery House.

Bennett, M. (1997). *An ethnographic study of HIV infected male-to-female transgendered clients.* Paper presented at the XI International Conference on AIDS. Abstract retrieved January 4, 2003, from http://aegis.org/pubs/aidsline/1997/jan/m9714364.html

Bockting, W. O., Robinson, B. E., & Rosser, B. R. (1998). Transgender HIV prevention: A qualitative needs assessment. *AIDS Care, 10,* 505-25.

Bockting, W. O., Rosser, B. R. S., & Coleman, E. (2001). Transgender HIV prevention: community involvement and empowerment. In W. Bockting & S. Kirk (Eds.), *Transgender and HIV: Risks, prevention, and care* (pp.119-144). New York, NY: Haworth Press.

Boles, J. & Elifson, K. W. (1994). The social organization of transvestite prostitution and AIDS. *Social Science and Medicine, 39,* 85-93.

Clements, K., Katz, M., & Marx, R. (1999). *The Transgender Community Health Project: Descriptive results.* (Available from the San Francisco Department of Public Health, 25 Van Ness Ave., #500, San Francisco, CA 94102).

Clements-Nolle, K., Marx, R., Guzman, R., & Katz, M. (2001). HIV prevalence, risk behaviors, health care use, and mental health status of transgender persons: implications for public health intervention. *American Journal of Public Health, 91,* 915-21.

Cornell University Empowerment Group (1989). Empowerment and family support. *Networking Bulletin, 1,* 1-23.

Darbes, L. A., Kennedy, G. E., Peersman, G., Zohrabyan, L., & Rutherford, G. W. (2002). *Systematic Review of HIV Behavioral Prevention Research in African Americans.* UCSF AIDS Research Institute & Cochrane Collaborative Review Group on HIV/AIDS.

Diaz, R. (1998). *Latino gay men and HIV, culture, sexuality, and risk behavior.* New York: Routledge Books.

Diaz, R. M., Ayala, G., Bein, E., Henne, J., Marin, B. V. (2001). The impact of homophobia, poverty, and racism on the mental health of gay and bisexual Latino men: findings from 3 US cities. *American Journal of Public Health, 91,* 927-932.

Elifson, K. W., Boles, J., Posey, E., Sweat, M., Darrow, W., & Elsea, W. (1993). Male transvestite prostitutes and HIV risk. *American Journal of Public Health, 83,* 260-262.

Gagne, P., Tewksbury, R., & McGaughey, D. (1997). Coming out and crossing over: Identity formation and proclamation in a transgender community. *Gender and Society, 11,* 478-508.

Grimaldi, J. & Jacobs, J. (1997). *HIV/AIDS transgender support group: Improving care delivery and creating a community.* Paper presented at the XI International Conference on AIDS. Abstract retrieved June 10, 2001, from http://198.77.70.150/nlmabs/SFgate.cgi

Human Rights Watch (2001). *Hatred in the hallways: Violence and discrimination against lesbian, gay, bisexual, and transgender students in U.S. schools.* New York, NY: Human Rights Watch.

Imbarrato, A. & Sandonnini, M. (1997). *HIV testing and counseling program in a non-institutional community health center.* Paper presented at the XI International Conference on AIDS. Abstract retrieved June 10, 2001, from http://198.77.70.150/nlmabs/SFgate.cgi

Israel, G. E. & Tarver, D. E. (1997). *Transgender Care: Recommended guidelines, practical information, and personal accounts*. Philadelphia, PA: Temple University Press.

Kelly, J. A. (1995). *Changing HIV risk behavior: Practical strategies*. New York: The Guilford Press.

Kenagy, G. P. (1998). *Exploring an oppressed group: A study of the health and social service needs of transgendered people in Philadelphia*. Unpublished doctoral dissertation, University of Pennsylvania.

Kim, B. S. K., Atkinson, D. R., & Yang, P. H. (1999). The Asian values scale: Development factors analysis, validation, and reliability. *Journal of Counseling Psychology, 46*, 342-352.

Krammerer, N., Mason, T., Conners, M., & Durkee, R. (2001). Transgender health and social service needs in the context of HIV risk. In W. Bockting & S. Kirk (Eds.), *Transgender and HIV: Risks, prevention, and care* (pp. 39-58). New York, NY: Haworth Press.

Kreiss, J. L. & Patterson D. L. (1997). Psychosocial issues in primary care of lesbian, gay, bisexual, and transgender youth. *Journal of Pediatric Health Care, 11*, 266-274.

Lombardi, E. (2001). Enhancing transgender health care. *American Journal of Public Health, 91*, 869-872.

Lombardi, E., van Servellen, G. (2000). Building culturally sensitive substance abuse programs for transgendered populations. *Journal of Substance Abuse Treatment, 19*, 291-296.

Namaste, V. K. (2000). *Invisible lives: The Erasure of transsexual and transgendered people*. Chicago, IL: University of Chicago Press.

Nemoto, T., Iwamoto, M., & Operario, M. (2003). HIV risk behaviors among Asian and Pacific Islander male-to-female transgenders. *The Community Psychologist, 36*, 31-35.

Nemoto, T., Luke, D., Mamo, L., Ching, A., & Patria, J. (1999). HIV risk behaviours among male-to-female transgenders in comparison with homosexual or bisexual males and heterosexual females. *AIDS Care, 11*(3), 297-312.

Nemoto, T., Oggins, J., Operario, D., Keatley, J., & Soma, T. (in press). Ethnic group differences in health status and HIV risk behaviors among male-to-female transgenders. *AIDS Care*.

Nemoto, T., Operario, D., Oggins, J., Keatley, J., & Soma, T. (2002). *Critical health issues and HIV risk behaviors among male-to-female transgender women of color*. Manuscript submitted for publication.

Nemoto, T., Operario, D., Soma, T., Bao, D., Cristosomo, V., & Vajrabukka, A. (2003). HIV risk and prevention among API men who have sex with men: Listen to our voices. *AIDS Education and Prevention, 14*, S53-65.

Ross, M. W. & Williams, M. L. (2002). Effective target community HIV/STD prevention programs. *The Journal of Sex Research, 39*(1), 58-62.

San Francisco Department of Public Health (1999). *The transgender community health project: Descriptive results*. San Francisco, CA: Author.

San Francisco Human Rights Commission (1994). *An investigation of discrimination against transgender people: A report by the Human Rights Commission*. San Francisco, CA: Author.

Sausa, L. (2003). *HIV prevention and educational needs of trans youth.* Unpublished doctoral dissertation, University of Pennsylvania.

Schilder, A. J., Kennedy, C., Goldstone, I. L., Ogden, R. D., Hogg, R. S., & O'Shaughnessy, M. V. (2001). "Being dealt with as a whole person." Care seeking and adherence: the benefits of culturally competent care. *Social Science and Medicine, 52,* 1643-1659.

Sexual Health and Family Planning Act (2002). *Safe sex.* Retrieved December 13, 2002, from http://www.familyplanningact.org.au/safesex.html

Strecher, V. J. & Rosenstock, I. M. (1997). *The health belief model.* In K. Glanz, F. M. Lewis & B. K. Rimmer. San Francisco, CA; Jossey-Bass.

Stokes, J.P. & Peterson, J.L. (1998). Homophobia, Self-esteem, and Risk for HIV among African American men who have sex with men. *AIDS Education and Prevention, 10,* 278-292.

Sykes, D.L. (1999). *Transgendered people and HIV: An "invisible" population at risk.* Sacramento, CA: California Department of Health Services, Office of AIDS.

Waldo, C. R., & Coates, T. J. (2000). Multiple levels of analysis and intervention in HIV prevention science: Exemplars and directions for new research. *AIDS, 14,* S2, 18-26.

Warner L, & Hatcher, R.A. (1998). Male condoms. In R.A. Hatcher, J. Trussell, F. Stewart, W. Cates, G. K. Stewart, F. Guest, D. Kowal (Eds.), *Contraceptive Technology* (17th ed., pp. 325-355). New York: Ardent Media.

Xavier, J. M. (2000, August). *The Washington, D.C. transgender needs assessment survey.* Washington, DC: Gender Education and Advocacy & Us Helping Us, People into Living, Inc.

Index